TOMMY

TOMMY

MY JOURNEY OF A LIFETIME

TOMMY G. THOMPSON
AND
DOUG MOE

The University of Wisconsin Press

The University of Wisconsin Press
1930 Monroe Street, 3rd Floor
Madison, Wisconsin 53711-2059
uwpress.wisc.edu

3 Henrietta Street, Covent Garden
London WC2E 8LU, United Kingdom
eurospanbookstore.com

Printed in the United States of America

This book may be available in a digital edition.

Library of Congress Cataloging-in-Publication Data
Names: Thompson, Tommy George, 1941– author. | Moe, Doug, author.
Title: Tommy: my journey of a lifetime / Tommy G. Thompson and Doug Moe.
Description: Madison, Wisconsin: The University of Wisconsin Press, [2018]
Identifiers: LCCN 2018011384 | ISBN 9780299320805 (cloth: alk. paper)
Subjects: LCSH: Thompson, Tommy George, 1941– | Politicians—Wisconsin—Biography.
| Governors—Wisconsin—Biography. | LCGFT: Autobiographies.
Classification: LCC F586.42.T47 A3 2018 | DDC 977.5/043092 [B] —dc23
LC record available at https://lccn.loc.gov/2018011384

TO THE PEOPLE OF WISCONSIN

TOMMY

I was sitting in my office in the Wisconsin State Capitol, alone at night, thinking about the recent presidential election, which was weeks past but not yet over. I was conflicted. Part of me was hoping the man I had worked so hard for wouldn't win.

It was an unusual feeling, but that was an unusual time.

By then—early December 2000—I was the longest-serving governor in the history of the state of Wisconsin, having first been elected in 1986.

Like the rest of the country, I was riveted by what was going on in the state of Florida. The presidential election on November 7, 2000, between George W. Bush and Al Gore had been extremely tight, close enough that it all came down to Florida and its twenty-five electoral votes. Bush won Florida by 1,784 popular votes, a number so small it triggered, by statute, a recount in the state. With the legal and political maneuvering on both sides, and with the highest possible stakes, the Florida result, and the presidency, remained up in the air.

I had campaigned hard for Bush. I first met him through his dad, President George H. W. Bush, in 1991. George W. had gone to Washington to help in his dad's 1992 reelection campaign. He knew his dad was in trouble. I had gone to Washington to talk with the president about the potential of welfare reform as a campaign tool in the 1992 presidential race. We were making national headlines with welfare reform in Wisconsin. It was in Washington that I met George W.

The Bushes, father and son, are close, but they are different personalities, with contrasting leadership styles. George H. W. is personable, outgoing, and upfront. George W. is more tactical, and tougher.

In 1994, a few years after I first met him, George W. ran for governor of Texas against incumbent Ann Richards. I was head of the Republican Governors Association at the time, and I went down to Texas and campaigned and raised money for George W. No one thought he was going to win, but I saw something in him. He was so driven. He was doing all the right things. Nobody gave him a chance, just as few people gave me a chance when I sought the Republican nomination for governor of Wisconsin the first time, in 1986. To that end, I sympathized with George W. Bush. He won his race for governor, as I had.

When George W. decided to run for president in 2000, his father called me. I was thinking of running for president myself.

George H. W. said, "Tommy, I know you're thinking about running. I know you know that you're one of my favorite governors. I would never ask you not to run. But if you decide not to run, would you support George?"

I said, "Yes, Mr. President." In the end, I didn't run for president, not then, and I supported George W. Bush.

In November 2000, I took it personally when Gore won Wisconsin, in a race nearly as tight as Florida. We thought we had won. It was so close—fewer than six thousand votes—that I wanted the Bush campaign to ask for a recount in Wisconsin. They said they needed to put all their resources into Florida, and I suppose they were right. But it was a bitter pill to swallow.

Everyone remembers different things about those wild weeks when the 2000 presidential election was undecided. Books have been written of that time, and movies made.

What I remember is that night alone in the governor's office in Madison. Nothing had been promised, but I knew there was a very good chance that if George W. Bush carried Florida and won the presidency, he would ask me to come to Washington as a member of his cabinet.

We had shared a foxhole kind of experience on an extraordinary night just five days before the election in November. Bush made his eleventh visit of the campaign to Wisconsin on the evening of Thursday, November 2. There was a rally in West Allis at the Wisconsin State Fair Park's Dairy Cattle Barn. Some fifteen thousand people showed up, one of the largest crowds of the whole campaign, everyone shouting and cheering. The Oak Ridge Boys played first, and then I spoke, introducing the candidate. Bush gave a good speech—at one point he ridiculed Gore for having said "I'm against big government" during a debate—but the real fireworks came afterward, when we went out the back of the barn and a group of reporters confronted Bush with questions about a drunk-driving arrest in 1976 that had just been made public, virtually on election eve.

Bush answered a few questions. "I was pulled over and I admitted to the policeman I was drinking," he said. "I am not proud of that. I've oftentimes said that years ago I made some mistakes."

We managed to keep the chaos and questions to a minimum, and got Bush into a car for the airport within a few minutes. He exhaled, looked at me, and said, "Thanks for the help." A little later, one of Bush's aides said, "If we make it to Washington, we're going to want you to come with him."

George W. himself hadn't discussed the cabinet with me at all before the election. I'm not sure he thought he was going to win. Maybe he was afraid of jinxing his campaign. He was very tight lipped about it. But without any real discussion, I sensed that I was being considered.

On that night alone in my office, the controversy over the recount still in full frenzy, I thought to myself, "If he loses, I won't have to make that decision." I hated the idea of having to choose between Wisconsin and Washington. Part of me that night was hoping Bush wouldn't win.

As much as anything, it speaks to how much I loved being governor of Wisconsin. I love the state, I love the people, and I loved being governor. In that fall of 2000, I felt I was still making things happen. Two years earlier, I had won reelection to a fourth term with 60 percent of the vote. In the past fourteen years, we had built $2 billion worth of buildings on University of Wisconsin campuses alone. Our Corridors 2020 plan had upgraded and connected our vast state highway system to an unprecedented degree. We had also acquired more public land for conservation than any previous administration. We had accomplished welfare reform, school choice, and BadgerCare, which helped more Wisconsin citizens afford health insurance, and we had assisted in getting the Packers and Brewers modern stadiums. We had accomplished a great deal.

Being governor was in a very real sense a dream come true for me. My sister, Juliann, remembers a time in our small house in Elroy, growing up, when she, our brother Ed, and I were sitting around talking about what we might do as adults. She and Ed were making jokes about it, but Juliann recalls that I looked her straight in the face and said, "I think I'd like to be the governor of the state." I was a freshman or sophomore in high school at the time.

The political bug came from my dad, Allan Thompson, who ran a grocery store in Elroy, a city of some fifteen hundred people along the Baraboo River in Juneau County. Elroy is where I was born and where I have a farm that is one of the great joys of my life. People are surprised by how beautiful the land is around Elroy, but then it is not the kind of place people find if they're not actively looking for it. When I was running for governor the first time, I found out even Wisconsin residents weren't too sure about Elroy's location. People would ask, "Where is it?" I would say, "Elroy is the center of the universe. It's between Kendall and Union Center, north of Wonewoc and south of Hustler." It always got a laugh.

My dad and I had a complicated relationship. He was harder on me than on my brothers and sister. I was the first boy, and, looking back, I believe that he felt he needed to toughen me up. I was intimidated by him. As a young kid, when I asked for a bicycle, he said I could earn it by cleaning eggs in the basement under the grocery store. I did it, but I didn't like it. There were no windows. I sat down there and at first I broke more eggs than I cleaned. To this day, I can't stand eggs.

But it was in that grocery store on Friday nights that I first became fascinated by politics. My father was vice chairman of the Juneau County Board and chairman of the roads and bridges committee. Many people wanted him to be board chairman. He didn't want to be chairman—he liked the roads and bridges committee.

On Friday nights at Thompson's Grocery, my dad would put out ring bologna and summer sausage, and men—farmers and shop owners, everyone knew everyone else—would stop by to chat. There would be coffee and beer. Someone would be trying to get a road built. That would start a discussion. Someone else would say, "What if it went through here, instead of there?" My father was a central part of it. He loved the wheeling and dealing, the deal making, the negotiating. Overhearing on Friday nights, so did I. To this day, I love to make deals and negotiate. Those lively Friday nights in the grocery store put me on the path to politics.

On December 12, 2000, just a few days after that night alone in my office, the US Supreme Court voted 5–4 upholding the previously certified vote total in Florida, which meant George W. Bush was going to be president.

Two or three days later, Bush called me. During that phone conversation, he never offered me a specific cabinet position. He said, "Tommy, I want you

to come to Washington and be part of the cabinet. I want you on my team."
A short time later, Andy Card, who became Bush's chief of staff, called, and
we arranged for me to fly to Washington before Christmas for a face-to-face
meeting.

There were two cabinet posts that made sense to me: the Department of
Health and Human Services, because of my record with welfare reform and
BadgerCare, and the Department of Transportation, which was the job I really
wanted. I thought there was a reasonable chance that if I got transportation, I
could help George W. Bush become the high-speed rail president. I knew the
turf, having been on the Amtrak board under George H. W. Bush and board
chairman under Bill Clinton. I knew from reading history—I love history—
that it was a Republican, Ulysses S. Grant, who helped complete the transconti-
nental railroad across America. A century later, Dwight D. Eisenhower, another
Republican, championed the interstate highway system. I thought, as a Republican in the first years of the twenty-first century, I could go to Congress and
convince them that high-speed train corridors were the wisest investment of
our transportation dollars.

I never got the chance. I flew to Washington on December 19—it was a
Tuesday—and met with Bush and his team. It was all pretty secretive. They
had a suite in a hotel, and I remember seeing the press set up across the street,
trying to see who was going in to see the president-elect. When I came out of
the hotel, several reporters rushed up and someone said, "Are you going to be
in the cabinet? What did he offer you?"

I said, "I don't know what you're talking about. I was just there to have a
cup of coffee and congratulate him."

In fact, Bush had said, "Tommy, I want you to be secretary of health and
human services."

I wasn't really surprised, by either the offer or the fact that he hadn't solicited
any input from me first.

When you are first elected governor, the National Governors Association
appoints another, senior governor to be a kind of pledge brother, or mentor,
for you. I was George W. Bush's. When I was first elected, Bill Clinton was
mine. There is no real function to it, other than having someone to call if you
have a question that another governor might be able to help with. I used to call
Bill Clinton once in a while. He was very good to me. I consider Bill a friend. I
went down to Arkansas to see him a couple of times. But George W. Bush

didn't reach out to me, not in that role. I suppose he thought he knew how to do it. He called me once or twice. But as a new governor, I spoke with Bill Clinton a lot more than George W. Bush spoke with me.

In the hotel room in Washington, President-Elect Bush said, "I will give you secretary of transportation if you really want it. But I want you at health and human services. It's bigger, you have the expertise, and I need someone there I can trust and count on."

I said, "Do I have to make a decision now?"

Bush said, "No. Go back and talk to your family. But I do have to move. I have to know before the first of the year."

As it happened, my family had planned a trip to Mexico over Christmas. It was unusual for us. We had on occasion taken the week between Christmas and New Year's and driven up to the Upper Peninsula of Michigan for downhill skiing. Once I became governor, we would do the same thing, only fly to Colorado. We hadn't taken a warm weather trip around the holidays before, but my wife, Sue Ann, had found us a condo on the beach in Puerto Vallarta. She and our kids—our daughters, Tommi and Kelli, and our son, Jason—flew to Mexico on December 21. It was a Thursday, and I was going to join them on Saturday. Christmas was the following Monday.

I was still terribly conflicted about whether to go to Washington. It was clear that if I was going, it was going to be as secretary of health and human services. That's where the Bush team wanted me. I would have been more comfortable, and more inclined to go, if it was secretary of transportation. In talking with friends, and with my family before they left for Mexico, I had pretty much decided to stay in Wisconsin. There was still a lot I wanted to do. We had worked hard to reform the relationship between the state and local governments, but there was more to do. We were finishing the expansion of State Fair Park. I had a plan for making Wisconsin completely energy independent. I felt I was still hitting high marks as governor. My family was in Wisconsin. Why would I want to leave all that? I didn't want to, and yet, somewhere in the back of my mind was the nagging thought that if the president of the United States personally asks you to serve, you shouldn't turn him down.

Flying to Mexico on Saturday, two days before Christmas, I fully expected my family to give me the out I was looking for. My daughter Tommi was living at the Governor's Mansion and going to graduate school in Milwaukee—along with helping her mother start the Wisconsin Women's Health Foundation—

and we spoke on many evenings between Thanksgiving and Christmas, making lists of the pros and cons of my going. Tommi had concluded it would be best if I stayed in Wisconsin.

It was rainy and chilly when I joined the family in Puerto Vallarta. Someone made a joke about the Thompson family still not having taken a warm weather vacation. We went out on a fishing boat on Sunday, and I mentioned that I had made up my mind: I was going to continue as governor. Nobody said much about it, but later that afternoon Tommi and I decided to go for a walk. We ended up down at the small swimming pool located between the condominium complex and the ocean. We must have talked for nearly an hour. I have a fair amount of nervous energy, and we walked in circles around that small pool as we spoke. Tommi surprised me. She had changed her mind. She felt the people who were urging me to stay in Wisconsin, many of them, had their own best interests in mind, rather than mine. She and her mother were dedicating themselves to women's health, and here I had the opportunity to oversee health care in America. Sure, it would be more comfortable to stay. Often the right thing to do is the harder thing to do.

Then the next day, Christmas, Sue Ann and I spoke and she said some of the same things. Never in my political life had she really taken a strong position where my career was concerned. She doesn't care all that much for politics. But that day she said she didn't want to live with me a decade from now and have me wondering what might have been if I had gone to Washington when I had the chance. She wanted me to join the Bush cabinet.

My family, then, cast the deciding vote. I was going to Washington.

I phoned the president-elect when I got back to Madison, prior to the New Year's deadline he had set.

"I am honored to come to Washington and be your secretary of health and human services," I said.

"Good," George W. Bush said, and that was about the extent of our conversation.

Time would tell if it was a good decision or not, but the president's cabinet was certainly a long way from the little house and grocery store on Academy Street in Elroy, where everything started for me.

I never stayed in the White House when I was a member of the cabinet, but earlier, when I was governor and George H. W. Bush was president, I had slept in the Lincoln Bedroom. That was among many kindnesses he showed me. For someone with a privileged background, George H. W. had a common touch. There are many stories of him spotting a tour group some distance away in the White House and making a point of going over to shake hands and pose for pictures. "It's your house," he would say.

Once when I was visiting him in Washington, while he was president, he took me out to lunch at the Alibi Club, a private club where he was a member. It was clear the staff there revered him. At one point, Bush took me into the kitchen and introduced me to the chef and the waiters. It was hard for me to imagine a president doing that, but he did. Leaving the kitchen, Bush said, "Never forget where you came from, Tommy."

I never have.

My dad, Allan Edward Thompson, built the house I was born in. It was at 1407 Academy Street in Elroy, and he built it for my mother, Julia Dutton, before they were married, with the intention they would live there and raise a family. They eloped to Iowa, a city called Waukon, just across the Wisconsin border, and got married on September 30, 1939. We had always heard they were married in Des Moines, but the record states otherwise. I think perhaps they went to the big city, Des Moines, for a honeymoon.

My sister, Juliann, was born August 14, 1940. Our parents were living in the home on Academy Street by then. My mother's doctor—Dr. Stella, they called her—had her practice in Elroy, but she delivered Juliann in the hospital in Sparta, thirty miles away. My mother was in the Sparta hospital for eleven days. The bill came to thirty-three dollars. That may have been too expensive for my father. I wouldn't say he was tight, exactly, but he was conservative with money. He always paid in cash, and for the most part I have followed that tradition. My father used to always keep a thousand dollars in cash in his billfold. Years later, I made a point of carrying a little more than that. It was my quiet way of showing I had done better than he had.

Soon after Juliann was born, my mother was pregnant again, and the decision was made to have the second baby at home. Dr. Stella made a house call to deliver me on November 19, 1941.

Early on, my parents had some difficulty with names. My older sister's name was supposed to be Julie Ann. We think it was my dad who in writing the name down for the doctor dropped the *e* and brought the two names together as Juliann. When I was born, they wanted to name me Thomas, with the idea of calling me Tommy, which was my dad's nickname. But my understanding is that after my birth, my dad announced, "We'll call him Tommy," and that's what the doctor wrote down: Tommy George Thompson. The middle name was for my dad's dad, George Thompson, a colorful guy whom I came to know and love very much.

That Tommy is my formal first name always surprises people, and it even played a small role in my first run for the state assembly. In the Republican primary for the assembly in 1966—I was just out of law school—I beat a fourteen-year incumbent named Louis Romell by some six hundred votes. He hadn't taken me seriously as a candidate. It was a Republican district—it included Juneau, Marquette, and Adams counties—and suddenly I was the upstart favorite to win the seat in the general election. Except as the campaign went on we began to hear rumblings about the Democrats having some sort of secret plan that would get their candidate—he operated a Mobil gas station in Adams-Friendship—elected. It was nothing we could pin down, but finally someone told either my dad or me about the rumor that I was going to be kicked off the ballot on a technicality. We drove ourselves crazy looking at the nomination papers, trying to figure out what they might have. Finally, the Democrats took some kind of action to the election board suggesting my candidacy was invalid because I was using a nickname, Tommy Thompson, on the ballot. According to law, a candidate's official name had to be used. I ended up taking in my birth certificate to show everyone that my name was really Tommy. I won the election, and my career was underway.

I have politics in my blood beyond my father. My mother's father, Charles Dutton, ran for the Wisconsin assembly in 1926, in the Republican primary. Being a Republican back then was a little different from today. My grandfather was a progressive and a disciple of Fighting Bob La Follette. Charles Dutton didn't win that assembly seat, but forty years later I did.

Charles's father, Thomas Dutton, my great-grandfather, was from County Offaly, Ireland. He married Margaret Clark, also from County Offaly, around 1845 (Thomas would have been thirty-one; Margaret, nineteen), and they immigrated to the United States a year or two later. They married at the beginning of Ireland's potato famine, when much of the crop failed and what was produced was claimed by England. Something like a million Irish men and women died; a similar number immigrated to the United States, my great-grandparents among them. It was anything but easy. Many of the potato famine immigrants came in the holds of cargo ships—lacking food, water, adequate sanitation—and by some estimates one in five of them died on the voyage.

Thomas and Margaret survived the journey. They did not come immediately to the Midwest. Thomas worked for a time on the Erie Canal, but by 1850 he was in Wisconsin. As the story has been passed down, my great-grandparents might have even been the first white settlers in the series of hills and valleys between what is now Elroy and Kendall, a village six miles northwest of Elroy. Thomas Dutton was taken, as people have been ever since, by the area's natural beauty, the colors and vistas. To him, it looked like Ireland. It looked like home. A few miles away, the first stirrings of what would become the village of Elroy were taking shape, as well. By 1860—although the village would not be officially established until 1879—the settlement had a sawmill, general store, blacksmith shop, livery stable, and an inn.

Two years later, the Homestead Act of 1862—signed into law by Abraham Lincoln—allowed my great-grandfather to acquire 160 acres of farmland between Elroy and Kendall for no cost, other than an eighteen-dollar filing fee. Something like 270 million acres of land—10 percent of the area of the United States—was settled under the Homestead Act. The actual deed for the land, however, was not forthcoming for another five years, during which time the homesteaders were required to live on the land, make a home and improvements, farm, and otherwise prove themselves worthy of the property.

Thomas and Margaret Dutton got their deed. They called their farm Mount Haven. The 1870 United States census shows them living with eight children in Juneau County. My grandfather Charles Dutton was their sixth child, born in 1861. He was working off the farm when his father died, of Bright's disease, in 1892. Charles came back to farm. In 1895, he married my grandmother, a beautiful woman with bright red hair named Ellen Murphy, eleven years his junior.

Charles took Ellen to live on the Mount Haven farm, an arrangement that proved difficult for his mother, Margaret, who lived another dozen years after their marriage.

Charles and Ellen Dutton would eventually have ten children of their own. My mother, Julia, was the eighth, born in 1908. What we know about life at Mount Haven—which, I should point out, is on the same property as my beloved farm today—comes in large part from my mother's sister, Eileen, two years older than my mother. Much later Eileen wrote an unpublished memoir that touched on life on the farm.

"The ten Dutton children all received their grammar school education at the Sherman one room schoolhouse," Eileen wrote. "This was quite a distance away and they walked most days, but on stormy days enjoyed the luxury of a sleigh or buggy ride. At the end of eight grades they went to the Mauston courthouse to take exams. If they received passing scores they were eligible for high school."

I probably needn't mention that there was no indoor plumbing. Charles Dutton had a third-grade education, but was, in Eileen's estimation, "a just and honorable man" who later educated himself, becoming a regular newspaper reader and subscriber to Bob La Follette's magazine, *La Follette's Weekly* (later, *The Progressive*).

My grandmother Ellen—she was called Nellie—kept a vegetable garden on the farm and handled the cleaning and cooking. My aunt Eileen's memoir noted that Nellie was also accomplished at sewing, crocheting, and knitting.

"Mother took great pride in keeping herself and her family looking as nice as possible," Eileen wrote. "We took turns getting new coats, hats, etc. and I have been told that the Dutton girls were the envy of other large families when we appeared at church on Sundays."

The church my mother attended as a girl in the early twentieth century still stands in Elroy. Saint Patrick's Catholic Church was built in 1895 in a prominent position on a hill at the south end of town. There were also a Methodist church and a Lutheran church, for Elroy was growing. It was on the railroad line, a turnaround station for trains out of Minneapolis. Roundhouses were built and had to be staffed. By the late nineteenth century, according to Wilbert C. Clare, in his 1976 history titled *The Story of Elroy*, "There were two express trains and three freight trains each way between Elroy and St. Paul."

Saint Patrick's, or, more specifically, its new pastor, Father Murphy, was responsible for turmoil in my mother's family in the 1920s. In family lore, he was a tyrant, rigidly conservative to the point where lipstick and short-sleeved shirts on women were looked on unfavorably. Dancing was the gateway to great sin, and the company of fellow Catholics was preferred over all others.

Well, my mother's brother Charles Dutton Jr., who decided to work on the farm rather than attend high school—and who, it was assumed, would one day head the farm's operation—fell in love with a Lutheran girl named Mildred.

When Father Murphy learned that they planned to marry, he was so incensed that he forbade my grandmother to attend the wedding. In fact, no one from our family attended the wedding, which was held in Mildred's home with a Lutheran minister officiating. It got worse. My grandmother and several of her children had moved from the farm into Elroy, following the death of my grandfather Charles Dutton, in July 1929, from a ruptured appendix, leaving the farm in the capable hands of Charles Jr. and Mildred. Father Murphy, as the story is told in our family, could not abide that. He threatened my grandmother with some grave consequence—possibly excommunication—if Charles and Mildred remained in charge of Mount Haven. My grandmother and my mother moved back to the farm, and Charles and Mildred departed. By that time, my mother, Julia Ellen Dutton, had her own story to tell.

My mother had an early first marriage to a young Elroy native, Kenneth Bernard "Curly" Roche. They had a son, Charles Patrick Roche, and a second son, Edward Louis Roche, who was born in May 1929. But by 1930 the marriage was over.

It was very tough for my mother. Before she moved back to the farm, she was living in town with her two little boys, working as a waitress at a place called the Beanery, at the railroad exchange. She cooked, too. I heard later that the Catholic priest—whether Murphy or another—didn't like her working there, and that may have been a reason she moved back to the farm with my grandmother. It's also quite possible she just couldn't make it in town alone with two boys; feeding and clothing them was never going to be easy for a single mother.

Now back at the farm, she returned to school and earned a teaching degree at Juneau County Normal. My mother was putting her life back together when an unthinkable tragedy occurred in August 1933. Back then, a feed truck from a farm cooperative went from farm to farm on a regular basis to mix feed for the cattle. You would have the corn and oats that you had harvested during the year, but then you'd have it mixed together to make better feed. Men from the cooperative would come and do the mixing, and the farmers would give them a few bucks. Maybe they came every other week. That summer morning in 1933, my mother's younger boy, everyone called him Eddie, came out of the house to see what the noise was. It was the feed truck, a big truck without good mirrors, and that day the driver just backed up and ran over Eddie. He was four years old. The official cause of death was a basal skull fracture. My mother was devastated. She saved a lock of his hair—he had thick curly hair—until the day she died. Juliann has it still.

My mother's other son with Curly Roche, Charles, served with the marines in Korea and was wounded in action in August 1950. He received the Purple Heart and the Bronze Star Medal for heroic action against an armed enemy. Charles Roche died in April 1969, two months shy of his forty-second birthday, in a hospital in Vernon County, of lung cancer that had metastasized to his brain.

In the late 1930s, my mother was teaching at a two-room rural school outside of Elroy called Fowler Prairie. She taught the first four grades, while another teacher, who was also the principal, taught the upper four grades. His name was Allan Edward Thompson. I'm pretty sure they knew each other before sharing that schoolhouse. They were the same age, and the Elroy area isn't that big. But the school is where they really got to know each other, and before too long, they were dating. In 1939, they were married.

My father's family came from England and Germany. My great-grandfather Isaac Thompson was born in Cambridgeshire, England, in 1832 and immigrated to the United States in 1854. He landed in New York and went to Walworth County, Wisconsin, where his uncle had a farm. Two decades later, at forty-two, he married Elizabeth Fuller. My grandfather George William Thompson was their third child, born in 1884.

The other side of my father's family was German. My great-grandfather Edward Lange was born in Prussia, now Germany, in 1853. He immigrated to the United States with his family as an infant and became a naturalized citizen in Jefferson County, Wisconsin, in 1870. In 1879 he married Delia Brockman, in a Catholic church in Tomah, in Monroe County. Their fifth child, Lenah Rose Lange, was my grandmother.

I don't know how George William Thompson and Lenah Rose Lange, my father's parents, first met, but I have seen a photo of them on their wedding day, August 28, 1907, in New Lisbon. It is a handsome portrait that shows George seated and looking a little away from the camera, the suggestion of a grin beginning to form on his face. Lenah stands beside him, in her full white dress, looking serious, if not quite solemn. From what I know of their relationship—and it lasted a long time—the photo kind of presaged things. My grandfather was a character, and I am not sure my grandmother always appreciated it.

Before they were married, and for a short time after, my grandfather lived in Clifton, and my understanding is he was chased out of town. He was a trouble-maker, good looking, and not averse to taking a second drink. In one version of the story, he was tarred and feathered as a way to encourage him to exit Clifton. In the version my grandfather told it was his buddy who was tarred and feathered, at which point my grandfather decided he had enjoyed enough of Clifton. In any case, he came to Elroy, fifteen miles south, far enough, apparently.

The stories may have been embellished, but my grandfather George was a great guy. He couldn't have been too irresponsible, because he got a job as a US mail carrier and kept it for thirty-five years. Eventually he and my grand-mother lived almost right next door to us on Academy Street in Elroy. While I never knew my mother's parents, I spent considerable time with my father's. Dada and Gramp, we called them. We had a small cabin in Juneau County, and it was there that my grandfather—along with my uncle John, my dad's adopted younger brother—taught me how to hunt, which became one of the great passions of my life. My father never hunted, but I went deer hunting with my grandfather every year. It was an exciting time, deer season. I think I first started in the eighth grade. All these decades later, I still enjoy hunting, but I don't shoot anything, if that makes sense. I have made my quota for life, as I look at it. Now I will carry a gun into the woods without ammunition. I like being out there.

My father was George and Lenah's first son, born July 23, 1908, in Clifton. My uncle John was adopted quite a few years later. My father graduated from high school in Elroy and then attended the University of Wisconsin in Madison. He got his undergraduate degree in 1930 and then enrolled in law school at UW. After completing his first semester, my father came home to Elroy, and one morning my grandfather asked him to harness one of the horses, which my grandfather would use to deliver the mail. I recall that the horse my father sad-dled that day was named Nell—it's funny what you remember. My father must have told me the story. As my father was harnessing Nell, something spooked her and she took off running. My dad was caught in the harness and wound up being dragged a considerable distance. By the time they got the horse stopped a bone was protruding from his leg, and he had suffered a multiple-compound fracture. From that time on, one of his legs was an inch or so shorter than the other. It made it difficult for him to run and kept him out of World War II. He couldn't move very well, but he was a big guy, still a physical presence.

My dad didn't finish law school. In those days, if you had a college degree, as my dad did, you could get a job teaching. He needed a job and was hired to teach at the two-room Fowler Prairie school, eventually serving as principal as well, and meeting, or getting reacquainted with, my mother. When they ran off to Iowa to get married in 1939, the school board told them that one or the other would have to give up the teaching position. My father was the one who left. He decided to build a gas station and auto repair shop in downtown Elroy. He didn't know much about the business, but he was a determined guy. You didn't necessarily want to get between him and what he had in mind. He told me that he opened for business even before he completed the building, so he could generate some income. He slept overnight at the gas station for six weeks, protecting the inventory, until doors and locks were installed and he could go sleep in the house he had built for himself and my mother.

My father made some money during the war, buying and selling tires, and eventually sold the service station and began to acquire some farm properties outside of town, often getting them at a reduced price. The Depression was not long past.

I remember it was a huge day when his brother, John, came home from the war. I went with my dad to New Lisbon, or perhaps Mauston, to pick John up. Everyone was so happy. John hadn't been home long when he talked to my dad about going into business together. There was a grocery store for sale, with a couple of gas pumps out front. John didn't have any money, but my father bought it and they formed a partnership. Thompson's Grocery was where the men in town gathered on Friday nights, and where, as I said, I learned to hate eggs and love deal making.

The grocery store was open from early in the morning until nine at night, six days a week. We were a traditional family, in the sense that my father worked long hours and didn't really help much around the house. He would come home for lunch at noon, take a little nap, and go back to the grocery store. When my mother was teaching, my sister would cook most of the meals, stopping by the grocery and getting whatever meat hadn't been sold to fix with boiled potatoes. We ate a lot of boiled potatoes, and we ate as a family. On Sundays we would have fried chicken for dinner, and my grandparents, who lived next door, would join us. As we were finishing dinner, my father would ask us what we wanted to do, and then, most of the time, we did what he wanted to do, which was take a drive out into the country so he could check out the roads and bridges that were his responsibility on the county board. There would be eight of us, including my grandparents, in the big Buick Roadmaster my father drove. In strawberry season, he used to take us out to a place where you could pick your own berries, and we'd all be put to work picking. We picked apples, too. Anything that was growing, we picked.

My father was demanding, especially of me, but the fact is that both of my parents had good hearts. If people came into the grocery and couldn't pay, my father would first try to see if they could barter something, and if they couldn't even do that, often he would just give them what they needed and take an IOU. When he died, we went through the store's records and found thousands and thousands of dollars in charge slips that were eventually just forgiven. He was tough, but a soft touch, except with me.

My mother, who had gone through some very tough times, was unfailingly compassionate and kind. She was always helping people and encouraging us to do the same. As unreasonable as the Catholic Church, or at least one or two pastors, had been with her and her family, she never turned away from it. I doubt she ever considered it. My mother was an integral part of Saint Patrick's across decades. In 1980—my mother would have been seventy-two—a local paper ran a story about her, headlined "Jewel of the Parish," that told about her cooking meals for people who were ill or on hard times and helping prepare children for their First Communions.

Religion was important to me as a boy in Elroy, and certainly part of that came from her. My father was a Methodist but didn't go to church. My mother insisted that we go, and I found myself embracing it, much more so than my sister and brothers. Starting in about sixth grade, I was either serving or attending daily Mass, which meant getting up at dawn or earlier, trudging up the hill to Saint Patrick's, then turning around and walking back past our house to go to school. I did that for three years. Beyond my mother's encouragement, I think part of it was that I was bullied and pushed around as a kid because I was physically small in my class. I became an introvert and found some solace in religion. It used to irritate my sister and brothers, who didn't take it as seriously. At summer church camp, I always won the prize for knowing every prayer. During Lent, if my mother was late getting home, I would make my sister and brothers get down on their knees and say the rosary. Juliann thought I was going to become a priest, and I considered it. Why didn't I? The line I use is, "In eighth grade I kissed my first girl, and that was that." The fact is, I am still religious. I go to church every week.

Christmas was a big deal when we were kids. On Christmas Eve my dad would load us in the car and take us out to see if we could find Santa Claus. It was a tradition that started when Juliann was just old enough to understand who Santa was and continued with the rest of us. Driving around, my father would always claim he had spotted Santa. "Over there, don't you see?" Of course, none of us ever did. We would come home and open presents, then go to midnight Mass.

One Christmas Eve when I was maybe eight or nine years old, we went out for the drive and Juliann stayed home. She had probably figured out the hard truth about Santa. Unbeknownst to me, while we were out driving, she and my mother walked over to my grandparents' house and brought back a tiny German shepherd puppy. It was all I wanted for Christmas, but every time I had brought it up my parents said I couldn't have it. I suppose I was pretty much resigned to not getting it, but I wasn't happy. When we came home from not seeing Santa, I glanced under the tree and stormed upstairs saying I didn't want any presents. Well, the puppy was there, probably in a small box. Juliann had to call up and tell me to come downstairs. I wound up apologizing. I got my dog. I named him King.

Every family has its traditions, and we had ours. That included vacations. For a while our big annual vacation was a one-day trip to the Wisconsin State Fair outside Milwaukee. We would get up at five o'clock, load my grandparents and all of us kids into the car, and drive to the State Fair. Those are the first few vacations I remember, eight of us in the car, maybe seven—my younger brother Artie might not have been born yet. But we were up before dawn to go to the fair, and then after a long, hot day in the sun my dad would have planned it so the Milwaukee Braves were playing a home game that night, and we'd go to County Stadium for the ball game. None of us really wanted to go, but he did, so we went. That was my father. Now, my kids chuckle and say they see the same thing in me.

One year the eight of us drove to Canada for a fishing trip. I don't know if my dad underestimated how long the drive would take, but I remember that it was a day or two after we had arrived that he announced we needed to head back. My grandfather was pretty mad because he had packed a variety of fishing equipment and was really looking forward to some time on the water. It didn't matter. We were on my father's schedule. It's kind of funny now. I think our best vacations probably were the times we borrowed a cottage not far from Hayward that was owned by a friend of my father's in Elroy. It was on a lake called Little Lac Courte Oreilles. It was less expensive real estate than properties on Big Lac Courte Oreilles, which was connected to the little lake by a channel and was ninety feet deep with twenty-six miles of shoreline. We didn't care, we liked the little lake. We learned to water ski. My grandfather got to fish, and my grandmother fried up what he caught for meals. At night, we played cards. It was at Little Lac Courte Oreilles that I once saved Juliann from drowning. As she tells the story now, she was going down and my brother Ed and I were on the shore arguing about who should jump in and save her. I don't remember it quite that way. A man had spotted her and came running down shouting, "She's in trouble!" I went in after her and brought her to shore. Juliann will vouch for that much.

On occasion, my dad would surprise us. One day, after Juliann and I had started high school, he drove up to the house in a green 1948 Chevrolet.

"Tommy!" he said. "I got you a car!" Well, it was a nice gesture, but the car had seen better days. I think he may have won it in a poker game. It was supposed to be for Juliann and me, but she couldn't drive a standard shift, so I had it most of the time. If it didn't come out of a card game, it may have been repossessed. We named it Sputnik, after the Russian space satellite that was launched in 1957.

It wasn't a Cadillac, but it was fun to have a car in high school. The other fun was sports. I grew up playing all the sports. My father owned a vacant piece of property between our house on Academy Street and my grandparents' house. The neighborhood kids would gather there and play baseball, football, every sport in season, and hide-and-seek at night. While there were some tough things about my growing up—overcoming my shyness and dealing with my father's relentless expectations—in the end Elroy was a good place to be a kid and a teenager. We went where we wanted. You could jump in anybody's car. People weren't afraid, because for the most part they had no reason to be.

There were fifty-five kids in my 1959 graduating class of Elroy High School. The year I graduated, the adjacent Kendall School district voted to consolidate with the Elroy district, moving their students to Elroy, and eventually a larger school was built on land west of Academy Street. The name of the new school,

Royall High School, was devised from the last letters of Elroy and Kendall, and it opened in September 1961.

A class of fifty-five students meant that if you went out for a sport, you made the team, whether or not you were any good. I was best at baseball. I lettered in baseball my freshman year, playing left field, and then played short-stop my sophomore and senior years. Junior year, I played third base, and a kid named Billy Singletary played short. My senior year, we thought we were one of the better teams in the state. I played short, my friend Ed Brown played third base, and we had a southpaw pitcher named Warren Hanson whose family had just moved to Elroy that year. Warren had a terrific fastball and curve. I remember one game when word circulated that there were some professional scouts in attendance. I doubt they lasted past the third inning; we weren't that good, although it was fun to think we were. We made it to the sectionals that year, and as far as I know nobody from our class ever saw Warren Hanson again.

I ran for class president my senior year, so I must have been getting over being introverted to some extent. I didn't win, though. Ed Brown beat me. Ed was and is a good friend. He later became mayor of Elroy and a county super-visor. For a long time after I got into politics, I would occasionally see Ed at an event or rally and point him out as the only one to ever beat me in an election. If I didn't point it out, Ed would.

Ed recalls that I finished third academically in our senior class; my recollec-tion is that I was in the top ten—no great achievement, in any case, in a class of fifty-five. But I was a good enough student that it was always assumed I would go to college. My father went to the University of Wisconsin in Madison, and that's where I wanted to go. A guidance counselor at Elroy High School spent quite a bit of time trying to talk me out of it. His name was Wilbert C. Clare, and he had been at the school since 1929, starting as a science teacher. He was a graduate of what was then called Platteville State Teachers College—now UW–Platteville—and for some reason he was bound and determined that everyone graduating high school in Elroy should go to Platteville, especially me. He thought young people in Elroy should not try to jump to a big city like Madison and a big school like the University of Wisconsin. "You have to go look at Platteville," he told me. He thought I would be able to play sports there, but not at Madison. He kept giving me material about Platteville and calling me into his office to talk about it.

It didn't work. I wanted to go to Madison, and I did. (In 1976, the country's bicentennial year, Wilbert C. Clare published a small paperback titled *The Story of Elroy*, which in about seven thousand words does a nice job tracing the history of the city. Funny, even though I had been representing Juneau County in the state assembly for a decade by then, Clare didn't mention me. He had some nice things to say about my father, though.)

Before I enrolled at Madison in the fall of 1959, I spent most of the summer working construction—hard, tough, hot work that paid for my tuition. My father got me the job. From his position on the county highway committee he was well acquainted with a man named Chuck Mathy, who ran a company called Mathy Construction. Mathy was based in La Crosse, but it did blacktopping all over, including Juneau County. Founded in 1945 by Chuck's father, Aime Mathy, the company is still going strong today.

My father asked Mathy to give me a summer job, and he did. I worked for Mathy paving roads. Blacktop is poured at 285 degrees, and if you're not careful it can burn you pretty easily, but the pay was unlike anything I had ever seen. We started on a county road in Mauston, then went to Fox Lake, a little community in Dodge County, where we redid the streets. It became clear early that I didn't mind hard work, and they started contracting me out—they gave me an air hammer and sent me to local farmers to break up cement. Mathy always had all the work it could handle and was always on a tight schedule, so we worked ten to twelve hours a day and were paid time and a half for the overtime. I was making several hundred dollars a week.

That August, we started a job for the federal government at Volk Field, the Air National Guard Base outside Camp Douglas, in Juneau County. I didn't get to see it finished. One Friday night, the foreman, Earl Welch, took me aside, handed me my paycheck, and said, "Tommy, you can't come back to work Monday."

"Why not?"

Earl told me the union had learned I wasn't eighteen years old—I would turn eighteen in a few months—and that violated the union contract. I wasn't too upset. I was getting ready to go down to Madison to school anyway. But then Earl said, "You're the best damn worker we've ever had. You come back next summer."

I think that because I was only seventeen and had never really been away from home, my father insisted that I live with a guy from Elroy, Wayne Johnson, when I first went to Madison. Wayne was a couple of years older than me, a junior when I was a freshman, and I guess my dad felt he would look after me and make sure I studied. I would much rather have been in a dorm. We lived in an upstairs flat of a house on Madison Street, off Monroe Street, not far from Camp Randall Stadium. The place was pretty small. Two beds, two desks, not much else. Wayne was a good guy, very bright, an electrical engineering student who later had a distinguished career with the Ford Motor Company. We became good friends, and back then he did try to look after me and suggested I go into engineering. That was never going to happen. Advanced math like calculus was not my strong suit. I gravitated toward history and political science.

I lived with Wayne only one year. Summers, I worked for Mathy, still earning good money, and when I went back to school I had a series of roommates and apartments. I worked during the school year, too, including bouncing and bartending at a legendary State Street establishment called the Varsity Bar. Many stories came out of the Var Bar, and I will share a few, but the most meaningful job I had was at the state capitol. It was after I got my undergraduate degree and enrolled in the University of Wisconsin Law School. The Wisconsin Legislature had received some grant money—I think it may have come from the Ford Foundation—to hire college students to work on committees and see how the legislature functioned, as legislatures across the country were doing. My dad suggested I go to Louis Romell, a Republican who represented Elroy in the assembly, and see if he might hire me as part of the new program. My dad didn't have to ask twice, because by that time I was interested in government and politics. Well, Romell wouldn't hire me. He was very curt. It got back to me later that he sensed that if I got inside the capitol, I might not stop at helping with committee work. He was afraid I might eventually run against him for the assembly. Romell's instincts were pretty good. By the time I was in law school, the political bug hadn't just bitten me, it had pretty well devoured me.

It had started all those years ago when I listened to the men wheel and deal in my father's grocery store in Elroy, but it really took flight in my senior year as an undergraduate. I had read *The Conscience of a Conservative* (1960) by Arizona senator Barry Goldwater (ghostwritten by his longtime speechwriter, L. Brent Bozell Jr., brother-in-law of William F. Buckley) and liked it a lot. I wasn't the only one inspired by Goldwater's message—preserving and extending freedom was at the core—but I was one of few on the campus in Madison, I can assure you of that. Goldwater's ideas were much in my head when I took a political science course my senior year from Ralph Hewitt, who was regarded by some as the leading congressional scholar of his day. He taught a class on Congress, among other courses. I remember we had to write a paper, and mine took a conservative point of view. It took some guts, because Hewitt's own politics were liberal. My take was the opposite of his, but to his credit, in my estimation, he gave it back to me and said, "I don't agree with your conclusions, but I like your passion and how you presented things."

Not long after that, Professor Hewitt asked me into his office for a chat.

"Have you ever thought about going to study in Washington?"

I said, "I think I might like that."

Hewitt smiled. "Well, you're the only Republican I know of in the class."

I was proving I could be a contrarian and was beginning to get over my shyness.

It turned out that Hewitt was involved with an internship program that allowed him to choose two students each year who would spend the summer with elected officials from Wisconsin in Washington, one Democrat and one Republican. That year, 1963, Hewitt assigned a young black woman—I think her name was Marilyn Mitchell—to the Washington office of Senator William Proxmire and me to the office of Vernon Thomson, a Republican from Richland Center. Thomson had been governor of Wisconsin and was now serving in the House of Representatives. My dad knew him. Thomson had another young guy, from Platteville, interning that summer, William "Denny" Dennis, and we have stayed in touch. He later headed a taxpayers group.

The best thing about the internship program was that we got a chance to hear prominent speakers, about once a week, usually at night. One exception was Jimmy Hoffa, who spoke one Friday noon at the Teamsters national headquarters building. The auditorium was packed, and it wasn't just students. Hoffa, of course, was the president of the Teamsters. I have vivid memories of that day. The atmosphere was electric. I was sitting about five rows back, on the right side, at the end of the row. Hoffa got up in front, no lectern, just kind of planted himself there. He looked like he could have played linebacker for the Packers. Everyone knew who was in charge in that room. I was spellbound. You could tell he was one tough guy, but he turned out to be quite articulate. He spoke briefly about the Teamsters but quickly moved on to the subject of Bobby Kennedy, who was then attorney general. Hoffa spent the better part of an hour criticizing Kennedy and his Justice Department, which at the time was mounting an aggressive corruption investigation of the Teamsters. Hoffa was convinced that Bobby Kennedy was out to get him.

When Hoffa was finished, he took a few questions and that was it. I walked up front because I wanted to shake his hand and compliment him. Not everyone in the audience had appreciated his attack on Kennedy, but I liked the speech. I didn't get to shake hands. He did nod at me as he walked past, and then he was gone.

The other speaker who really impressed me was Barry Goldwater, whose book, of course, had made a great impact on me when I read it back in Wisconsin. One of my hopes in going to Washington was to meet Goldwater and encourage him to run for president. He was as impressive in person as he was on the page, at least to me. When I got back to Madison, I knew I wanted to do what I could for Goldwater's presidential hopes.

Just before I left to come home, however, I managed to be present at a remarkable moment in history. On August 28, 1963, I was on the National Mall in Washington when Martin Luther King Jr. gave his famous "I Have a Dream" speech. Vern Thomson had forbidden the student interns to go because of concern there might be violence. That alone was enough to ensure I was going to be there. If something happened, I wanted to see it. It was orderly. I was about halfway down on the right side of the Mall. The number of people, many more than anticipated, was impressive, but I can't say that I saw the occasion as momentous at the time. No doubt that was a failing on my part. The speech and Dr. King grew in stature with time. I'm very glad I was there.

Back in Madison, preparing to start law school, I was ready to get more involved politically. My roommate, a guy named Dick Wright—Richard Wright, later a judge in Marquette County—had been active for some time, writing articles for a magazine called *Insight and Outlook*, always very conservative, much more so than anything I might have written. Compared to Dick, I was moderate. In any case, we were both for Goldwater for president. In early 1964, Dick was president of the Dane County Young Republicans. I helped start a unit on campus called Collegians for Goldwater. Both groups were dedicated to getting Goldwater elected president, as well as unseating Bob Kastenmeier, the liberal Democrat who had represented Madison and the Second Congressional District since 1959. I remember going down to Memorial Library once when Kastenmeier was making an appearance, along with a few other guys, and we held up signs accusing Kastenmeier of something like being soft on communism. A

Wisconsin State Journal photographer took a photo of us protesting, and it ran in the paper. It's worth noting because years later, when I was governor, occasionally people would show up with protest signs at an event where I was appearing. I didn't like getting picketed. I used to say, "What is it with these people? Can't they get a life?" Somehow someone on my staff found that old *State Journal* photo of me with my protest sign and showed it to me, grinning. What could I say? I was a kid. It certainly didn't do much damage to Kastenmeier. That spring the Dane County Young Republicans endorsed Carl Kolata, a Watertown radio station owner. Kastenmeier not only won that election, he won every election for more than a quarter of a century, finally losing in 1990 to Scott Klug, a television anchor.

Between the state Republican Party, Dick Wright's Young Republicans, and my Collegians for Goldwater, we somehow convinced the Goldwater campaign to bring the candidate to Madison. That was unusual, a Republican presidential candidate making an appearance in a bastion of liberalism, although Madison's liberal reputation—which would spike with the Vietnam War protests—was not yet in full flower. Goldwater flew into Madison on September 24, 1964. He didn't stay long. He arrived a little after noon and spoke outside the capitol a short time later. The crowd was estimated at around eight thousand, and more than a few of them were chanting "LBJ" and trying to interrupt him. By midafternoon, Goldwater was back on his plane and off to the next campaign stop.

The *Capital Times*—Madison's liberal afternoon daily paper, which would later be consistently rough on me as governor—nearly went berserk in its coverage of Goldwater's visit. One headline pointed out that the candidate's plane was forty minutes late getting into Madison. Another noted that Goldwater was critical of his Madison audience for being "noisy." Finally, above the fold on page one, the *Cap Times* published an open letter to Goldwater—"Where *Do* You Stand Sir?"—as well as this reference to a Walter Lippmann column on the op-ed page: "Demagogue Goldwater Seeks to Build GOP as Party for Rich White Racists."

Subtlety was never a strong suit of the *Capital Times*.

Back when my father encouraged me to try to get a job in the state capitol and Louis Romell turned me down—concerned, rightly, that I might have my eye on his seat—my father then suggested I go to see Jess Miller, a Republican senator from Richland Center. My father knew Miller, too, though by the time I contacted his office Miller wasn't coming in much. He was ill, dying, actually. But his office called him, explained that I was looking for a job and grant money was available, and Miller hired me. He never interviewed me, not even over the phone, but he hired me. I wish I had had a chance to thank him. When he died, in 1965, John Wyngaard, who would soon become the dean of the capitol press corps (if he wasn't already), wrote a tribute that included this: "Sen. Miller was a rural conservative in the classical mold and gloried in the identity. His resolute skepticism about impulsive proposals for change became his hallmark."

I was assigned to Allen Busby, who since 1959 had chaired the Judiciary Committee in the senate. Busby was an attorney and a Republican out of West Milwaukee, which was highly unusual—once he left, no Republican held the seat—but then Busby was an unusual Republican. He was first elected to the senate as a Progressive in the 1930s. He switched and ran as a Republican in 1940, but he remained a maverick and voted with the Democrats a fair amount, which was probably why he hung on to his seat for so long. He was the longest-serving senator—thirty-six years—when he decided not to run in 1972, at age seventy-two.

When I worked for him, Busby was still practicing law in Milwaukee, so he would be in Madison only a few days a week, arriving Tuesday and leaving Thursday. Busby was a small man, with a pencil-thin mustache and glasses. What he most wanted from me was research on bills. Before he held public hearings on a bill, he wanted a memo from me on what the bill was all about. Not that he didn't read them—he did—but my memos gave him some additional perspective on the bills. Then I would take notes when people came and testified. Truth is, more than Busby, I really worked for the marvelous woman who ran his office, Helen Grant. She took a liking to me, and I spent a lot of time with Helen.

When Busby was there, he would sit and talk to me. He was bright but quiet, soft spoken, and definitely well-to-do. He gave me one piece of advice. He looked at me intently one day and said, "Tommy, get into stocks. Buy stocks, and never sell." He kind of paused, and said, "I just buy stocks and put them away, never sell anything, and I've done very well."

I was a year or two into law school when it became clear that it would be a lot easier for me if I could work evenings in the capitol, giving me more time for classes and study on campus during the day. It happened that the assistant sergeant at arms for the senate had two positions that were almost like night watchmen. Every two years the senate elects its sergeant at arms, who is basically responsible for seeing that things run as smoothly as possible, not always an easy task. At this time, the sergeant at arms was Harold Damon, and his assistant was Harry Levander. They had a staff of clerks and messengers to help too. Levander eventually become sergeant at arms himself but did not serve long in the position. He suffered a fatal heart attack in November 1967.

In his last year or two in the assistant's job, Levander was well aware that the senate does not necessarily shut down at five o'clock, so he wanted a couple of us to work five to nine, getting meals, bringing around cars, running errands, whatever the senators wanted. He picked me and a guy named John Gable, a tall, thin, good-looking graduate student in history. John and I kind of became Harry's boys. He could count on us to take care of what was needed. If a senator wanted something, we got it. John and I became very close friends. He later became a highly successful business executive in Chicago and a generous contributor to the University of Wisconsin, active in the alumni association.

As I said, we were kind of like night watchmen. When we started, Harry said, "I know you guys are in school. If there's nothing going on, feel free to study." We were often able to study and get paid for it, because Harry saw that when something came up, we handled it. Our work shift—from five to nine— included the cocktail hour, and it was an era when many of the legislators at times took a second drink. Certainly that was true of Leland "Packy" McParland, a Democratic senator serving Milwaukee County's south suburbs who spent fourteen years in the assembly before being elected to the senate in 1954. Packy wasn't the only one, but occasionally he would go missing when the senate was having a roll call vote, and Levander would send John and me off to find him. They would be holding the roll open in the senate. One time we found Packy in the bar of the old Park Hotel across the street from the capitol.

Packy had left sobriety behind and didn't want to go. "Senator, they're voting," I said.

He kind of grumbled, shrugged, and didn't protest too much when John and I got on each side of him, took an arm, and walked him out of the hotel and onto the Capitol Square. We crossed the street, and he still didn't say anything. Then, just as we were stepping over the curb, heading for the capitol lawn, Packy got his right arm free from John, turned in my direction, and threw a big roundhouse punch. I saw it coming and ducked. Packy went around in a circle, lost his balance, and fell flat on his back in the gutter. He was out, not from hitting his head, I don't think, but from the booze. John and I kind of shook him awake, got him back on his feet, and walked him in. He still wasn't happy, but he wasn't as aggressive or cantankerous. Levander saw us and his eyes got wide. We got Packy in place and he cast his vote. Then we took him to his office and got him in a chair, where he fell asleep. It couldn't happen today, not a chance. Back then, I didn't make a big deal of it, Packy taking a swing at me. We were pretty protective of the senators.

The thing is, we all drank a bit. I know I did. It was part of the deal in college, and it was fun. At my job at the Varsity Bar, I fit the hours around my obligations in school and at the capitol. I bounced and bartended at the Var Bar, which was a great college bar in the tradition of the Kollege Klub or the Pub in Madison. It was located adjacent to the Pub, in the 500 block of State Street, on the left as you faced the capitol. I was a customer first. I started going to the Varsity Bar after I got thrown out of Chesty's, which was across the street, for getting in a fight. My Young Republican buddy Dick Wright worked at the Var Bar, so I'd go in to see him. One day when I was in there, a guy named Francis Doane—everyone called him Bob—spotted me and said, "You're Tommy Thompson." Doane was running the Var Bar for the owner, Tony Plescia, and he recognized me from Elroy. He'd had my mother for a teacher and liked her a lot.

"You want to go to work?" Doane said.

"Sure," I said.

There was quite a cast of characters at the Var Bar. The story was that Plescia won it in a poker game. It wasn't that big of a place, but it had picture windows facing State Street, great for people watching. The bar and grill were on your left as you came in, with booths on the right. The first Monday of every semester, Tony had something he called Paint Night. I made a point of working it. For three hours, from six to nine, the bar was open only to female students, and the idea was they could come in and paint whatever they wanted on the walls and the booths of the bar. They'd paint the name of their sororities or their boyfriends or just something they thought was funny, and Tony knew that they would make a point of coming back often and showing everyone what they had painted. It was a good gimmick. The guys working were the only men allowed. I got more than a few dates out of Paint Night, I assure you. One of my coworkers, and a guy I eventually roomed with, was Peter Salg, a cousin of

Pat Richter, the great athlete and later UW athletics director. There were a couple of former college boxing champions, Jim Mack and Jerry Turner, working at the Var Bar, and an unforgettable character named Charlie Lanphear, whose older brother, Dan Lanphear, was a tremendous football player and All-American for the Badgers. Charlie was probably tougher than Dan, but undisciplined. We called him Towel, because he always had one hanging around his neck. I got along fine with Charlie, but he was pretty wild, and he left Madison in the late 1960s. Much later, it turned out Charlie Lanphear and I had something in common beyond having worked at the Varsity Bar: we were both on the cover of *Madison Magazine*. I was on the cover in February 1987, after first being elected governor, and Charlie appeared a few years later, under the title "The Last Pirate." The story detailed Charlie's adventurous life after leaving Madison, which included being busted for running guns in Singapore. It took some money, in the form of bribes, to get him out of that one. Later, Charlie settled down, spent time in Aspen and Hawaii, worked building houses, and, last I heard, was living in Arizona, writing his memoirs.

The picture windows in the Var Bar were the downfall of my friend John (we called him Super Pole—he was Polish), who would sit on a stool at the window and drink on Friday afternoons when I was bartending. After a few drinks, John had the bad habit of falling in love with one or another young woman who was walking by on State Street. He had the even worse habit, if he'd imbibed enough, of acting on it.

My senior year in law school, homecoming weekend, I spent a happy Saturday afternoon at Camp Randall Stadium, participating with several hundred of my law school classmates in the tradition of running the length of the football field prior to the start of a Badger game. The law students carry canes in their hands as they race from the north end zone to the south, in the shadow of the Field House, where they toss the canes between the goal posts. Legend has it that law students who catch their canes will win their first case. I honestly don't remember whether I caught my cane or not. What I remember is getting a call that night from my friend John, who said he had been arrested for disorderly conduct following an episode that day outside the Varsity Bar.

"You're going to be a lawyer," John said. "You can represent me."

He had a court appearance the following Monday, and I went with him. I remember announcing to the magistrate that we intended to plead not guilty.

"Have you read the police report?" the magistrate said.

"No, Your Honor," I said.

"You should read the report before you plead not guilty," he said.

I glanced at John, who looked away. Then the magistrate said, "In fact, allow me to read it for you."

The courtroom was crowded, but it got pretty quiet, and the magistrate read, "A large man, clearly intoxicated, came out of the Varsity Bar with a determined look on his face, leaned over behind a young woman, and with *teeth bared . . .*"

The courtroom erupted in laughter. I chuckled myself. Apparently John was unsuccessful in his effort to bite the young woman, but the attempt was enough to get him arrested. We didn't win the case.

I didn't graduate the spring of my last year in law school. I was three credits short, so I needed to take a summer course. That summer of 1966 proved to be one of the most memorable of my life. It was hectic. Sometimes it seemed like I was doing six things at once, and the first couple of months raced by. That last course I was taking was environmental law with a legendary professor named Jake Beuscher. He was a great conservationist, before anyone had ever heard of Earth Day, and I got my best grade of my entire law school career in his class, a ninety-three.

Meanwhile, I had three jobs. I was still working part-time in the capitol and bouncing and tending bar at the Varsity Bar, while living with some roommates in a house at the back of an alley that ran off State Street between the Var Bar and the Pub. That location did nothing to diminish our socializing. It's shocking we weren't evicted. It may have helped that my third job that summer was with Wisconsin Physicians Service, better known as WPS, located on Lakeside Street, downstairs from the State Medical Society. It was a busy time at WPS because Medicare had just been established, and my job was to review contracts. It paid well and helped keep me out of the State Street saloons. Still, by any measure, it was a wild summer, at least the first two months.

By July I had settled on a plan to enter the United States Air Force Judge Advocate General's Corps—better known as the JAG Corps—which is the legal arm of the air force. But that wasn't going to happen until November, or maybe even January, and that summer I heard a piece of news from Elroy that got me thinking, and eventually changed my life.

Louis Romell was the incumbent representative for the Wisconsin assembly district that included Juneau, Adams, and Marquette counties. Louis was from

Adams County and often faced opposition in the primary from Ben Tremain, a Republican from Juneau County. For a while it seemed as if they were trading the seat back and forth, and it was always close. In 1954, for instance, Romell won the primary with 2,474 votes to Tremain's 2,413. Four years later, it was Tremain's turn. He won with 1,958 votes to Romell's 1,867. It almost goes without saying that whoever won the Republican primary won the general election; it was a solidly Republican district.

Romell was back in office by 1966, and that summer the news I heard from the district was that Tremain had decided against challenging Romell in the September primary. I thought about it a bit, but I really didn't have to think too long. The hours I'd spent in the capitol had convinced me I could do the job as well as or better than the existing legislators. I felt I could make a difference. Besides, what did I have to lose? I figured that if I ran and lost, as would likely happen, I would have gained both experience and name recognition in the district. After my JAG Corps service, I could come back and run again. I figured Romell would probably have retired by then. (I was wrong about that. After I beat him he took the position of sergeant at arms in the assembly and eventually, after redistricting, ran for office again in 1972, losing an assembly race to Marlin Schneider of Wisconsin Rapids.)

All that was in the future in the summer of 1966, when I announced I was running for the assembly in the Republican primary in my home district. The announcement did not generate big headlines. Romell expressed his degree of concern about my candidacy by embarking, a short time later, on an Alaskan cruise.

3

I was twenty-four years old, with no money and no organization. On the plus side, I knew I could work hard. Since I was a kid, I had been able to pretty much outwork anybody. I didn't always like it, but I knew I could do it. Even when I was running wild for a time in college, I always had at least two jobs. I decided that the way to run against Louis Romell was to treat campaigning like a job. I would personally meet as many people as I could in the three counties: Juneau, Adams, and Marquette.

It wouldn't be easy for me. I had been fairly social the past few years in Madison, but there's a difference between going up to a girl in a State Street bar when you've each had a few beers and knocking on somebody's door at noon in Endeavor or Mauston and explaining you're running for office. I did it because I had no other way to campaign. The county boards and town boards across the district were going to support Romell. The Republican caucus in the assembly down in Madison was supporting Romell and giving him money. I needed to get out and introduce myself to people. It was all I had, and in hindsight it's clear it really helped me. I was the first candidate from the district who actually made a deep dive into all three counties. When Romell and Ben Tremain were trading the seat back and forth, Romell dominated Adams County and Tremain pretty much controlled Juneau County. They really didn't try to shake loose votes on the other guy's turf. Whoever did a better job getting out the vote in Marquette County and near home was the winner. I didn't see it that way. I knew I needed to go everywhere—and that's a mindset I kept throughout my political career.

The first thing I did was borrow five hundred dollars from the Bank of Elroy. My father had to cosign for the loan. I used one hundred dollars of that to buy a beat-up car with two hundred thousand miles on it. It was in sad shape, with bald tires and a floorboard with holes you could see through. I suppose it's ironic that one of my campaign issues was highway safety.

My dad also agreed to give me ten dollars a day, five dollars for gas and five dollars for food. That meant something back then, and I don't just mean that ten dollars could buy more in 1966. It was clear my dad was behind me, and proud of me. The maddest I'd almost ever seen him was during that campaign when a guy who had competed with my father for a time in the grocery business took out an advertisement in the local paper that essentially said, "Louis Romell is Elroy's friend, not Tommy Thompson." My dad was furious. It's not that he expected me to win, but any suggestion that we weren't friends of Elroy was going to set him off, and that ad certainly did.

Another member of my family, my brother Ed, helped in that first campaign by introducing me to Gene Delmore, who worked with Ed driving trucks and plowing snow for Juneau County. Gene volunteered to be my unofficial campaign manager in my run against Romell. His real name was Wayne Delmore, but everyone called him Gene. He was a nice guy and knew a lot of people. His duties as campaign manager basically consisted of going along with me when he could. Often that was in the evenings, when he got off work, but he spent some days with me too. In part because of Gene, people were glad to see us. Gene loved to barter. He loved restoring and reselling old things, especially toys, and I remember at one door where we stopped he walked away with a stamp collection that turned out to be worth quite a bit of money.

Early in the campaign, one morning when Gene wasn't with me, I stopped in at a bar in Montello—I think it was called the Town Tap—that was run by a guy named Bill Cotter, whose wife was the register of probate for Marquette County. Bill leaned Democrat and didn't much like Romell, so he decided he would help me. Bill pointed to a guy sitting by himself at the end of the bar, a day drinker who was obviously not going anywhere for a while. Bill said to me, "Introduce yourself and buy that fellow a drink. All day long, he'll be telling people how Tommy Thompson, who is running for the assembly, bought him a drink." I did that, and I started doing it other places, stopping in the local bars. Sometimes it worked better than others. One day I went into a little bar in far northwest Adams County that had a live goat. I started chatting with the bartender, and the goat came over and peed on my foot.

Gene Delmore and I went to weddings, funerals, bowling alleys—we went all over. I'd go door-to-door during the day, and then at night we'd hit all these other places. If it was a weekend and we saw a wedding party, we would stop and get a photo taken with them. We bowled or shot pool with people we met at bowling alleys across three counties. It wasn't easy for me, but it got easier. I was getting over my shyness, and my name was getting known.

I still remember the first time I saw Louis Romell that summer. It was on Labor Day at the Harrisburg Brat Fest in Marquette County. These days it's billed as the state's largest one-day brat festival—it celebrated its fifty-fifth anniversary in 2015. There's music and softball and a lot of people eating brats. I was shaking hands and talking to people when Louis came up to me. Recently back from his Alaskan cruise (the primary was about two weeks away), he had been told that I'd been blanketing the district, knocking on doors, and showing up anywhere a group gathered, for any reason.

"Young man," he said, "I have to tell you I've been hearing good things about you. They tell me you're campaigning hard. They said I had to get back here and defend myself."

I think I smiled, thanked him, and said something about only trying to establish myself in the district. He continued, "I am going to beat you, but I'm not going to be around that long. You may have a future."

I think he was trying to kind of feel me out. I'm not sure, maybe he was trying to intimidate me, although he was quite nice and respectful. After a minute, he went one way and I went another. From that point on, over the next two weeks or so, I saw him a lot. He began working hard. But it was too late.

Nobody knew that until the night of the primary. I felt good that day. I didn't expect to win, but I was hopeful that I could carry Elroy and do well in Juneau County overall. That was my goal. The first indication I had about the results wasn't until eight thirty or so that night. There weren't exit polls in those days, or hardly polls of any kind. I was standing in the kitchen of the house in Elroy when the phone rang. It was Buzz Kelly, the highway commissioner of Juneau County. My dad was chairman of the roads and bridges committee on the county board. Kelly not only reported to my dad, he liked him. So he called the house, I suppose about a half hour after the polls closed. I answered and he said, "I have some wonderful news."

He had called the highway commissioners in Adams and Marquette counties, who were keeping a close watch on the vote counting, and they told him that I was leading in both Adams and Marquette. "You're going to win," he told me.

I couldn't believe it, but Kelly was right. I beat Romell by 635 votes. It was a thrill. Then, of course, all the Republicans who had no time for me when it was assumed Romell would win began getting in touch and asking how they could help. One guy from the assembly caucus came up to Elroy a few days after the primary to meet with me.

"We didn't support you," he said. "We didn't expect you to win. But now we're here to help you."

My recollection is that he gave me a roll of stamps and a check for fifty dollars. I think that was the first money I received in the campaign, other than what my father gave me. After that I spent a lot of time meeting with different groups. We had to set up a campaign committee and get a treasurer.

The district was solidly Republican, but my upset of Romell gave the Democrats hope that they might have a chance in the general election. Their candidate was Steve Baumgartner, a gas station owner from Adams. He was a nice guy but really not that strong of a candidate, in part because he had a business to run. I was still in full campaign mode, even more energized than before. I went all over and saw everybody. It was an exciting time. There was a hotly contested senate race in the district between Jim Wimmer and Walt Terry. Terry beat Cy Bidwell in the Republican primary and then beat Wimmer in the general election. Wimmer and I became close friends, even though he was a committed Democrat and served for a time as chair of the Wisconsin Democratic Party. You could be friends across the aisle then. He later became a top lobbyist. When he died in 1998 at sixty-two, after a fall, I gave a eulogy at Jim's funeral.

My assembly campaign against Baumgartner was in the same vein. It wasn't contentious. I won handily—7,703 votes to 3,002—a couple of weeks before my twenty-fifth birthday.

The phone calls kept coming, this time from established assembly Republicans who were already jockeying for leadership positions, like Speaker, and wanted my vote. One of them, Harold Froelich, came to see me in late November. I think what I said during our conversation surprised him.

It was a big deal—and my vote was important—because the Republicans had retaken the majority in the assembly, a position they had lost in the 1964 elections after holding it the previous four years. The Republicans in the assembly would elect a Speaker, and the Speaker would make committee appointments and get his people in the key spots. Once again, starting in 1967, the Republicans held the cards. (The Republicans also held a majority in the senate, and the governor, Warren Knowles, was a Republican as well.)

As I say, a number of men wanted that Speaker spot. Besides Froelich, there was Curtis McKay, a lawyer from Ozaukee County; Paul Alfonsi, a schoolteacher from Minocqua; and Harold Clemens from Oconomowoc, who eventually became state treasurer. They all called me. Of course, each of them had supported Romell in the primary race. None of them had given me money, none of them had campaigned for me. I didn't owe any of them anything. Yet they all wanted my vote.

Only Froelich came to see me, a few weeks after the election. I was still living with my father and mother at 1407 Academy Street in Elroy. He arrived at about three thirty and sat in an easy chair to my right in the living room. Harold was a big guy, a navy veteran from Appleton who was at UW–Madison around the time I was. Harold got his law degree in 1962. He eventually ran successfully for Congress and later became a judge in Outagamie County. Back then—November 1966—he wanted to be Speaker of the state assembly.

"I hear you're a conservative," Harold said. "I'm the conservative candidate."

I smiled. "I am a conservative. But I don't really know you. The others have called me. They all want my support."

"They want you," Froelich said. "But I need you. If you support me, I can win."

I said, "That's nice, but if I help you, I want something in return."

Harold said, "What's that?"

"I want to be on Joint Finance."

I suppose it was an audacious thing to say. First-term legislators do not get appointed to the Committee on Joint Finance. I had been in and around the capitol enough to know that, but I also knew that Joint Finance was where the power was. If I was going to make any kind of mark, at twenty-five years of age, I needed to be on a powerful committee, and they don't come any more powerful than Joint Finance. It was the key committee because it controlled all the spending. It was the heart of state government. If you were on Joint Finance, you could influence policy to a great degree. Everybody had to come to you for their projects, so you were a power within the Republican caucus, and a power in the state. The University of Wisconsin needed to talk to you. Anybody who wanted something had to go through you. No one would come to talk to Tommy Thompson, freshman legislator, but they would come to see me—if I was on Joint Finance—before they would go see a fifteen-year legislator who wasn't on that committee. It was just hugely important. It granted instant power and credibility. That's less true now than it was in 1966. There are more rules and regulations today. It was more free flowing then.

That day in Elroy, Harold Froelich grimaced when I mentioned Joint Finance.

"I can't do it," Harold said. "No freshman goes on Joint Finance."

I spread my hands in front of me. "That's the price of my support."

Harold said, "Well, I can't do that."

He left on good terms. I walked him to the door. As we shook hands, he said, "Think it over."

"Think about my deal."

Harold shook his head. "I just can't."

Less than a week later, Froelich called back. "I will consider giving you Joint Finance." I said, "I appreciate it. That's still the deal. Let me know when you're certain."

A few more days passed. Another phone call. "I will put you on Joint Finance."

It was a wild time. With all those guys wanting to be Speaker, there was horse-trading and half-promises coming left and right. Eventually a few guys dropped out when it became clear they couldn't get the votes, and it came down to Froelich and Clemens, who was more moderate. John Shabaz, a conservative from the Milwaukee area first elected to the assembly in 1964— and already a force in the capitol for his intellect and work ethic—had originally backed McKay but swung early to Froelich. Then McKay dropped out and backed Froelich. Alfonsi went with Clemens. Having a correct tally was crucial—who was supporting whom, who had the votes—but it wasn't easy with all the maneuvering.

At one point right before the vote, Froelich called me. "Shabaz doesn't know if we should trust you, Tommy. Are you going to deliver?"

"Is the deal still on?" I said.

Harold said, "The deal's on."

The day of the vote, both Froelich and Clemens were certain they had the votes. Someone had to be wrong, and it was Clemens. Froelich won by one vote. Ody Fish, who ran Warren Knowles's successful campaign for governor in 1964 and was Republican state party chairman in the 1960s, told a friend, "Froelich could count, and Clemens couldn't." I don't think so. I think somebody lied to Clemens.

However it happened, Froelich was the Speaker, and for the next several years he was destined to be a thorn in the side of Governor Knowles, who was a moderate, especially compared to Froelich and Shabaz.

In my first two terms in the assembly, the friction between Knowles and the leadership in the Republican assembly caucus underscored everything.

Froelich set the tone early. On March 9, 1967, Harold gave a speech to the Kenosha Taxpayers Association.

"For those of you who were under the impression earlier in the year," Harold said, "that all our problems were solved with the election of a Republican governor and a Republican legislature—let me extend my apologies."

Harold continued, "We're still worrying about taxes. We're still concerned about spending, and although divided government—which we experienced for the few past sessions—contributed to our problems in Wisconsin, let me say for the record that one-party control has not miraculously eliminated our problems.

"The budget, as presented by the governor, it is true, calls for no new taxes, and I am happy about that. But the budget is closely hanging by a fine thread, and any additional weight that might be applied in the form of new spending proposals is going to put so much strain on that closely balanced budget that that thread is going to break, and in will pour the deluge of proposal after proposal to spend, spend, spend." Harold concluded, "I believe it's time to stand firm. I, for one, don't want the spenders to get one foot in the door."

I can't emphasize enough that Froelich was not talking about just the Democrats. He and Shabaz were already positioning themselves in opposition to Knowles, the moderate Republican governor. In a speech a month later, in April 1967, to the American Legion Auxiliary in Appleton, Froelich drew a line in the sand.

"It is our feeling that for all too long now," he said, "the legislature has been relegated to a secondary role in Wisconsin government." Harold continued, "Well, things have changed. We have a job to do at Madison, and we're going to do it."

It was clear to anyone paying attention that Knowles and the Republican assembly leadership were headed for a confrontation. It happened, too—a doozy—but it took a couple of years. It was a slow-burning fuse. Budgets are never easy, but my first in the assembly, passed in the summer of 1967, came together without a great deal of acrimony. It was the first billion-dollar budget in state history but pretty well held the line on taxes. The real controversy came at the very end of the session, when Knowles resurrected a highway safety package that had fallen apart in late June and got it in front of the legislature for a vote in late July, at the very end of the session. Knowles had decried the rising death toll on state roads and said the bill was his highest priority. It lost by one vote. At the last minute, John Shabaz—ever the thorn in Knowles's side—switched his vote, sided with the Democrats (as did three other Republicans), and that was that. The second paragraph of the Associated Press story said this: "The stunning, one-vote defeat was the worst setback ever for Knowles as governor."

That fuse I referenced a moment ago had begun to burn.

I had my own controversy to deal with that summer. With the budget finally passed, I had decided to make good on my earlier promise to serve my country—I had planned to enter the JAG Corps but then had been elected to the assembly—by signing up for the National Guard. My unit was the Red Arrow Division, the 732nd Maintenance Battalion of the US Army's 32nd Division. We were sent to Fort Bliss, in Texas, for two months of basic training. It was no fun. I can remember sharing a tent with another guardsman for four nights in the Texas desert. The daytime temperature was over one hundred. Worse, for me, was that Knowles had decided to call a special session of the legislature to make one last attempt to pass a highway safety bill. It would do things like raise the beer-drinking age, toughen drunk-driving laws, increase the size of the state patrol—a big, important bill, and eventually it passed. But I was in Texas and unable to go back for the special session.

I missed all those votes. While that is never a good thing for a legislator—even with an excuse as valid as mine—it might have slipped under the radar except that a colleague of mine in the Republican assembly caucus, James Devitt from Milwaukee, had a strong voting record and thought it would be a good thing if the assembly public information officer, Joe Phillips, put out a press release that detailed the roll call record of the entire assembly. Devitt thought the story would get picked up by the papers—he wasn't wrong—and make it appear that he was hard working and conscientious. He had the fourth-best voting record in the assembly. No surprise, John Shabaz was first. Out of 1,873 roll call votes that year, Shabaz did not miss a single one.

I missed 187 votes. Of course I did, I was in Texas. I wasn't the worst, but I was near the bottom. Devitt—who was later elected to the state senate, where he was convicted of a felony after a campaign contribution controversy—convinced Phillips to really trumpet the numbers. I let Phillips have it when I got back, and we never really got along after that. He wound up writing a letter to the newspapers in which the numbers appeared, but the damage was done. The letter that appeared in the *Wisconsin State Journal* in Madison carried a small headline that read, "Analyzing Assembly Attendance."

Phillips wrote, "While your written account of the report was essentially accurate, it did not elaborate on several factors important to any conclusions which might have been drawn from the report. Assemblyman Tommy Thompson is listed as missing 187 Roll Call votes. In reality, Thompson was absent with leave . . . at which time he was serving his country in the uniform of the National Guard."

That letter may have helped a little, but when the time came for my 1968 re-election campaign, I ran scared. My opponent, Leslie J. Schmidt of Friendship, brought up the missed-votes issue at every opportunity. To combat it I worked as hard as I had two years earlier when I upset Louis Romell.

It meant I was back in Elroy, and back in the district, quite often during the first half of 1968. I was fine with that. Wally Brady, who had been in practice in Elroy since 1947, had invited me to join him in November 1966, just after I was first elected to the assembly. We did general law out of the Elroy office. Fourteen months later, I opened the second office in Oxford.

The real reason I didn't mind coming back to the district was that, by early 1968, I was married, to Sue Ann Mashak. We were from the same part of the state, even had a high school class together, but we met in Madison, in the capitol. It was the fall of 1967 and I was back from National Guard duty in Texas. Sue Ann came to Madison to lobby the legislature for more money for Milwaukee Public Schools, where she was working. She ended up talking to me, and I asked her to lunch. What can I tell you? She was cute. She still is.

Sue Ann was born in Cashton, in Monroe County, but moved with her family to Kendall, six miles from Elroy, when she was three. Her father was a butcher and operated a meat locker in Kendall, and her mother inherited a tavern, the Longbranch, from her grandmother, who, Sue Ann said, taught her to play euchre and dirty clubs. Sue Ann and I were in the same grade through school, but it wasn't until our last year of high school, when the Kendall and Elroy school districts merged, that we had a class together. The new building wasn't constructed yet, but the Kendall students were transported to Elroy for a few classes. Sue Ann claims that, as a consequence, she thought the Elroy kids were stuck up, and maybe we were. We were the big city, twice as big as Kendall. Sue Ann had a trigonometry class in Elroy the first semester of our senior year, but it was second semester, in a literature class, that we were in the same classroom. We didn't really meet then, but six or seven years later, when she was in Madison to try to talk to the legislature, she recognized my name, and we met in the capitol.

Out of high school, Sue Ann decided to attend Viterbo College in La Crosse. She was interested in medicine, becoming a nurse or perhaps even a doctor, but she was told that women would stand a much better chance of getting a job teaching, and so she studied education. Viterbo is a Catholic liberal arts school affiliated with the Franciscan Sisters of Perpetual Adoration. Men weren't admitted until 1971; in 2000, Viterbo acquired university status.

After two years at Viterbo, Sue Ann, as she puts it, "walked across the street" and joined the adjacent convent, where she finished her education and prepared to become a nun. She was there six years and took one-year vows and three-year vows, but when it came time for her final vows, Sue Ann decided, after a great deal of thought, that it was not the life for her. It was a huge decision and a hard one, but as she told me later, she knew by then that she wanted to have children.

Teachers were in demand. Within a week of leaving the convent, Sue Ann was in touch with a friend who worked in administration for the Milwaukee school district, and she was hired two weeks later. Sue Ann was teaching language arts, and her union asked her to lobby the legislature in Madison for more money for Milwaukee teachers. She told me later she felt altogether like a fish out of water that day. Her family was not political. Her mom and dad would make a practice of purposely canceling out each other's votes. To them, that was fun.

I remember the day Sue Ann and I met in October 1967. As I recall it was a Tuesday, about eleven in the morning. In those days, a visitor who wanted to see a legislator sent a note in with a page. Sue Ann had arrived that morning, and the first thing she did was look down a list of the legislators. She recognized my name—mine was the only name she knew—and asked to see me. The assembly had a kind of sitting room off the main chamber, and I remember walking in and seeing her sitting by herself on a long couch. I walked over, introduced myself, sat down, and listened as she told me how much the teachers in Milwaukee needed and deserved better pay.

When she paused, I smiled. "Sue Ann," I said, "I come from a rural district, as you know. Those schools need money, too. Why would I want to send it to Milwaukee?"

Not long after, I visited Milwaukee's inner core and did eventually support state funds for that impoverished district. At the time, however, I made a palms-up gesture with my hands, telling Sue Ann that if I was going to go to bat for teachers, it would be back home. It certainly wasn't an unpleasant exchange. I liked her right away. So I said, "I can't give you the support you're asking for, but how about lunch?"

We went across the street to the Park Motor Inn, and lunch must have gone well, because when I asked her to the UW Homecoming football game, she accepted.

That date was pretty much a disaster. I suppose it was my fault. As a student, I had never been to Homecoming, so I didn't realize that the football game is only a prelude to dinner in a nice restaurant.

The Homecoming game was just a week or two after that first lunch. Sue Ann had taken a day off from school to go shopping and paid a lot of money for a nice gown and shoes. The day of the game she came over from Milwaukee and would spend the night with an aunt who lived in Madison. I took her to the football game at Camp Randall Stadium—we sat with some of my buddies who brought flasks to deal with their perpetual thirst—and we watched the Badgers lose to Northwestern, 17–13. The Badgers didn't win a game that season. You might consider that symbolic of our date. After the game we went to a party at my friend's apartment, where there was more drinking. At some point Sue Ann said, "Aren't we going out to dinner?" I hadn't made a reservation. I kind of shrugged.

"Take me home," Sue Ann said. She was angry.

Sue Ann told me later that she thought she would never speak to me again, but I was persistent. She eventually realized the disastrous date had been ignorance on my part, not malevolence. She hung on to that Homecoming gown, too, and years later our young daughters wore it to play dress-up.

Our subsequent dates went better, well enough that when I proposed marriage—while we were taking in a drive-in movie in Wisconsin Dells, I might add—Sue Ann said yes. We married quietly, not even telling our parents, in a Catholic church in Arcadia, in March 1968. A few months later, on a Sunday afternoon in early June, our folks hosted an open house at the Valley Inn in Elroy to celebrate the marriage. They put an announcement in the local paper: "Everyone is invited to attend. No invitations will be sent." Several hundred people showed up.

In those early days we found a variety of places to live in the Elroy area, sometimes on our own, sometimes bunking with family. I had a tough reelection campaign coming up—I was still haunted by the bad publicity from those missed votes. Sue Ann started teaching again right away. When a teacher died unexpectedly in New Lisbon, school superintendent Herb Juneau asked Sue Ann to take over the class, which she did, for two years, before moving on to a technical college in Mauston. For a time, we lived in an apartment over her mother's bar in Kendall, the one Sue Ann's grandmother, Bertha Kaus, had owned. I never knew Bertha, but Sue Ann recalls that she would sit in a chair by the potbelly stove in the bar. When a customer asked for credit, Frank the bartender would glance at Bertha and she would either nod or shake her head. Sue Ann told me that when she was growing up her grandmother would ask her to be her partner in the regular card games. When they won, her grandmother would give Sue Ann a shot glass of beer.

Sue Ann wanted a family, and that happened when we moved into my dad's old grocery store in Elroy, which had been more or less refashioned into a home. It wasn't very big, and the gas pumps were still in the front yard.

When our first daughter, Kelli, was born, I remember being there, at the Hillsboro Hospital, thirteen miles from Elroy. Sue Ann's recollection is that I was there only for the birth of Jason, our third child and only son. We both agree I missed the birth of our middle child, Tommi, and that it wasn't my fault. It was a Sunday, and there was a Packers game on television. I took Sue Ann to the hospital, where the doctor told me it looked like she wouldn't deliver until the following day. I went home to watch the game. Unbeknownst to me, by halftime they were wheeling Sue Ann into the delivery room. The doctor had left too. Tommi was tiny when she was born. We named her Tommi Noel Thompson. I liked that her initials were TNT, and I'm pleased to say she has lived up to those initials.

I feel like I wasn't a great father to the kids when they were young. I have since apologized, and I continue to. I was gone a lot, to Madison, and on occasional trips having to do with my position in the assembly. When I was home, I was often campaigning. Once they were old enough, the kids became part of that, too, showing up with me at parades, that kind of thing. They didn't much like it, and I doubt any of them will ever run for public office.

Sue Ann should get enormous credit for raising the kids and putting up, as they did, with my absences and all the campaigning. I was politically ambitious. I worked at my law practice too—it brought in around $15,000 in 1971—but I put my heart and soul into my political career, and that came at a financial sacrifice. After outgrowing the old grocery store, we moved into another house in Elroy, which my dad had bought. Once when I was gone on an extended work trip, Sue Ann hired a carpenter friend to add a room to the house. She didn't ask me, and I didn't complain. Another time when I was gone, she had someone put up an elaborate playhouse for the kids in the backyard. I had left suddenly on that trip and Sue Ann wasn't happy. I asked her if the backyard playhouse was my new quarters. She laughed. Still, it wasn't easy. We didn't have a lot of money. And as I said, I was often away.

I thought I was in the fight of my political life in that first reelection campaign. It seemed everywhere I went, the missed-votes issue came up. And even though I had maneuvered successfully to get myself on the Joint Committee on Finance, I think it's fair to say I wasn't heard from a lot in that first term. Joint Finance or not, I was still a freshman, and there were a lot of large personalities in the capitol.

I could take credit for a few things, though. In the spring of 1967 I coauthored a measure that appropriated $100,000 to repair the Montello Dam on the Fox River in my district. The dam forms Buffalo Lake, and the lake also needed major work—drawing down, dredging, and removal of invasive species. We got money for that too.

A year later I was at the Adams County courthouse when the transaction was completed to purchase land near Oxford for a youthful-offenders institution. It had been announced a month earlier, on April 11, 1968, and I got some good press, including this, in the *Wonewoc Reporter*, under the headline "Corrective Institution to Be Constructed": "Assemblyman Tommy Thompson stated today, 'It appears now that a youthful offenders institution, the first of its kind in Wisconsin, is just a step away from becoming a reality.' Thompson reported that the State Building Commission has authorized the release of $60,000 to purchase a 640-acre site in Adams County, where the institution will be constructed. The institution is an $11 million facility."

The publicity may have helped me in my reelection campaign that fall, but the story had, for me personally, a devastating ending a few years later. The institution was a big idea, maybe my first big idea, and big ideas have always motivated me: something big, something new, something exciting. In this case, a facility for just young men, ages eighteen to twenty-four, with an eye toward their rehabilitation—perhaps even including a vocational school on the property—seemed to me like something that could be a model for the rest of the country. I still think it makes sense.

The facility moved forward—there was a groundbreaking in May 1970— and everybody was happy. Its location wouldn't generate safety concerns. It was in rural Wisconsin, and it would provide jobs in an area of the state that needed them. What was not to like? Well, sometime after the groundbreaking, but before the institution was open, Patrick J. Lucey was campaigning for governor—probably in fall of 1970—and his entourage stopped at the site where the youthful-offenders facility was being built, and he threw a fit. That's how the story was later related to me, anyway. Pat—he was a Democrat—got out of his car, looked at this windblown plain in the middle of nowhere, and said, "This is the stupidest place to put a prison that I've ever seen." It was too big and too remote, he said. When he was governor, Lucey said, he would close it down.

He didn't have to close it down, because it never opened. It was finished and scheduled to open in 1972, but Lucey, governor by then, kept that from happening—he just let it sit idle—and in early 1973 he had his new secretary of the Department of Revenue, David Adamany, negotiate a deal with the US Department of Justice to sell the facility to the federal government.

I was going crazy. This was my baby. If the feds got it, the idea of it being a youthful-offenders institution would be scrapped. I did everything I could to fight Adamany and Lucey, but they held the cards. Along with Lucey's election as governor in 1970, the assembly had flipped heavily to the Democrats. I put out a press release that said selling the facility to the federal government was "asinine, ludicrous and foolish." It didn't work. The plan to sell it sailed through the senate and the assembly, where I led the fight against it, and we got trounced two to one. It was a done deal, and even some of my friends voted against me.

The federal prison in Oxford has done fine. It's still operating and it has had some famous residents, including Dan Rostenkowski, an Illinois congressman. It's just that it could have been so much more if the youthful-offenders institution had come to pass. How much more we'll never know.

Pat Lucey and I eventually became friends. When Pat died in 2014, I gave one of the eulogies at his funeral. I think I was the only Republican asked to do so. David Adamany, who after leaving Wisconsin served for fifteen years as president of Wayne State University in Detroit, was at the funeral and I couldn't resist taking a moment to chide him for what happened with the Adams County correctional facility back in the early 1970s. "I've been waiting forty years to get you back," I said, and everybody laughed. David himself passed away in November 2016.

All that was far ahead, of course, when the facility was first announced in 1968. Along with the Montello Dam, I hung my hat on it in my reelection campaign against Leslie Schmidt. I had helped the district get some money for new highway construction, too. I campaigned like I was afraid I was going to lose, which I was. In the end, I surprised myself. I beat Schmidt by better than two to one. It was becoming ever clearer to me that you could make up for a lot—maybe just about anything—if you were willing to work twice as hard as the people against you. And if you work extremely hard, whatever the reason—ambition, fear of failure, to prove the doubters wrong—and then you see results, you begin to believe in yourself. For me, right after the November 1968 election, that belief led me to consider running for Congress.

Richard Nixon was elected president in November 1968—beating Hubert Humphrey of Minnesota—and Nixon named Melvin Laird, the longtime (sixteen years) congressman from Wisconsin's Seventh District, as his secretary of defense, which meant there would be a special election in April to fill Laird's congressional seat. It's a large district, touching more than fifteen counties, with Wausau its biggest city. Dave Obey—he was thirty in 1969 and the assembly minority leader—was running for the Democrats in what had traditionally been a Republican district. I thought I could beat him. But a former television newscaster named Walter John Chilsen—some people called him "the Walter Cronkite of the North"—was a Republican state senator in the district (he lived near Wausau), and he wanted to run against Obey.

Walter John and I met, and he talked me out of running.

He said, "You could run, but you should wait. I've got the support of the party. It's a Republican area, and since I'm from Wausau, I can beat Obey there. You would have trouble doing that."

Walter John concluded, "You stay in the assembly. Then when I decide to retire, I'll support you."

That made sense, and in the end I didn't run for Laird's seat. Of course, Dave Obey turned our plan upside down by upsetting Chilsen. Walter John later admitted he thought he was a shoo-in, and that didn't help. Hubert Humphrey came to Wausau to campaign for Obey. Chilsen was also hurt by the decision of Nixon's Department of Agriculture to limit milk price supports. The announcement came just days before the April election. A Democrat then in the legislature, Bert Grover, later recalled that "the dairy farmers came storming out of their barns to vote for Obey." The election was close, but Obey prevailed, 63,592 to 59,512.

I don't know if Obey knew how close I came to running against him, but in May, a month after the election, he sent me a note: "Now that I am settling in here in Washington, I am writing to express my appreciation for the time we served together in the State Assembly." I suspect he sent notes to many in the assembly. Clearly Obey didn't make many wrong moves as a congressman. When he retired in 2011 he had served more than forty years.

Of course, when Obey went to Washington in 1969, plenty remained to occupy those of us who remained in the legislature, especially those of us on the Joint Committee on Finance. I was reappointed by Harold Froelich, as were the other eight members from the assembly (Joint Finance had nine assemblymen and five senators). My assembly colleagues on Joint Finance included six Republicans: Byron Wackett, who ran a Mobil gas station in Watertown and was the committee chairman; John Shabaz, from New Berlin and the true power on the committee—Wackett deferred to him; Merrill Stalbaum from Waterford; David Martin from Neenah; Russell Olson from Bassett; and Kenneth Merkel from Brookfield, who was a member of the John Birch Society. We were all very conservative. Shabaz set the tone. A *Capital Times* headline from March 1969 read, "Spirit of Joe McCarthy Seems to Pervade Finance Committee." The thing that really iced it for us was that although Froelich had to appoint two assembly Democrats to Joint Finance, one of them, Ron Parys of Milwaukee, was a Democrat in name only. Parys called liberal Democrats "fuzzies"—fuzzy thinkers. Most of the time he voted with us, which gave us an eight-vote majority on the fourteen-member committee. When the Joint Finance Republicans met in caucus, Parys would join us.

Quite often those meetings occurred in a private back dining room of Namio's restaurant in Madison. Joe Namio was a colorful restaurateur who was born in Palermo, Sicily, and came to the United States when he was twelve. He graduated from the now-gone Madison Central High School and operated the Village Bar, near Glenway Golf Course in Madison, before opening Namio's, the South Park Street supper club that became legendary during the thirty-four years Joe ran it. In my early years on Joint Finance we hammered out the state budget in a back room there while his daughters, who were the waitresses, served us steaks and wine. I remember one night—I don't recall if it was first or second term—when we had a split among the eight of us, the seven Republicans and Ron Parys, about a proposal to raise money for highway construction by slightly increasing the fee for an automobile license. I believe it was fifteen dollars and Shabaz wanted it to stay there. Byron Wackett thought we could move it to twenty dollars. We ended up split 4–4, at which point Joe Namio walked into the room to see how we were doing with dinner. Byron explained that there was an impasse. I guess we'd all had enough wine that he asked Joe, "How would you vote?"

Joe said, "I think twenty dollars is too high, but at fifteen, I can see the need to raise it. Why not seventeen fifty?" In the end, that's what we decided on— not that figure exactly, but a compromise. It became known as the Namio amendment.

That was probably my first term. By 1969, and my second term, any tax or fee increases had become a major issue and a point of great acrimony between the assembly leadership, Froelich and Shabaz, and the Republican governor, Warren Knowles.

Knowles and Shabaz didn't get along at all politically. Shabaz simply would not agree to spend any money, and he wasn't pleasant about it. Bill Kraus, a Republican strategist who eventually became a top aide to moderate Republican governor Lee Dreyfus, tells a story of how Paul Hassett, Knowles's chief of staff, approached him sometime in the late 1960s and said, "You're about Shabaz's age. Can you get him off our backs? Take him out for a drink and reason with him."

Kraus and Shabaz toured the watering holes on Capitol Square. The next day, Kraus called Hassett. "I got a hangover and you got nothing," Bill said. Shabaz was not about to compromise, even within his own party.

I got along with Shabaz and learned quite a bit from him. He was formidable, made so by his personality and intellect. He could be mean and sometimes a bully. He could embarrass people. You did not want to get Shabaz mad, especially in those assembly days. He became mellower later in life. Back then, he was tough as nails. In the 1970s, when the Republicans lost the majority in the assembly, Shabaz was minority leader and I was assistant minority leader. We were entitled to two offices. Shabaz was so conservative he wouldn't allow himself a private office. He said it didn't matter what the Democrats did. They could have separate offices. We would not. Shabaz, myself, two secretaries, and two aides shared an office. That was my friend John Shabaz.

The people who fought against him—and at times that included me—invariably ended up respecting him. A notorious "insiders poll" published in 1980 in *Isthmus*, a Madison alternative weekly newspaper, purported to tell what *really* went on in the legislature, and in it Shabaz was called "the monster that haunts the Assembly." That referred to his personal style as much as anything. The same story said there was no more effective lawmaker in the capitol than Shabaz. He read every bill and was a master of parliamentary procedure. There was no one better at keeping things he didn't like from being passed into law. Especially later, it was hard for even his opponents not to respect him, what he stood for, and how he did it. Former governor Tony Earl, a Democrat's Democrat, tears up when you mention Shabaz these days. Tony was invited to deliver a eulogy at John's funeral.

Back in 1969 Shabaz was still in "monster" mode, and the rest of us assembly Republicans followed his lead, especially when it came to taxes. It had been making life miserable for Warren Knowles, and, unbeknown to a lot of people, Knowles considered not running for reelection in 1968. Ody Fish, who ran the Republican Party in the state in those days, talked him into it. Warren won reelection—he beat Bronson La Follette by 53–47 percent—but 1969 was a tough year for him. Knowles had to call out the National Guard that February to deal with disruptive Vietnam War protests on the UW–Madison campus. And the Republican assembly caucus was adamant about not passing the 1 percent sales tax increase that Knowles felt was necessary.

Wisconsin first imposed a sales tax in 1962, a 3 percent tax that targeted specific goods and services, among them household furnishings, cars, jewelry, tobacco (except cigarettes), alcohol, food sold in restaurants, hotel rooms, and tickets for athletic events and entertainment. In 1969, Knowles wanted to raise the rate to 4 percent and make it a general sales tax, with very limited exemptions. As you might guess, it was not popular in our Republican assembly caucus.

So one day, Warren Knowles came and appeared in front of our caucus. His express purpose was to sell the sales tax. I was impressed that he came; I think it was the first time he met with us. Looking back, I think it probably was not his idea. I think Hassett, his top aide, talked him into it. Knowles came in—Hassett was with him—and I can still remember where everyone was sitting. Knowles sat down next to Shabaz and Froelich. I was down at the end of the table. Russ Olson, a farmer from Kenosha County who later became lieutenant governor, was off to one side, under a window.

Knowles gave a passionate presentation about why we needed to increase the sales tax. He thought he could reason with us, which may have been a reasonable assumption but it was dead wrong. You could feel the tension in the room. People were on edge. And when Knowles finished speaking, Russ Olson said, "Governor, can I ask a question?"

Knowles nodded at him.

Russ said, "Not only don't we like this, we think passing it will come back to haunt us. Why is it so necessary to raise the sales tax?"

There was a moment of quiet, and then Warren Knowles exploded. He was on edge, too. I had never seen Knowles lose his temper. He did this time. He slammed his fist on the table.

"That's it!" Knowles said. He began gathering his papers. "If you don't want me to govern, I won't, and I won't run again. I am out of here." He stalked out of the room with Hassett scurrying after him.

We were all stunned. Finally Russ said, "What did I say that was so wrong?"

In the end, Knowles honored his pledge not to run for reelection. But he got his sales tax through, and Pat Lucey, the Democrat candidate, hung it on the Republican legislators and the Republican gubernatorial candidate, Wisconsin Dells businessman Jack Olson, who had been chairman of Richard Nixon's presidential campaign in Wisconsin in 1968. Lucey managed to portray the Republican Party of Wisconsin as tax and spenders! Olson had been doing pretty well a few months before the election, but then he proposed a zero-based budget plan that Knowles ridiculed—pretty soon they weren't speaking—and then Lucey put an ad on television that was enormously effective. It said, "Do you realize the Republicans put a tax on your Christmas tree?"

In the end, we got crushed. Lucey beat Olson, 54–45 percent, and in the assembly we lost twenty seats. It was a disaster. I won against an uninspired opponent, Justin Tarvid, by campaigning as hard as I always did. In December, a few weeks after the 1970 elections, I wrote a letter to a friend of mine, Pat Hahn, who had moved to California. The letter summed up what happened: "I am sorry it has taken me so long to write you, but I have been conducting a very vigorous campaign for reelection. I was reelected, but can't say the same for many of my colleagues in the Republican Party, as we certainly took a shellacking. This happens to be the major defeat suffered by the Republican Party in Wisconsin history. We will have a minority of thirty-three Republicans in the Assembly."

We were destined to remain in the minority for more than two decades. In 1973 Shabaz became minority leader of the assembly and I became assistant minority leader. As I noted earlier, Shabaz decreed that we would share an office. I had just survived, in fall 1972, what I thought would be a tough election that pitted me—due to redistricting—against another incumbent member of the assembly, Democrat Robert M. Thompson. In 1972 my old district of Adams, Marquette, and Juneau counties was expanded into the Seventy-ninth Assembly District. In the old district, which was strictly rural, Mauston was the largest city, maybe four thousand people. I had cemented the district quite nicely. I worked it very hard. People knew and liked me. The new district added parts of Sauk and Columbia counties that included Wisconsin Dells and Portage. Robert Thompson had represented Portage in his old assembly district and he was a popular, conservative Democrat. The new district was split pretty evenly between people in the old Bob Thompson district and people from my old district. I was worried about Portage, and he had done some things for the Dells community. There were Republicans in those areas who supported him. Then there was the fact that our last names were the same. To makes things even more complicated, his nickname was Tommy!

I ran scared, which meant I ran hard, and to my surprise, I won big—12,027 to 7,519.

I became the assembly's assistant minority leader in 1973 and held that post for eight years, until Shabaz was appointed a federal judge in 1981 by President

Ronald Reagan—an interesting story that I will relate momentarily—and I became minority leader.

There were perks to those leadership positions, even as assistant minority leader. One night in May 1976, Sue Ann and I were invited to the White House for a reception in honor of King Hussein of Jordan and his wife, Alia. Gerald Ford had become president with the resignation of Richard Nixon, and Ford was looking at a tough campaign in 1976. He was facing a serious primary challenge from Ronald Reagan. The state of Wisconsin was in play, which is why I got asked to the White House.

Sue Ann and I were excited and a little nervous. I had to rent a tuxedo—we still didn't have much money—and Sue Ann had been told that whatever she did, she needed to wear long white gloves to a White House dinner. Where do you buy long white gloves in Elroy? Sue Ann wound up borrowing a pair from my mother.

We took a cab from our hotel in Washington to the White House. It's funny in hindsight, our yellow cab pulling up in the midst of all these black and white stretch limousines. Once you're inside, you wait in line and the woman is escorted by a service officer, usually a marine, and the man walks in immediately behind them. We walked in and the first thing Sue Ann noticed was that there wasn't another woman in the room wearing long white gloves. She was mortified. We began circulating on the perimeter of the room and as soon as she got the chance, Sue Ann slipped the gloves off and put them in the base of a potted plant.

When we started circulating for real, of course we didn't know anybody. I saw a man and woman standing off by themselves, and figured they didn't know anybody either. I kind of steered Sue Ann toward them, and I stuck out my hand. "I'm Tommy Thompson," I said. "Assistant minority leader of the Wisconsin assembly." The man was gracious, he shook my hand.

"What's your name and what do you do?" I said.

"I'm David Rockefeller," he said. "I'm president of the Chase Manhattan Bank."

I felt a little foolish, but I recovered. It ended up being a wonderful evening. It is White House protocol to split up husbands and wives for the dinner seating, and Sue Ann was seated between Henry Kissinger and Donald Rumsfeld. She told me Kissinger was a little hard to understand at first, but very friendly. She made a connection with Rumsfeld because he talked about owning some property in Wisconsin.

Sue Ann was always great in those situations, because she never tried to be anyone but herself. Years later, in May 1990, toward the end of my first term as governor, we were invited to a White House dinner at which the guest of honor was Soviet president Mikhail Gorbachev. I was the only governor invited. As was custom, we were split up for dinner. I found myself at a table with, among others, *Washington Post* publisher Donald Graham and Secretary of State James Baker. I have to admit I was thinking about how it was all pretty remarkable for a kid from Elroy, and about then I thought to look around to see where Sue Ann was sitting. They were just introducing Gorbachev. I glanced over at the Soviet president, and there was Sue Ann, seated at his table. I couldn't believe it. George H. W. Bush's wife, Barbara, was at that table, too. Sue Ann was seated next to the actor Morgan Freeman, but she got a chance to talk to the Soviet president. He asked her about teaching in Elroy, and Sue Ann was able to say she had visited a series of Russian schools in the late 1980s. That surprised Gorbachev. "What did you think?" he asked. Sue Ann had not been impressed, but she wasn't going to say that. "I was treated very graciously," she said. At the end of the dinner, Sue Ann passed a menu around her table and asked everyone to sign, which they did, happily.

Sue Ann likes to talk about having that menu signed, but she also tells a story about what happened after our first White House dinner, the one in 1976. The next morning, we woke up in our hotel and Sue Ann realized that the long white gloves she had put in the potted plant belonged to my mother. She called the White House. Would it be OK if she came back and collected her gloves from the plant? There was a brief silence on the other end, and she was put on hold. We laughed later thinking about the conversation we weren't hearing. Gloves? A potted plant? Who is calling? In any case, the potted plants—and the gloves—were gone. "Maybe they took them to the Smithsonian," Sue Ann said.

In 1978 I decided I wanted to try to go to Washington on a more permanent basis. I had won reelection to the assembly by a huge margin that November. My opponent, George Lytle, ran a strange campaign in which he basically refused to talk to reporters or appear on television or radio programs. If a reporter called him, he wouldn't discuss the race. Finally a reporter for the *Portage Daily Register* approached him in person and asked, essentially, what was going on. Lytle said, "The telephone doesn't bring people together." It turned out his unorthodox campaign brought people together—for me. I received over twelve thousand votes, and Lytle got fewer than four thousand. I was feeling confident, and then, just a month after the election, Bill Steiger, the congressman from Wisconsin's Sixth District, suffered a fatal heart attack in Washington. He was forty. There was a special election to fill his congressional seat and I decided to take a shot. In hindsight, I probably shouldn't have run. It's a big district, and my home in Juneau County was out on the edge of it, away from where most of the votes were, in Oshkosh, Manitowoc, and Sheboygan. But I figured that if I outworked everyone, as I always did, I could win. So I ran in what quickly became a very crowded field. There were seven of us in the Republican primary. I worked hard but it was a miserable campaign from a physical standpoint, traveling around that big district in the snow and ice. In the end, I finished second. Tom Petri, a Republican in the state senate, won the primary, and eventually won the seat in a close general election. I took some lessons from my loss about the need for grassroots organization, because in a race contested over a large geographic area, you can't do it alone, no matter how hard you work.

As I noted earlier, another Wisconsin Republican got a call from Washington during my assembly years, and it had the effect of reinvigorating my political career. When Ronald Reagan was elected president in 1980, there was a federal judgeship open in the Western District of Wisconsin. Presidents fill those vacancies, and John Shabaz, my friend, mentor, and occasional foe—Shabaz's personal style in those days meant he occasionally clashed with everyone—decided he wanted it.

A lot of people were surprised that Shabaz would put his name out for a federal judgeship, but I was not. I thought I knew what was going on, and it had to do with fathers and sons—in particular, demanding fathers and their sons, a subject I knew something about. John's dad, Cyrus Shabaz, was an attorney who had always wanted his son to join him in the practice of law. That happened—Cyrus and John shared offices in New Berlin—but of course John won his assembly seat and devoted much of his time to state government. John told me that his father always wanted him to be a lawyer-lawyer, as opposed to a legislator-lawyer, to the extent that he insisted John pay half the law office expenses even though he was in Madison much of the time. John told me that for a time he had to take work serving summonses for other attorneys to make ends meet. When he complained, Cyrus said, "You need to make it on your own."

My impression was that John respected his father but felt frustrated that Cyrus didn't appreciate what John was doing in Madison. Cyrus just didn't see it as a high calling, no matter that John was getting his name in the newspapers all the time. I don't believe Cyrus ever came to visit his son in the capitol. Maybe at his swearing-in, but I'm not sure. I never met Cyrus. So John always felt he had not measured up to what his father thought he should be. By 1981, and Reagan's inauguration, Cyrus Shabaz had passed away, and I believe John felt an appointment to the federal judiciary would validate him in his late father's eyes.

Even though Reagan was a Republican, it wasn't going to be easy to get Shabaz the appointment. In 1979 Wisconsin's two US senators, William Proxmire and Gaylord Nelson, had established the first Wisconsin Federal Judicial Nominating Commission, with a goal of taking politics out of the appointments of federal judges. It was a noble goal, but hardly realistic. You might as well try to take the politics out of politics. Those of us who were helping Shabaz met in the assembly office he and I shared and tried to figure out how we could get him enough votes from the commission. We had a chance because Bob Kasten, a Republican, had defeated Nelson in the same election that won Reagan the presidency. The way the commission was set up, Kasten appointed seven members. Proxmire appointed three, the State Bar appointed three, and the last member was the dean of the UW–Madison Law School.

Democrats had issues with Shabaz, but he was also highly respected for his intellect and work ethic. We convinced all the Kasten members to support him. That got him the most votes, if not a clear majority—the non-Kasten members of the commission announced themselves aghast at the clearly political bloc voting for Shabaz—and Kasten recommended him to the president. Reagan nominated him, and Shabaz was confirmed as a federal judge in January 1982.

I think John turned out to be a wonderful judge. I know there are certain criminal defense attorneys and their clients who would disagree. He gave tough sentences. But right from the start he began clearing up a long backlog of cases in the district, and the civil law attorneys who had feared him came to respect both how fast they could get their clients to court and how well versed the judge was in the law. During the infamous, interminable O. J. Simpson case, someone said that if Shabaz had been the judge, it would have been over in a month and the lawyers would have been in jail. Shabaz did not put up with shenanigans, and he also read all the briefs in a case, something not all judges routinely do. He worked hard. And, to a degree, I think he mellowed. He had a loving second marriage with his wife Patty. John was profiled in *Madison Magazine* a few years after he became a judge, and near the end of the interview he handed the writer a crumpled note from inside his desk in the courthouse. It contained three words: patience, understanding, and compassion. "I keep the note here to remind me," John said. "I sometimes don't remember as well as I should, I suppose." He was trying.

One other thing struck me in that profile. It mentioned that at a small celebratory dinner after Reagan called John to say he was nominating him, there was a quiet moment in which John said, "I just wish my father could have been here with me today."

A few years later, when I was elected governor for the first time, I had a similar feeling. My own father had been demanding; he seemed to expect so much more of me than of anyone else. As I got older, I realized it was his way of helping me succeed, but it led to some tough times and tough words between us. I recognize that is not unusual in families.

On the night of April 16, 1971—it was a Friday—I drove home to Elroy after working that day in my law offices in Oxford and Mauston. When I passed my parents' house, the home I was born in, I saw Dr. Roy Balder's car in front and just had a feeling that something was terribly wrong.

My father, Allan Thompson, had recently undergone nine hours of surgery at Madison General Hospital to remove a blood clot and have the varicose veins stripped from his legs. He had never paid attention to his health and it caught up with him. He always did the opposite of what the doctors said. After the surgery the doctors urged him to consider a vegetarian diet. He may have considered it, but that Friday evening he went out to the Elroy American Legion Hall and ate a bunch of fried smelt and french fries. I'm sure he was smoking. When he came home he suffered a heart attack. It must not have been long before I arrived on the scene.

I parked and ran in. My father was lying on the bedroom floor, gasping for breath. Dr. Balder was preparing a hypodermic, and I remember taking my father's head in my hands and telling him to breathe. My mother was standing beside us. We were both crying. Dr. Balder gave him two hypos right in the chest, but he never regained consciousness. He was sixty-two.

My father was buried in the Elroy cemetery on April 20, 1971. I can remember the day he died like yesterday. Even though we had difficult times, the fact of the matter is he loved me dearly, and I loved him, too. He wanted the best for me, and it led him to push me. It would have been great if he had been able to see me elected governor.

4

When John Shabaz joined the federal judiciary, the Republican assembly caucus needed a new minority leader. I ran and won. I wanted very much to be minority leader. Actually, I wanted to be Speaker, but that required getting enough Republicans elected to have a majority in the assembly. That became a goal of mine.

In the meantime, I loved being minority leader. First of all, Shabaz was gone. I think I have made plain how much I respected him, but his personality was so dominant that it was hard for anyone else in his orbit to feel able to make a significant contribution. His absence allowed me to show what I could do. And the post itself—minority leader—gave me the chance to make decisions for the minority. I learned how to lead and persuade members of the caucus, and I had the opportunity to reward my allies with key committee appointments, further building alliances.

Even though people called me a breath of fresh air after Shabaz—I was not as conservative, combative, or intractable as John—I pretty quickly got the moniker "Dr. No" for my ability to keep the Democrats from racing their bills into law. My politics weren't nearly as antigovernment as Shabaz's had been, but I needed to show the Democrat leadership, Tom Loftus and Ed Jackamonis, that they still had Republican opposition. I took a lesson from Shabaz and basically memorized the rules of parliamentary procedure. I knew those rules better than anyone in the assembly. I think in the end I knew them as well as Shabaz did.

I became the amendment king. I had a sheet of amendments, and I would kill a bill by writing up amendments, right on the assembly floor. They seldom use floor amendments anymore. I used to have floor amendments on everything. It meant they always had to deal with me, because I was always figuring out ways to sidetrack their legislation.

The difference, I suppose, was that they *could* deal with me, at least to some degree. When Shabaz was around, any disagreement was liable to turn into an all-out war. I could talk to the other side.

My politics had changed a bit by then. During my first two terms in the assembly, my views were closely aligned with the highly conservative agenda promoted by Shabaz and Harold Froelich. But by the early 1970s, I had figured out that being for state aid to schools was not a bad thing. I was from a poor district; Shabaz and Froelich were not. Elroy could not survive without school aid. The whole district—Adams, Marquette, and Juneau counties—was among the poorest in the state. My views were evolving. I realized government could perform a service. I probably would not have seen that—would not have grown as I did—if I had come from a more affluent county. I could see the need for school aid and highway and transportation aids. We were getting two-thirds of our money for schools from the State of Wisconsin. My views had to grow.

Being minority leader helped with that, too. To build the Republican majority I wanted in the assembly, I needed to make sure the Republicans who were already in office got themselves reelected. That required that they take care of their districts. I told them they needed to get back to the district at least once a week, travel around, let people see them. They needed to write letters and issue press releases. I told them that, a few days after every election, I used to write letters of appreciation to the county clerks and radio stations in my district, the ones I called for the early returns on election night. In November 1974, I wrote a letter to Natalie Sampson, the Columbia county clerk, that began, "Dear Natalie, Now that the election is over and the dust is beginning to settle, I wanted to write and thank you for your patience on Tuesday and for telling me the updated returns as they became available. I realize that my persistent calls may have complicated your procedures during a busy time." People in the district appreciate little touches like that.

I told my caucus that I really didn't care what they did while they were in Madison, but that was true only up to a point. There was one Republican assemblyman—I won't name him—who was partying on a nightly basis. I told him, "It's going to get back to your district." He said, "My district loves me." Not enough to reelect him once the stories got back, as it turned out.

I was building a base. I knew that when running for statewide office it would serve me well. All of those legislators who were campaigning back in their districts would also be campaigning for me. Meanwhile, I needed to continue as minority leader. In 1978, when Lee Sherman Dreyfus, a maverick Republican and chancellor of the University of Wisconsin–Stevens Point, was elected governor, people assumed that Steve Gunderson, a Republican assemblyman favored by Dreyfus, would run for minority leader. Steve—who eventually ran successfully for Congress—came to me and said, "I am not going to run for minority leader. But I would appreciate you supporting the governor."

I liked Gunderson—we're friends to this day—and I liked and supported Dreyfus. I got along with the Dreyfus people and we grew to trust each other and work together over time.

I can still remember Dreyfus calling me into his office and telling me he wasn't going to run for reelection in 1982. I was surprised, and the first thing I said was, "Governor, what can we do to change your mind?"

Lee said, "My mind is made up. I am way beyond reconsidering." He then said he would appreciate it if I was by his side when he made his public announcement.

Dreyfus, over time, gave a number of reasons for not seeking reelection. Most people believed he was weary of battling the Democrats in the legislature, that he didn't enjoy being in office and governing as much as he had enjoyed traveling the state campaigning in his signature red vest. But he actually enjoyed being governor more than everyone thought. He liked meeting people, being a cheerleader and goodwill ambassador for Wisconsin. He was very good at it— red vest and all.

The real reason Lee didn't run in 1982, one he never made public, was that his wife, Joyce, had not enjoyed being the state's First Lady and was strongly against another term. They had been bothered repeatedly by supporters of Jack Pickens, a convicted sex offender who had some kind of eerie hold over his followers. They would show up at the Governor's Mansion and elsewhere, proclaiming Pickens's innocence and acting strange. They were vaguely threatening and Joyce couldn't stand them. At the same time, word came to Lee that the top job at Sentry Insurance was waiting for him if he wanted it. He told friends later that the decision not to run was an easy one.

The same couldn't be said for me. When Dreyfus opted out, I felt I should run for governor. In May of 1982 the *Wisconsin State Journal* did a straw poll of its readers asking who they wanted to see as governor. It drew more than five hundred responses. Jim Wood, a Democrat who worked for Pat Lucey when Lucey was governor, led with 181 votes. But I was second, with 134. A second Democrat, Tony Earl, an attorney who had headed the Department of Natural Resources, was third.

I wanted to run for governor. I was ambitious and thought I could win. In the end, a long talk with a good friend, Jim Klauser, led me to reconsider. By that time, 1982, I had known Klauser for fifteen years. When I was a freshman legislator in 1967, Klauser was a young lawyer working on a project in the legislature. We met each other then, but didn't really spend much time together. Over the next many years, we got to know each other a little better, came to respect one another, and by the time I became minority leader in the assembly Jim was chief of staff for the senate Republicans. We worked closely together. I quickly realized that the senate Republicans—people like Clifford "Tiny" Krueger and Gerald Lorge—trusted Klauser completely and relied on him to a great extent. He devised their plans and ran the senate. If I had a question for the senate leadership, they would say, "Talk to Klauser. He'll straighten it out." He had a complete mandate. In my dealing with him it was evident he was not only very bright, he knew politics.

The day Dreyfus officially announced he was not running for reelection, in spring 1982, Jim and I talked in my assembly office. He was a lobbyist by then, with big clients—Exxon, Union Carbide, the Minnesota Twins. I was generally probusiness, so he never had to lobby me very hard.

"No Republican is going to be elected governor in 1982," Jim said, when I told him I wanted to run. "Position yourself for 1986," he said, and in the end, that's what I decided to do.

When Earl beat the Republican candidate, businessman Terry Kohler, in November 1982, I had my eye on 1986, but what I said publicly, what I pledged I would do, was raise the number of Republican seats in the assembly in the 1984 election. We trailed the Democrats, 59–40. I pretty much said, early on, that if we couldn't raise that number in 1984, I wouldn't run for governor in 1986. People called it a gamble. Earl, the new Democratic governor, and the new assembly Speaker, Tom Loftus, said I was overreaching. They thought I would fail to get more seats and then be faced with either not running for governor or essentially going back on my earlier promise. I knew it wasn't going to be easy. The Republican Party was more inclined to give money to senate candidates. I was on my own, looking at two years of traveling the state to raise money and recruit assembly candidates. What kept me going was knowing that if I did succeed, if I raised the Republican numbers in the assembly, my colleagues there would be devoted to me and, once I was running for governor, would help me capitalize on my grassroots support in all those counties and towns I had visited over the preceding two years. It would be a gamble, but if I secured the seats in 1984, the potential was there for an even bigger win two years later.

I wasn't totally on my own when I began touring the state. I had a team of three women helping me. They were Diane Harmelink, who was chief of staff of my assembly office; Barbie Benson, from Portage, finance chairman of the Republican Party of Wisconsin and a flamboyant character; and Ave Bie, who had run the Governor's Mansion under Dreyfus and whom I recruited to direct the Republican assembly caucus when Dreyfus decided not to run again. Ave was the daughter of Helen Bie, a longtime Republican Party activist who had worked for the Dreyfus campaign and cochaired a couple of Reagan campaigns in the state. These three extraordinary women helped me organize the state.

The four of us spent more than a year making almost weekly trips—we would generally leave on a Thursday—to the farthest reaches of Wisconsin. Barbie would usually land a day ahead, and then Ave, Diane, and I would drive up together. Ave usually drove while I read newspapers or went through paperwork. No place was too far away, no function too small. We would try to combine a couple of events on a far northern swing. Early on, I wondered how Barbie would play up north to an audience of farmers and lumberjacks. She always dressed like she was going to the opera, or maybe the Kentucky Derby. High heels and big hats. A man named Butch Johnson had organized an event in Hayward, and he had his doubts about Barbie.

"If you bring that woman with the big hat in here," Butch said, "I'm going to disown you."

Barbie walked into that room full of flannel, and inside of five minutes, everyone loved her. She had a contagious enthusiasm.

We were raising money, and I developed an eye for candidates. If I could get a potential assembly candidate one on one, I could usually get them onboard.

Ave and Diane would follow up, helping them develop a plan for their campaign. We even put together teams that would be ready to act in the event of a close race and a recount. By early 1984 I had a hunch we were going to do pretty well come November. The assembly numbers were 59–39 at that point, with a vacancy in a Republican-leaning seat.

The 1984 state Republican convention was held at the Americana Resort in Lake Geneva in early June. All the talk was about who was going to run for governor in two years. I didn't deny it was on my radar, but I continued to stress the importance of the assembly races. I spoke to the convention, and the *Wisconsin State Journal* noted that I "brought nearly 1,000 to their feet with a rousing speech condemning Democrats and urging a legislative push."

State Journal political reporter Tom Still cornered me afterward, and I said again that any run for governor on my part depended on adding Republican seats in the assembly.

"If the Republican Party doesn't make gains in 1984," I said, "with all we've got going for us, then I will have to reconsider my plans for 1986."

Two months later, at the Republican National Convention in Dallas, I said it again. By that time, there was some speculation that Tony Earl wouldn't run for reelection and would instead run for the US Senate against Bob Kasten, whose term was up in 1986. I said that whether Earl was in or out (in the end, he ran again for governor) would not influence my decision about running; how we did in the assembly would. If I increased the Republican seats, it would be an indication that I knew what I was talking about in politics, that I was developing a statewide brand, and that the Republicans were coming back. I said it was also important for Reagan to carry Wisconsin in his run for reelection.

Election night came, and we added eight Republican seats to the Wisconsin assembly, putting the numbers at 52–47 for the Democrats. Reagan carried the state easily, as well. It was both a great victory and vindication for me. People began paying attention. A week or so after the election, a group of journalists called MORE (Madison Organization of Reporters and Editors) had a forum in Madison and invited two former governors, Lee Dreyfus and Pat Lucey, to share the platform. Dreyfus went out of his way to praise me.

He said, "I think the most underreported and underestimated part of the election in this state was the role of Tommy Thompson in bringing change to the assembly."

Dreyfus mentioned that a *Milwaukee Journal* political reporter had written a column over the summer essentially writing me off as a potential candidate for governor.

"I don't know if it's a matter of bias on the part of the capitol press corps," he said. A number of capitol reporters were in his audience. He continued, "Only you can answer that. But Tommy may be one of the best political engineers that has moved into my party in recent years."

Dreyfus concluded, "I am not endorsing anyone. I'm simply saying Tommy Thompson has not been given credit for being the political technician and engineer he really is."

Some weeks later, in early 1985, I got a telephone call from Terry Kohler, who had run and lost to Tony Earl in 1982. Terry and I liked each other. I knew he appreciated that I had stayed out of the race in 1982 and instead worked hard for his campaign. Now Terry was asking if I would meet him and his wife, Mary, for lunch at the Madison Club.

Shortly after we were seated for lunch, Terry looked me in the eye and said, "You're going to be the next governor."

I was flattered, and almost certainly planning to run—after twenty years in the assembly, it was time, everything was lining up for me to run—but I think my immediate response to Terry was to say I thought I could get a Republican majority in the assembly in 1986.

Terry said he had the results of a poll he wanted to show me. The numbers were very bad for Tony Earl in key performance areas like jobs, taxes, and business development.

"Tony Earl can't win," Kohler said. "Right now his negatives are so high, that whoever runs against him will be governor of the state of Wisconsin."

I said, "I don't put much stock in polls, Terry." I remembered that when Dreyfus first announced for governor, a poll to determine his name recognition came in at 3 percent.

"I do," Kohler said. "Tony Earl can't win. I am not going to run again. I will support you."

That was a big moment, the former candidate saying he would back me. The next important date on the calendar was in June, for the state Republican Party convention in Cable. My grassroots team—largely Diane Harmelink and Ave Bie—started cranking up, working out of Diane's place in the Camelot apartments in Madison. We still didn't have any money. They put together hundreds of handmade Thompson for Governor signs, pasting and stapling into the night, and we took them up to Cable and had a successful convention. At that point the viable candidates seemed to be only me and George Watts, who owned a retail store and tea shop in Milwaukee and had some money. His signs were professionally printed. But the convention buzz was about me. Tom Still, on hand again for the *State Journal*, wrote that I "earned loud applause at virtually every turn on the convention floor." I wonder if he saw Diane and Ave and a few kids from our campaign running up and down the aisles at the end of the convention, gathering all the handmade signs so we could use them again.

Money would continue to be an issue. I hadn't really been able to tap into the Milwaukee area, and so that fall we decided to have an event in the city to coincide with my birthday, November 19. It is important to note that by then another, possibly formidable, candidate had surfaced. In September, Dane County executive Jonathan Barry announced that he was leaving the Democratic Party. The following month, he became a Republican. He hadn't announced for governor—neither had I, officially—but there was a perception in some quarters that Barry, who was good looking, articulate, and polished, might be a great gift to Wisconsin Republicans and just the guy to head the statewide ticket in 1986. I didn't agree. I knew that in the past few years when I had been making myself the face of the Republican Party in the state, Jonathan Barry was a Democrat, attacking Republicans. I wasn't as worried about him as some, though he was certainly on my radar.

Barry's presence was another reason for me to introduce myself to the establishment Republicans in Milwaukee. My friend Fred Luber, owner of the Super Steel manufacturing company, helped us organize a "birthday party" at the Grain Exchange, a majestic, ten-thousand-square-foot room in the Mackie Building downtown. Fred packed the place. There was just one problem. There was no contribution required to attend. We were throwing a fundraiser that would raise no funds and, instead, cost us money we didn't have.

Fred said, "Tommy, nobody is going to pay to come to your birthday party. They don't know you here."

The evening went well, and my speech drew rousing applause. "Now I can go raise money," Fred said later. "They heard you speak and were impressed."

We began to have events in other areas of the state, where all the travel I had done and the network I had built really paid dividends. One early event was in the central Wisconsin village of Port Edwards, in Wood County. It was hosted by my good friends Gary and Kathy Vanatta (Kathy later became chair of the Wood County Republican Party). Again, there was no set contribution. The understanding was that I would speak, and if people wanted to donate, they could. I think there were a hundred people packed into the Vanattas' house. None of them really knew me, but I spoke, and I left with $5,615. I had never raised that much money. It was an indication that what I was saying was resonating with people. That was a big night for me. It gave me confidence I could be successful.

Around that time—December 1985—Kenyon Kies, who was managing director of the Wisconsin Utilities Association, had a holiday party at his office in downtown Madison, and across the room I spotted Jim Klauser, who had encouraged me to forgo a run for governor in 1982 and position myself for 1986. At that moment there was probably no one in Wisconsin whose political abilities I respected more.

I waited until I saw Jim walk into the kitchen to refresh his drink. I followed him.

"Jim?"

"Yeah, Tommy."

"I'm running for governor, and I need your help."

"Tommy," Jim said. "You don't want to run."

What Jim was really saying was that he didn't want to get involved in another political campaign. His lobbying business was becoming very successful. He had just helped push through an important bill for Exxon, and new clients were knocking on his door. Jim was tired, looking at even more work, and felt the last thing he needed was to sign on to my run for governor.

I knew all that, but I also knew I needed him. We had received a report the first week of December from Brian Sweeney, a Republican campaign consultant, essentially an analysis of what my campaign for governor needed to be successful, and his top recommendation was that it needed to be run more professionally.

That evening in Kies's office, I said, "Yes, Jim, I am running." I said again I needed his help.

Klauser began to list the reasons why he couldn't help, and I stopped him. "Think about it over Christmas. I know I can win, but I can't win without you."

In early January, Klauser came to see me in my assembly office. "I've made my decision," he said. "I am going to support you. I think you can win. What do you want me to do?"

I said, "I want you to run my campaign."

"I am not going to run the campaign, Tommy. I don't have time."

Instead of pushing him, I figured it would be better to just get him onboard in some capacity. If that happened, knowing Klauser, he might end up running things anyway.

I said, "You know what I would really like you to do? Make damn sure I don't go into debt."

I knew that would resonate with Jim. He had talked to me about Jack Stein-hilber, who ran in the primary for Bill Steiger's congressional seat—the one Petri won and I finished second—and Jack had been caught up in the race and found himself something like $35,000 in debt when it was over.

I told Klauser, "I don't have any money. Very few assets. I'm putting it all on the line with this race. I won't have the assembly seat anymore. I won't have much of a law practice, after spending a year campaigning. If I'm in debt, I don't know how I will ever pay it off. I've got three kids. They're my first responsibility. I can't go into debt."

Klauser nodded. "OK, that's my job."

Jim was onboard.

He and his wife, Shirley, were in my assembly office the morning I made the official announcement of my candidacy. Jim has said since that I was nervous, but I think it was more that I was excited. It was April 6, 1986. I was practicing the speech in my office. Marlene Cummings, who later became my secretary of regulation and licensing, introduced me on the assembly floor at the capitol. I gave my speech and then I was off on a whirlwind two-day tour of the state.

That first day, after the announcement, we hit Mauston, La Crosse, and Milwaukee and wound up at Cliff and Ceil's, a restaurant and ballroom in Green Bay that has since closed. A group of builders—builders were among my earliest supporters—was meeting there that night. The next day I was in Rhinelander, Wausau, Superior, Eau Claire, and finally back in Madison, for a rally of my supporters at the Badger Bowl.

It was a great two days. I enjoyed it and fed off the energy of the people who came to see me. I was an official candidate for governor. We had crisscrossed the state in those two days, and that would continue. Occasionally a private plane would be made available for the campaign, but more often we drove, and therein lies a tale.

Back in December, I had received a letter that meant a lot to me at the time and later had a greater impact on the campaign than anyone could have then known.

It was written by John Tries, president of the Milwaukee Police Supervisors Organization. He was writing to tell me his organization was supporting me.

"Our organization has never given its endorsement to any candidate in the past," Tries wrote. "We are extremely impressed with your past accomplishments and your plans for the future."

I was grateful, and Tries was to become an important part of that first run for governor. John was a big, tough guy, a Milwaukee police sergeant who was a native of Austria. He had recently injured his back to the extent that he went on disability from his police job. As I remember it, he was tossing his riot gear in the trunk of his car, moved the wrong way, and ripped some vertebrae in his back. In any case, he wasn't working, and he said, "I've really got nothing else to do. I will be your driver."

I said, "You're kidding me."

"No," John said. "I want to help you win."

He helped, all right. I had a 1984 Buick with maybe twenty-five thousand miles on it when we started the campaign. It was the only asset I had that was paid for. By the end of the campaign it had over two hundred thousand miles on it. John put most of those miles on that Buick, and I read or slept in the seat next to him. He was a warrior.

He was also fun to travel with. John liked Jimmy Buffett songs, and there is a Buffett lyric that describes "good days, bad days and going half mad days." That's what a campaign is like. I recall we arrived late one night at a motel in Sheboygan—we always slept in one room with two beds to save money—and John was checking us in, using my credit card. I came shuffling in as they were finishing up.

"Who are you?" the desk clerk asked.

"I'm Tommy Thompson."

The desk clerk looked at John, pointed at me, and said to John, "Do you know his name is on your credit card?"

Another time, in Racine, the campaign had booked us into a terrible hotel that was located above a tavern. A band was playing and we couldn't sleep. There was no question of going somewhere else—there wasn't money for that. So we got through the night, and in the morning, when John was taking a shower, the bathroom ceiling collapsed. Everything, including John, was covered with plaster.

I think John's favorite moment in the whole campaign came in a motel room in Waupun when he noticed a little laminated card next to the phone that said, "Please do not pick up this receiver unless it rings." I don't know what it meant unless they didn't allow outgoing calls. John thought it was the funniest thing he had ever seen. Don't pick up the phone unless it rings! John took the card with him when we left and kept it with him in his wallet until the day he died, which came too early, in 2006. John was just sixty and had battled some health problems. I liked and respected John Tries enough that once I was elected governor I appointed him secretary of the Department of Employment Relations. You log the kind of miles together in a campaign together that we did, and you feel a kinship. John's memorial was at Turner Hall in Milwaukee. They served Beck's, his favorite beer, and played Jimmy Buffett songs.

While John and I were bouncing around the state, we also managed to get a small campaign office open in Madison. Jerry Mullins was a businessman who owned quite a bit of property in downtown Madison, including the Park Motor Inn, later the Inn on the Park. He didn't want to contribute to my campaign, but he liked the idea of a Republican governor. He said there was a basement office in a building adjacent to the hotel that we could use if we cleaned it up. It took some cleaning. We didn't have any kind of storefront presence—you entered from a side door—but the place had its advantages. Ave Bie and Diane Harmelink could walk across the street from the capitol on their lunch hours or after work, and it was also close to Jim Klauser's law office. At first Klauser stopped by once a week or so to check the books, but then, as I had hoped might happen, he got more involved despite himself.

One spring day—it was probably late April—we were both in the campaign office one noon when Jim suggested we go next door to the Park Hotel coffee shop for a hamburger. After we ordered, Jim said he thought the campaign needed to bite the bullet and do some heavy spending on advertising leading up to the state Republican convention in Milwaukee in early June. He said we had around $100,000 on hand.

"How much do you want to spend?" I said.

"All of it," Jim said.

I'm sure I gave him a look. Klauser explained that he felt we needed to win the straw poll at the convention. Despite my statewide grassroots efforts over the past several years, some of the big-money Republicans, the country club Republicans, were either backing Jonathan Barry outright or taking a wait-and-see position. Jim felt a big win for us at the convention would pop Barry's balloon. And if we won—even though the straw poll was not a formal endorsement—money would not be an issue. We'd be able to raise money. If we lost, well, at least we had given it our best shot.

We didn't lose. We spent all but a few hundred bucks on a radio and TV blitz, and even though some party regulars tried to sabotage me—they moved the straw poll to Sunday, because some of my rural supporters had to leave Saturday night—we won big. I got 62 percent in the straw poll. Barry got 20. Many of our people stayed an extra day. There was a backlash against the effort to stack the vote against me.

The radio and TV campaign helped, too, but Klauser was not happy with the advertising firm we were using. I found that out a short time later, after giving a speech at the La Crosse Club. I remember a couple of things about that night. Jerome Gundersen and Charles Gelatt, two of the leading citizens in La Crosse, were in attendance. Gelatt approached me after the speech, shook my hand, and said, "I really like you. How much can I contribute to your campaign?"

"Well," I said, "you can contribute $10,000. That's the individual limit."

He was shocked. "I'm not giving you that much!" he said. He shook his head. I don't know why he even asked me. In the end, I think he wrote me a check for $1,000.

At some point I looked across the room, and there was Jim Klauser. That was unusual. Klauser didn't get out of Madison much. He said he needed to talk to me. I was going to catch a plane to Superior to give a speech the next morning, and Jim said he would walk me to my car, which he did.

"Good speech, Tommy," he said. "I wanted to let you know that we released most of the campaign staff today."

I stopped walking and looked at him. I was shocked.

"You campaign, and I'll take care of it," he said. As it turned out, it wasn't everybody. But a couple of things were going on. Jim was unhappy with the quality of our television spots in the run-up to the convention and went so far as to change the imagery in the last six or seven seconds. They had me looking funereal, Jim said. He found something brighter and spliced it in at the last minute, before the spots aired. Klauser was also unhappy with our campaign manager. They had tussled over the organization of the field staff. Klauser wanted it more hands-on, and the guy said, "I talk to them on the phone. It works." Jim told me he was intending to fire him, but never got the chance. It turned out the campaign manager was in a romantic relationship with the head of our campaign ad agency. When Klauser said he was changing agencies after the convention, the campaign manager said, "Then I quit."

Klauser was running things anyway by then, and he was tough. Around this time, one of our fundraisers made the mistake of telling Jim she was wasn't going to turn over the money she had raised until she was paid. "That money is not yours," Jim said. "If it is not in the Madison office by noon tomorrow I will get an arrest warrant from the district attorney." She brought it in. Klauser paid her, and fired her.

We could get by without any particular fundraiser, but we needed a campaign manager. Klauser had talked to Gerald Whitburn, who was involved with Kasten's Senate reelection campaign, and Whitburn had suggested we get in touch with a guy named Robert "Buzz" Buzinski, a Wisconsin native who had worked as a field representative for the Republican National Committee in states across the country. Klauser flew to Washington to meet with Buzinski. It was almost like destiny. They were having lunch in a D.C. restaurant when a camera crew from a local TV station showed up and said they were trying to do a piece on the "entertainment deduction" on tax returns, which had become controversial. The three-martini lunch was on the way out. The TV crew offered to buy Klauser and Buzinski martinis if they could take some shots of them sipping from the glasses. They didn't have to ask twice. Jim and Buzz, as it happened, both enjoyed martinis. Buzz signed on to the campaign.

We still didn't have much staff, or money either, but we gained momentum as the summer went on. Our campaign circulated a three-page memo that pointed out how liberal Jonathan Barry had been during his many years as a Democrat. The ultraliberal *Capital Times* had given Barry its third highest score out of ninety-nine members of the assembly in assessing his votes on select key issues. The memo was pretty devastating—true, but devastating—and Barry was outraged. It was while he was addressing it in an interview with the

Milwaukee Sentinel editorial board that Barry called me "a two-bit hack from Elroy." I think he knew he was in trouble.

By the day of the primary—September 9—I was feeling confident we would win. Sue Ann and I had dinner that night at the University Club in Milwaukee with Jim and Shirley Klauser and John and Peggy MacIver and afterward went to the Astor Hotel, where the victory celebration was being held. The early numbers were very positive and Klauser was telling me I needed to talk to the television reporters even though my opponents hadn't conceded yet. I wasn't sure, but Jim insisted. It worked out well because at one point during the interview, Tony Earl came on and we were together via a split screen. Tony congratulated me and said he was looking forward to the campaign. It was a classy thing to do but a bad move from the standpoint of political strategy: it served to put me on equal footing with the governor. I held my own in the conversation. I think maybe Tony and his people were relieved that Jonathan Barry didn't win the Republican nomination. They had become obsessed with him, and I was an afterthought. It was probably why their campaign didn't advertise for several weeks after the primary, another terrible move in hindsight. They still weren't taking me seriously.

That night at the Astor, after Jonathan and the others had called to officially concede, I addressed my supporters and pointed out that there was still much work to do. "We've won the pennant," I said. "We are now moving on to the World Series."

They liked that.

"Ladies and gentlemen," I said, "we are going to sweep the Series."

We needed money to do it, and Klauser had once again talked me into spending almost all our cash on hand in the weeks before the primary. It had worked at the convention, and it worked again. But while money started coming in—victories tend to do that—it wasn't enough for the TV buys we wanted to make. That year public financing was available in the governor's race—nearly a quarter of a million dollars—but we hadn't seen the check, and Klauser was just suspicious enough to worry that maybe the Earl administration had put it in a drawer somewhere. Actually, it had been sent to me in Elroy. It took a few days, but we tracked it down.

I did well in our first debate, October 4, which was sponsored by the League of Women Voters. I think the Earl people felt the debates—Tony and me talking side by side—would give them a boost. Maybe I would stumble. Instead, I got off the line of the night. Tony was talking about state services, how I wouldn't fund them sufficiently.

"Sometimes I think my opponent would rather be governor of Mississippi than Wisconsin," Tony said.

"I won't have to run for governor of Mississippi, Tony," I said. "With what Wisconsin pays in welfare, everyone in Mississippi is moving up here."

I kept hammering away on jobs and the economy. I think it was the polls that finally woke up Tony's team. We were consistently running even or ahead of the incumbent. I remember going down to Monroe one sunny fall day to campaign at the Cheese Days festival and picking up a *Wisconsin State Journal* that had a front-page headline about a poll that gave me a sizable lead. I spoke to Klauser that day, and while he was happy with the numbers, he felt it would energize the Earl campaign.

In addition, another November election in the state had begun to monopolize all the attention, because it had turned especially nasty. Ed Garvey, a Wisconsin native who returned to the state to work for Bronson La Follette in the attorney general's office, was challenging Bob Kasten, the incumbent Republican US senator. Garvey had a quick wit, a sharp tongue, and an occasional mean streak. He had served as executive director of the National Football League Players Association and led a strike against the owners prior to returning to Wisconsin. Kasten used Garvey's time at the NFLPA to launch an extremely negative television ad, suggesting that Garvey had mismanaged $750,000 of the players' money while heading the union. Garvey demanded the ads be pulled; Kasten refused. Garvey brought Gene Upshaw, his successor at the NFLPA, to Madison for a mid-October press conference to refute the charges. Then Ralph Nader showed up in Wisconsin and called Kasten a "chronic drunk." The day before Halloween, Garvey sued Kasten.

It was ugly, all right, and all that attention to the senate race may have hurt the Earl campaign's efforts to reinvigorate itself. On October 19 — the election was just over two weeks out — the *State Journal* ran a front-page story headlined, "Ardent Supporters Back Away from Earl." The gist of the story was that some crucial factions within the Democratic base — environmentalists, labor leaders — were not actively campaigning for Earl, for various reasons. Some felt he hadn't delivered on what he had promised. He had supported road building and had a Republican, Lowell Jackson, as his secretary of the Department of Transportation (DOT). Also — and I was at a point where I could smile at this—many of them did not think Tommy Thompson was a legitimate threat. Tom Loftus, the Democratic assembly Speaker, was quoted in the story: "They assumed Tommy couldn't be governor. I think they made a crucial error in their judgment."

Jim Klauser remained worried that the voters were fixated on the Kasten-Garvey race. He felt we needed something to shake things up, give our people one last reason to get to the polls. He found it—or rather Buzz Buzinski and his media people did—in a television ad that criticized Earl for his plan to build a state prison in the vicinity of County Stadium in Milwaukee. It was a great ad. It may not have been entirely fair—can any thirty-second ad on any issue ever be truly fair?—but it was a great ad. It was a color spot that showed a big, unseemly, black-and-white prison dropping out of the sky into the parking lot of County Stadium. It looked ridiculous, which, of course, was the point. The tagline was, "Tony Earl—What will he think of next?"

Milwaukee mayor Henry Maier was aligned with me against the Milwaukee prison, to the extent that he encouraged John Bilotti, the mayor of Kenosha, to meet with me and consider giving me his support. It provided one of the more amusing episodes of the campaign, at least in retrospect. At the time, it was exasperating.

Bilotti was a Democrat in a strong union city. In fact, Kenosha—and its troubled American Motors plant—would loom large in the early months of my administration. But while I was still campaigning against Earl, Bilotti—who had first won election as mayor in 1980, by one vote, after a recount—was not excited about meeting with me.

He finally agreed to have lunch, but we couldn't meet in a restaurant because he didn't want to be seen with a Republican. Instead, we would eat in Kenosha's city hall.

"Wait in the parking lot," Bilotti said. "I will come out for you."

It was comical. John Tries drove me into the parking area, and a man emerged out of city hall with his collar pulled up and his head kind of hidden. It was the mayor. As I got out of the car, he stopped me.

"I'm going to go back inside," Bilotti said. "I will leave the side door open"—he pointed to it—"and I want you to come up the stairs. Don't talk to anybody. Give me five minutes."

He said his staff would bring in sandwiches. It was clear he was deathly afraid someone would accuse him of consorting with a Republican.

After a few minutes, I walked over to the side door and went in. There were people inside and I wasn't about to not introduce myself. I shook some hands and went upstairs.

When I got to his office, Bilotti said, "Did you talk to anyone?"

"A few people," I said.

"Please don't," he said. Then he said, "Now, how can I help you?"

He didn't really do much for me during the campaign—no surprise—but I liked him well enough, and the following year Bilotti came to work for me, in the Department of Revenue.

My last debate with Earl was on October 23, at Eau Claire North High School. There was an audience of four hundred people, and I sounded the themes I had carried throughout the campaign: welfare reform, jobs, holding the line on capital gains taxes, and reducing the inheritance tax.

We were feeling good, trying not to be overconfident. One day in Madison, maybe two weeks before the election, Klauser and I took a walk around the Capitol Square. It was a little after noon. Taking a walk was one of the ways we managed to have a private conversation.

I said, "Jim, I think we're going to win."

Jim said, "I think so, too."

"You're going to have to come with me," I said. It was an important moment. I had needed Jim to run my campaign and I needed him to help me govern.

A day or two later, in another private moment, Jim said, "I have been look-ing at the Department of Administration, and looking at the statutes, and I think I can make that into something I would be very satisfied with."

The last week of the campaign, we got some poll numbers—we couldn't afford polling, but the Kasten campaign was polling and sharing the results with us—that made us feel even better. A *Wisconsin State Journal* poll on Sunday, October 26, showed the race at 37 percent to 36 percent in my favor, with a significant number—27 percent—undecided. The subsequent Kasten poll indicated the undecided voters, who generally go 2–1 for the challenger, were beginning to break toward us at a rate of 4–1. That was a very good sign.

That last weekend, Vice President George H. W. Bush came to campaign for me in Eau Claire. We brought him in because we wanted to get the Minne-apolis press that weekend for the northwest quadrant of the state. President Ronald Reagan himself had come a week earlier, making an appearance in Waukesha.

I voted for myself for governor in Elroy on Tuesday morning, November 4. Right after voting, I went over to the county highway shop to chat with the guys working there, something I had done every Election Day since my first assembly race.

Sue Ann and I went down to Madison that afternoon, and we had dinner at the Maple Bluff Country Club with Jim and Shirley Klauser. After dinner we went to the Concourse Hotel, where we had a suite of rooms. Downstairs, my supporters were gathering. Pam Anderson, my scheduler, was working the phones and getting early results. Milwaukee County was among the first to come in, and we knew that if we got anywhere north of 40 percent in Milwaukee County—historically unkind to Republicans—we probably were in. My recollection is we got around 42 percent in Milwaukee. I remember I called Ave Bie, who was over at the assembly caucus in the capitol, monitoring the other races.

Ave said, "Tommy, how are you feeling?"

"Ave," I said, "we are going to win." It felt good to say it.

Downstairs, it was bedlam. The Concourse ballroom was just packed. I've mentioned this before, but it's funny what you remember about any given situation. My son, Jason, was then twelve, and earlier he had been running loose on State Street, which is a block or so from the Concourse. I worried about him until he was back in the hotel and up in our suite. The fad at the time among young teens, for reasons adults aren't supposed to understand, was for the boys to leave the laces of their tennis shoes untied.

I said, "Jason, in a little while we are going to go downstairs, and I want you to tie your shoes, and keep them tied."

When I walked onto the stage to address the crowd and declare victory—a moment so many thought would never happen for me—I looked over at my family and there was Jason, with his shoes untied. I said, "Jason, tie those shoes." He shook his head no. So much for the power of being governor-elect.

I clasped hands with Scott McCallum, the lieutenant governor–elect, who would serve the state well in that capacity. We raised our arms and I called out to the crowd from the stage. "We are looking for a better Wisconsin!"

Among the celebrants at the Concourse that night I think there were probably a lot of next-morning headaches. But that did not include anyone in my inner circle. We got right to work. I had been determined to hit the ground running, and we met Wednesday morning in a suite on top of the Inn on the Park across from the capitol. We decided that Buzz Buzinski would be assistant transition director and my friend Chuck Thompson, a Wisconsin Dells business-man, would be transition director. My driver, John Tries, would be personnel director during the transition.

I had known Chuck Thompson since 1972, when, after redistricting, I found myself in a tough assembly race against another incumbent, Robert Thompson, a Poynette Democrat. I went to the Dells and introduced myself to Chuck Thompson (none of us Thompsons were related) and asked for his support. Chuck was involved with restaurants, hotels, and tourism in the Dells, and we hit it off immediately. He supported me in 1972 and he was a good fit for transition director fourteen years later. As governor, I appointed Chuck to the Public Service Commission, and later, in 1992, I made him the DOT secretary. Off hours, we hunted and skied together. Chuck was my very close friend until his death in 2012.

We wanted to make news that day—the Wednesday following the election—and we did it that afternoon with a press conference at the capitol in which I appointed my first cabinet member, Jim Klauser, to head the Department of Administration.

The following day, Thursday, there was a parade for me in Elroy. Sue Ann and I rode in a Duesenberg—which was manufactured in Elroy by my good friend Dick Braund—and enjoyed being around the friends and neighbors who seemed just as excited as we were about what had happened. Then it was back to business. Chuck Thompson had a place in the Florida Keys, and a few of us—Chuck, John Tries, Republican assemblyman Dick Matty, Klauser, and myself—flew down there for several days, kind of a working vacation, to talk about the transition and what my administration and first months in office as governor would look like. A year or so into my time as governor, there would be news stories and opinion pieces expressing surprise at my early success, or at any rate how energetic and focused my administration was right from the start. What people forgot, I suppose, was that I had had twenty years in the assembly to formulate ideas on important issues like welfare, education, and taxes, ideas that never went anywhere, never had a chance to go anywhere, because I was in the minority in the assembly.

Before I was elected governor, during the campaign, I put together a group of men and women from both business and government who would meet once a week or so, usually Saturdays in John MacIver's law office in Milwaukee, not only to assess how our campaign was doing and plot strategy but also to formulate some policy initiatives I might advance in the event we won. I didn't always attend those meetings myself—I was often somewhere else campaigning—but I would tell them what I was hearing around the state, what people were concerned about. Klauser would be at those Saturday meetings, along with Ave Bie, legislators like David Prosser and Betty Jo Nelsen, and Bruno Mauer, Mary Kohler, and Tom Hefty from the private sector. We continued to hold those meetings, maybe four times a year, after I was elected. The cast varied over time but it was always helpful for me to get that kind of input.

Much of what we advanced in our first budget in early 1987 had its seeds in those weekend gatherings in Milwaukee.

First, before we could draft a budget or anything else, a team had to be put in place. A few days after we got back from Chuck's place in Florida, I spoke to the Republican assembly caucus and made a point of referring to Jim Klauser as "the second governor," a phrase that was picked up and widely used from that time on. I also had some fun that day with Ben Brancel, who had just won election to my old assembly seat. "Don't be afraid to vote no," I told Ben, and everybody laughed.

Chuck Thompson had the transition director title, but Klauser had a hand in, too, and he and I interviewed and selected the cabinet secretaries and other top job candidates. Klauser and I attended a conference for new governors, and one thing we took away was how acrimonious some transitions could be. Ours went well, and all credit to the Earl people for that. Klauser was given an office in the GEF II state office building by the woman he would be succeeding at DOA, Doris Hanson. We also had space on the fourth floor of the capitol. I did most of my interviews that November and December in my old assembly office. I was continually amazed at the difference between being a legislator, even one in a leadership position, and being the governor-elect. It seemed a hand was reaching for me everywhere I went. A microphone would suddenly appear. Everyone wanted to talk to me. It was overwhelming. I couldn't help but think how I had spent two decades as a legislator trying to get attention and publicity.

My cabinet came together fairly quickly. We named Marlene Cummings secretary of the Department of Regulation and Licensing before Thanksgiving, and soon after that Bruno Mauer as head of the Department of Development. Klauser and I had worked it out that when we settled on a choice for the cabinet, he would let the outgoing secretary know what was happening and the name of the successor. There was one cabinet position where it didn't happen quite that way.

Lowell Jackson was Earl's DOT secretary, an unusual choice because Jackson was a Republican. First appointed DOT secretary by Lee Dreyfus, Jackson was a civil engineer who had long been politically active. He was involved in the Dreyfus campaign, and then Lee put him in the cabinet, first at DOT, and then, in 1981, as secretary of the Department of Industry, Labor and Human Relations. Jackson resigned that post in May 1982 to run for governor, but lost in the Republican primary to Terry Kohler. When Earl won the governor's race in the fall, he once again named Jackson to the DOT post.

I really liked Lowell's wife, Joni Jackson, who had been my secretary when I was minority leader in the assembly. I was less sure about him. I had found him arrogant, and when he came in to interview with me, after I was elected governor, it was almost as if he was interviewing me. He essentially said I didn't have to worry about the DOT, he would take care of it. He had stopped by to see if I was going to be worthy of serving. Did he want to spend his time being my DOT secretary? I may be overstating how blatant it was, but not by much.

After our interview, I talked to Klauser. "We're not going to keep him," I said. Jim responded, "There will be trouble if you don't." There was no question Jackson was an insider with a lot of friends in Wisconsin politics and government.

"I don't care," I said. Klauser didn't get the chance to let Jackson know he wasn't being reappointed. I made the phone call myself. When I gave him the news, Jackson hung up on me.

By then, I knew I wanted Ron Fiedler at DOT. I had always liked Ron, whose late father, Vere Fiedler, had been a member of the State Highway Commission—a predecessor of DOT. Ron had been a district officer for DOT until 1978, when he resigned to take a job as vice president of marketing for Donahue and Associates, a large and prestigious engineering and architectural firm in Sheboygan.

In early December I talked to Ron about coming into my cabinet as head of DOT, knowing full well he would have to take a healthy pay cut to do it.

"I want to build this state," I told Ron, "and I want you to be my point person."

He said, "I like what I'm doing. Why would I want to come back into the government?"

I suspected he might say something like that. Bruno Mauer, who was president of the Tool Service Corporation in Waukesha, said pretty much the same thing when I offered him the Department of Development job. I got Bruno to agree by saying he needed to stay at DOD only a year. (He wound up staying three.)

When Ron asked why he should return to state service, I said, "Because your father would want you to."

Vere Fiedler had been a friend of my father way back when my father was head of roads and bridges in Juneau County.

I reminded Ron of that, and added, "I want you to be my secretary of transportation."

"I need to think about it," Ron said, but he called me a couple of days later to accept the position. "It does sound interesting," he said. "I would like to build Wisconsin." We made the announcement on December 10.

The cabinet announcement that really rocked the capitol, though, came a week later. Early on, in the days following the election, Klauser and I spoke about the possibility of getting a Democrat or two into the cabinet. It made sense to me from a pragmatic standpoint. Both the senate and assembly had Democratic majorities. If my administration was going to succeed, I needed help from the other side of the aisle.

At one point during the transition, Jim said, "What about Tim Cullen?"

My immediate response was to say, "Why would he do it? He's going to run against me for governor in four years."

Cullen was a Democrat's Democrat, a seasoned pro from Janesville who was the majority leader of the senate. Obviously he was respected by his colleagues, but Republicans and others in the capitol—lobbyists, reporters—looked at him as honest and straightforward, a strong advocate for what he believed in, but also someone willing to listen. As is typical in the capitol, even though I hadn't been sworn in yet as governor, there was already speculation about who the Democrats would run against me in 1990. Cullen and assembly Speaker Loftus were at the top of the list.

Klauser knew Cullen better than I did. They spoke, and Cullen did not reject out of hand the idea of joining our administration. They spoke some more. The discussion moved to which department Cullen might head, should he decide to come onboard. Transportation was in play—we hadn't yet named Fiedler—but pretty quickly they focused on the Department of Health and Social Services

(DHSS). It was a massive agency, with 10,500 employees and an annual budget of $2.6 billion. Welfare reform was near or at the top of the policy initiatives I wanted to tackle once I was inaugurated. It was going to be complicated and likely controversial. Having a highly respected Democrat in charge of the department that oversees welfare would lessen the kneejerk outrage any attempt to change the system would provoke in liberals. Cullen knew that welfare as it was being administered wasn't working. He wanted reform, too, but he wanted to make sure people weren't hurt in the process. Once he and Klauser had arrived at an understanding, I assured him my plan would find a way to put people to work while also providing them with assistance. He said he wanted to be able to disagree with me without worrying about getting fired. I told him I wouldn't want him for the job if he wasn't going to speak his mind. In the end, I think it was a gut feeling on both our parts. We didn't know each other well, but we liked, respected, and, I think, trusted one another. Tim proved to be an excellent secretary; we became good friends and remain so.

We made the announcement on December 17 in the assembly parlor. People were shocked. Tim told me later he had consulted with a few close friends, including his senate colleague Joe Strohl and Bill Bablitch, who was Tim's mentor in the senate before Bill ran successfully for the Wisconsin Supreme Court. But Tim didn't tell either Earl or Loftus beforehand, so they were surprised along with everybody else, including the press corps, some of whom may have been at a loss for words for the first time in years. "Stunned," is how the *Wisconsin State Journal* described the audience in the assembly parlor, adding, "The Thompson announcement was a blockbuster."

I got a lot of credit for bringing Tim into the cabinet, but Klauser and Tim are really more deserving. They worked it out. The pundits pointed out how savvy it was politically, and there was no point denying that. It removed a prominent Democrat from the senate (and, in all likelihood, from a run for governor in four years); it set a moderate tone for my administration, especially opening the eyes of the critics who regarded me only as "Dr. No"; and it put welfare reform on a front burner with a reasonable chance of success. "Rep. Shirley Krug," the *State Journal* noted in a story the day after the announcement, "a Milwaukee Democrat, said Cullen's selection enhances Thompson's chances of winning support for his welfare proposals in the Legislature." The *Capital Times* wrote that I "clearly pulled off a political coup" with the Cullen appointment.

It was more than that for me. Tim proved to be just who I thought he was, a smart politician but one who saw public service as a high calling. What mattered was what was best for the people of Wisconsin.

Tim also had humor and hard-earned wisdom where politics and governing were concerned. His mentor, Bablitch, once told him—Tim shared the story with me—that a cardinal rule of politics and legislating is, every answer other than yes is no. It sounds simple, but it's profound. If someone tells you, "I really like the concept behind the bill," it is almost guaranteed they're not going to vote for it. It's not a yes, therefore it's a no.

The day after I was inaugurated, Tim sent over a memo on DHSS stationery.

Handwritten at the top was this: "Tommy—I made these notes for you before I accepted DHSS. Thought I would give them to you."

Tim began by telling me not to get a big head over winning: "I believe 1982 and 1986 were largely rejection of the loser." He counseled me to encourage my staff to offer advice even when I hadn't asked for it. He said I should listen more and talk less in meetings. I was particularly struck by a passage in which he told me not to get too excited by how I was going to be received when meeting people across the state. "People lie to governors," Tim wrote, adding that Tony Earl thought he was highly popular. Of course he did. Face-to-face, everyone told him how much they liked him.

My friend Tony was helpful and supportive during the transition, which didn't surprise me. The day of my inauguration—January 5, 1987—I found a handwritten note from him in the top drawer of the desk in the governor's office.

Tommy—

Every good wish—I hope you will enjoy this office as much as I.

Your friend,

Tony

I made a point of calling Tony a "class act" during my inaugural speech, and stepped off the podium to shake his hand. I'm not sure any other governor has done that, before or since.

The Earls moved out of the Executive Residence—more commonly referred to as the Governor's Mansion—the weekend before my Monday inauguration, so we didn't have much time to settle in prior to the festivities. Sue Ann taught up in Elroy that Friday, then came down to Madison. Sheila Earl showed her around the mansion. I spent much of Sunday moving boxes from the West Washington Avenue apartment I had shared with some legislators for the past decade over to the Governor's Mansion in Maple Bluff.

I still have a newspaper page that includes a photograph of me walking into the Executive Residence with several cardboard boxes in my arms. The mansion was built in 1920 as a private residence and acquired by the state in 1949. One point of trivia: it's one of only a handful of governor's residences not actually located in the state capital. Maple Bluff is a village adjacent to Madison. The mansion is on the shore of Lake Mendota, so there are beautiful views, along with a beautiful interior, thirteen bathrooms, seven bedrooms—more than sixteen thousand square feet.

It was quite a transformation for us, coming from our small house in Elroy. I had never been upstairs in the mansion until that Sunday. Just strolling around, taking in the grandeur of the place, I had one of those "what in the heck am I doing here" moments. Sue Ann and the kids would return to Elroy to finish out the school year, but they were at the mansion Sunday and would spend the night, in advance of Monday's inauguration. I think the staff at the Executive Residence was afraid the Beverly Hillbillies were moving in. We did wind up keeping nearly everyone who worked for the Earls, although we eventually hired our own chef, a big guy named Joe Dodge. Chuck Thompson knew him in the Dells and liked him. That first Sunday, the mansion staff was trying to be nice, but you could tell they were apprehensive. They had really liked the Earls and probably had not read much that was positive about me in the Madison papers. Then my son Jason and his cousin started throwing a Nerf ball around inside and managed to get it lodged on top of a beautiful, expensive, and rare chandelier. It's said to be one of only two of its kind ever made; the other is in the White House in Washington. I think it is fair to say that until that Sunday, a ball had never come to rest on either one.

The mansion staff was apoplectic. One came up to me and said, "Mr. Thompson"—they wouldn't call me governor, and I wasn't, not yet—"we must get the ball out of the chandelier."

We retrieved the ball without causing any damage and established a rule: no playing ball inside the Executive Residence.

Inauguration Day itself ran on a tight schedule. There was a Mass, a brunch at the mansion in the morning, a party for donors and campaign staff at the

Concourse in the afternoon, and the inaugural ball at the Dane County Coliseum that night.

The inaugural ceremony was at noon at the capitol, on the first floor of the east wing in front of the bust of Robert La Follette. The chief justice of the Wisconsin Supreme Court, Nathan Heffernan, read me the oath of office. Warren Knowles and Lee Dreyfus were there. Aside from the dignitaries, it seemed like the entire population of Elroy had made its way to Madison. People were caught up in the moment, and it was hard to blame them. I had invited a minister friend—he had campaigned hard for me—to say a prayer during the ceremony, but he ran on and on and was threatening to turn it into an entire sermon. I had to gently ask him to stop.

I began my own address by recalling my first swearing-in at the capitol.

"It was twenty years ago," I said, "as a newly elected representative to the assembly. I walked up the marble steps of the west wing of this magnificent capitol building, and there where I had once served as a page, raised my right hand and was sworn in as a legislator to be of service to the people of Wisconsin.

"I've never forgotten the shivers that moved up my spine that cold day in January 1967, but it wasn't the weather that made me shiver. It was the realization that I had been given the opportunity to be of service to a great people. I told myself that I didn't have to move mountains, but only to do my best. I told myself to never forget that it was the people who put me there.

"Today, as I become your governor, I once again have that body- and mind-shaking sensation of great responsibility. It's a challenge I accept."

By the time I delivered my inaugural address, I was fully aware of the challenges of being governor. You don't need a sign on the desk to know where the buck stops. My first big challenge—it eventually became a crisis—began weeks before I took office.

During my time as governor, Sue Ann founded the Wisconsin Women's Health Foundation, and its ongoing success is a great tribute to her. (Thompson family)

Juliann and me sharing a fun moment. (Thompson family)

I'm in the middle between my sister, Juliann, and brother Eddie. (Thompson family)

With my father, Allan Thompson. He pushed me hard, but he did it out of love. I wish he could have lived to see me elected governor. (Thompson family)

My mother, Julia, grew up on a farm that is now part of my property outside Elroy. She had a great heart and was always finding ways to help others. (Thompson family)

Warren Knowles signing a bill while I look on. I believe this was the youthful-offenders institution bill that I championed. Though Knowles signed the bill and the institution was built, Governor Patrick Lucey sold the property to the federal government before it opened. (Department of Special Collections and University Archives, Marquette University Libraries)

Governor Patrick Lucey signing a bill in the Wisconsin State Capitol. I'm looking on, second from the left, in my role as a member of the assembly. (Department of Special Collections and University Archives, Marquette University Libraries)

Moving the government around the state every summer was a great idea, and we always played a softball game against the locals. (Thompson family)

Tommy~ Friendship!

9-4-87

On the boat with Vice President George H. W. Bush in Kennebunkport in 1987. We developed a good friendship that I treasure. (Thompson family)

On the capitol's lantern observation deck, Election Day 1990. We were feeling confident about defeating Tom Loftus. Standing at the far left is Scott Fromader. To the right of Fromader is Peter Helland. Kneeling and wearing a white glove is Bob Brandherm. Immediately behind Brandherm is Dale Dumbleton, and behind Dumbleton is Dean Stensberg. I am at the lower right with my thumb up. Immediately behind me is my son, Jason, and behind Jason is Patrick Osborne. (Thompson family)

I really enjoyed leading a couple hundred people on a Harley-Davidson motorcycle ride during many of the summers while I was governor. (Department of Special Collections and University Archives, Marquette University Libraries)

My beloved daughters and son, who didn't always like politics but always showed up. *From left*: Kelli, Tommi, and Jason. (Thompson family)

On board a French train with legal counsel Stewart Simonson (*left*) and top aide Jim Klauser. (Thompson family)

An official portrait while governor. (Thompson family)

At some point not long after I won the election for governor—around my birthday, November 19—I got a phone call from Joe Cappy, president of American Motors Corporation (AMC). Cappy wanted to brief me on the ongoing negotiations between AMC and the union, Local 72, at its Kenosha manufacturing plant. AMC had been struggling—though Cappy said things were turning around—and he believed there was a role for both a new governor and the State of Wisconsin not only in the union negotiations but in securing a brighter future for AMC and Kenosha for a long time to come. Even though I wasn't yet governor, I agreed to meet with him.

The ups and downs of AMC in Kenosha—lately, it had been mostly downs—had been well publicized. In 1985 AMC—and the company's majority owner, the French carmaker Renault—had threatened to close the Kenosha plant if the union would not agree to concessions on wages and other issues. The negotiations were heated, but in the end the union agreed to most of the concessions, and a new contract was signed. That close call led Tony Earl to appoint former governor Patrick Lucey to lead an effort to make sure AMC stayed in Wisconsin. Plans were discussed for a new, state-of-the-art plant for Kenosha that would include a large incentive package of state money in return for increased production and thousands of new jobs.

The plan was put on hold the following year when Chrysler Corporation, a much larger car company than AMC, entered the picture with an offer to have the AMC Kenosha plant manufacture some of Chrysler's luxury vehicles. It was a welcome offer for both management and employees at AMC, but before proceeding with the arrangement Chrysler wanted some additional union concessions having to do with job classifications at the plant. The union was skeptical until it was determined they could be done without reopening the 1985 contract. A compromise was struck.

That summer—while I was busy campaigning for governor—Chrysler made AMC still another offer. This time the company wanted to move production of two of its subcompact cars, Dodge Omni and Plymouth Horizon, from its Belvidere plant in Illinois to Kenosha. There would be bountiful new jobs, but AMC management wanted to reopen the 1985 labor contract because small cars meant smaller profits. Local 72 and its president, a tough, fiery, crewcut guy named Rudy Kuzel, were not interested in revisiting the terms of a contract for which they had already made serious concessions.

My understanding is that things had pretty well stalled until the November election, at which point I received the call from Cappy. They needed help bringing the two sides together, and they also needed—if their larger plans were to succeed—some significant financial help from the state. They wanted to talk to the incoming governor. I wound up going to Kenosha before my inauguration, meeting with AMC executives, their counterparts at Chrysler, Kenosha city officials, and union leaders, too. I got along with Rudy Kuzel.

Those negotiations went well enough that on January 6, the day after I was inaugurated governor, I talked to reporters about what we hoped to accomplish. The top headline on the front page of the *Wisconsin State Journal* the next day read, "Auto Jobs Could Double." The package we were putting together included the additional production of Chrysler vehicles in Kenosha that had already been discussed, but it also called for a loan—the figure was around $200 million—from the State of Wisconsin to help build a new plant. Chrysler was agreeing to launch a new Jeep line at the refurbished Kenosha facility, beginning in either 1988 or 1989. The number of new jobs this could generate was eye-popping—somewhere between sixty-five hundred and eight thousand. While this pleased the union leaders, they were less excited about AMC's insistence that the 1985 contract needed to be reopened and amended.

All the while I was involved in the negotiations, through January and into February, I had mixed feelings, mostly related to the $200 million in state assistance we were promising. I wished at the time there was some kind of set policy for what the state could and couldn't do in assisting job development, but there was no policy. I got the call from Cappy in late November, and off we went. I did believe that if we failed to reach a deal, AMC wouldn't be in Kenosha by the time I ran for reelection in 1990.

We worked hard into early March, and all the pieces were in place except one: a new deal with the union. I got word in Madison one day that management and union officials were close. Meeting at the Pfister Hotel in Milwaukee, they negotiated into the night and asked me to come to the hotel the following morning. I think they felt that my presence might help push them across the finish line, or at least keep things on the rails if the talks got heated at the last minute. I agreed to go to Milwaukee.

It was there, that morning in March 1987, that we received the stunning news: Chrysler was buying American Motors—the 46 percent owned by Renault—for $1.5 billion. It meant all deals, including the proposed Kenosha expansion, were off, at least temporarily. Nobody had seen it coming, and the union was furious. Rudy Kuzel looked like he was ready to eat nails and hit something.

Still, at first, Chrysler and its high-profile chairman, Lee Iacocca, sounded all the right notes for Kenosha. In my conversations with him he indicated no desire to stop or reduce production at the Kenosha plant. That summer Chrysler went ahead with the shift of the Omni and Horizon models to Kenosha, and the town rejoiced. Four thousand plant employees were called back to work. But in hindsight, there were some ominous signs. Some one hundred mid-management employees at the Kenosha facility were laid off in a corporate re-structuring. The union was approached about reopening negotiations a year before the 1985 deal was up. (They refused.)

Yet nobody foresaw the announcement that came in late January 1988. Chrysler released a statement saying it would stop making cars in Kenosha before the end of the year. This time I was furious. I felt like Iacocca had lied to me. At one point, he had told me the plant would stay open at least five years. Iacocca gave a press conference in New York a week later saying he hadn't lied. He had never promised anyone anything, he said, and besides, they were going to continue making engines in Kenosha and employ around one thousand people.

Kuzel and the union wanted us to sue Chrysler, and we weren't ruling it out, though I thought of it as a last resort. I wanted to negotiate with Iacocca. If it turned out we couldn't convince him to keep making cars in Kenosha, we could at least work out the best possible deal from Chrysler as it exited.

I met face-to-face with Iacocca—in early summer 1988, as I recall—and it was memorable. Jim Klauser and I traveled to Washington, D.C., for the meeting, which was held in Les Aspin's congressional office in the Rayburn House Office Building. Les represented Kenosha and, as chairman of the House Armed Services Committee, had some clout with Iacocca, or should have, since Chrysler had government contracts to produce military vehicles. Les was a Democrat, and I appreciated his willingness to help.

Klauser and I got there first, and Les parked us on one side of a big rectangular table. A few minutes later we heard some commotion in the hallway. It was Iacocca and his entourage. Iacocca is a large man. He came in and kind of grunted at us. There had been harsh words exchanged back and forth in the press. At one point, a Detroit paper quoted Klauser as calling Iacocca "a strange man." That day, Les was trying to smooth things over. He got us to shake hands, reluctantly, across the table.

But Iacocca and I were not going to get along. Within a few minutes we had each pounded a fist on the table, and then I said something that must have really set him off. Iacocca stood up, pushed back his chair, and lunged across the table—but not at me, at Jim. He shouted, "I am not a strange man!" Jim pushed back from the table, Iacocca kind of rebounded back into his own chair, and things quieted down. I am not sure why he went after Jim. Either that "strange man" quote really bothered him, or he didn't want to attack a governor and chose Jim by default. In any case, I think Iacocca was rattled by that exchange. In the end, Kenosha got a very good deal, the best we could get under the circumstances. There were many more meetings and discussions, with less theatrics. Chrysler finally agreed to pay $25 million—much of which went to job training and benefits for displaced workers—in return for our not filing a breach-of-contract lawsuit. The deal was announced in September 1988. Kuzel was terribly upset. The union had wanted us to sue. I still think it was as good a deal as any city in a similar circumstance ever received.

Later, Jim and I would chuckle about that meeting with Iacocca. It was one of many memorable moments we shared in the decade he worked with me in state government. I've noted earlier he was really much more than a cabinet secretary. I trusted him completely. I let it be known that his word was as good as mine, and my word is my bond. If Jim made a commitment on something, even if I didn't particularly agree with it, it was a deal, and I backed him.

For much of that decade, Jim and I started our days together. He lived in Maple Bluff, not far from the Executive Residence, and he would come by for breakfast. We would eat and then drive in together, discussing whatever issues were in front of us.

One morning, not long after I was first elected, an issue presented itself during our drive in. The route from the mansion to the capitol takes you up a long street called East Washington Avenue, and as we approached the Capitol Square I looked to my right and commented on all the cars that were parked on several nearby surface lots.

"Those are our cars," Jim said.

He meant that all the vehicles—and there were a lot of them—were owned by the state. They were covered with snow that morning, which was no big deal, but then we noticed they were covered with snow the next morning when we drove by, and again the next. Jim had someone go by and take photographs that ended up documenting that many of these state-owned cars hadn't been driven in a week. I had been elected in part to keep an eye on state spending, and it was pretty clear that state government might have too many automobiles. When Jim looked into it, he discovered the State of Wisconsin owned more than sixty-six hundred cars. They were scattered across agencies and there was no central accounting for them. We ended up getting them off the leased lots and onto state property. We monitored use closely and reduced new car purchases. Over several years, we saved taxpayers millions of dollars.

I remembered that episode sometime later when Kenneth "Buzz" Shaw, the University of Wisconsin System president, was in my office to talk about the budget, and the subject of the university's automobile fleet came up. I believe the president wanted a 5 percent increase in the system's allotment of vehicles. I don't recall the precise details, but I distinctly remember asking the following question: "How many cars do you have now?"

He frowned and looked over at his budget guy, who had accompanied him to my office. That fellow quickly developed an intense interest in his shoes. It was clear they didn't know how many cars the university owned. I suggested they come back when they did.

I relate this story to illustrate a bit of the common-sense mindset I tried to bring to the governor's office. If you think you deserve more cars, you should know how many you have to begin with. If you can let them sit a week without brushing the snow off to drive them, you probably have too many.

I'll admit that one of the perks of being governor that I appreciated from the beginning was having a car and driver of my own. It occasionally allowed me to catch a nap while we were on the road, but more often it allowed me to sit in the back and work, returning phone calls and catching up on the newspapers.

When I was first elected governor, I inherited two Wisconsin State Patrol officers, Jerry Baumbach and Jim Friedel, who had served as drivers and security for Tony Earl. I became very close friends with Baumbach. I also respected and befriended Friedel. Jim loved Tony. The only thing Tony asked me after the election—I think it speaks to the classy guy Tony is—was, "Please take care of Jerry and Jim. They will serve you well, Tommy."

He was right. They were different guys, though. Friedel was a cop's cop, a big man, serious about the job, and a union supporter. I think he was worried early on that I wouldn't keep him. His loyalty had been to Tony, and I had beaten Tony. I had to keep telling Jim I liked him, which I did.

We had a near-disaster soon after I was elected governor. Paul Weyrich, a conservative businessman originally from Racine—he cofounded the Heritage Foundation, and, with Jerry Falwell, the Moral Majority—invited me to speak to an elite gathering of conservatives at the Breakers, a fancy resort in Palm Beach, Florida. I think Weyrich, given his Wisconsin ties, kind of wanted to show me off. I was the only Republican to beat an incumbent Democrat governor in 1986. It was going to be my first major postelection speech outside of Wisconsin. It was a formal, black-tie event, and since I didn't own a tuxedo, I rented one before we left.

I flew down to Florida with Friedel and Diane Harmelink, my chief of staff. When we checked in at the Breakers, there was just enough time for me to grab a quick nap and a shower. When I got out of the shower, I opened my suitcase.

There was nothing in the suitcase but Hawaiian shirts.

Jim Friedel had gone to baggage claim and grabbed the wrong bag. In Jim's defense, the suitcase looked exactly like mine. But it wasn't mine, and that was a problem. I had worn jeans on the flight down. I had worked hard to cultivate a more sophisticated image both before and after the election, and I really didn't want to give a speech at the Breakers wearing jeans and a Hawaiian shirt.

I called Friedel over. "Jim! You picked up the wrong bag!"

Friedel was speechless. I think he was in shock. He was ashen. Finally he said, "I'll run back to the airport." He took the suitcase and left. I called Diane in her room, where she was going over my speech. I think she called the kitchen at the Breakers to see if they had an extra waiter's suit that might fit me. In the end, it wasn't necessary. Friedel must have broken all speed records getting to the airport, and there he found my bag, untouched. He replaced it with the bag he had taken by mistake, and he got back to the Breakers in time for me to dress and give the speech.

We got to the point later where we could laugh about it. Jim and I got along fine. He wound up retiring—his own decision—after a few years.

Jerry Baumbach, the other security man Tony asked me to retain, became like a brother to me. When Jim retired, I asked Jerry if he thought he could handle the job on his own, and he agreed to try. He later said it was the beginning of nine years of eighteen-hour days. Jerry was more than a driver—he handled all kinds of logistics, from airline tickets to hotel reservations—but that doesn't begin to explain our relationship. We were close. We celebrated together and helped each other through tough times.

We could kid each other pretty well, too. You'll recall I said Jim Friedel was a cop's cop. Jerry—and I say this with great affection—was not. I used to joke that I knew he had shot his pistol only twice. The only time the gun had ever been fired was when he shot twice at a skunk or a woodchuck under the porch of his house in Sun Prairie. I'm pretty sure he missed both times. When he retired, Jerry sold me the pistol. It was filthy. He had never cleaned it.

I always told him, "Jerry, if we ever get in trouble, and there's some shooting, just hand me the pistol. You get down and stay down. I'll take care of it."

Jerry said, "OK."

I think one of the Jerry's favorite moments in our time together came late one night when we checked in to a hotel and I just flopped down—I was exhausted—on a Murphy bed, while Jerry, after seeing me fast asleep, repaired to the luxurious master bedroom. I knocked on his door in the morning and said, "Tell me again, which one of us is governor?" He just smiled.

It was tough on both of us when Jerry retired from the state patrol in December 1997. I was gearing up for my last run for governor. We had dinner at the mansion.

"I really don't want to go through another campaign, Governor," Jerry said. "You wore me out. I can't take the pace any longer."

We remained great friends—and, of course, I got his pistol.

Campaigns *were* exhausting—my mantra was to always run as if we were behind—but I'm not sure we ever worked harder, my team and myself, than when we were putting a budget together in the early months of my first term. I had campaigned hard on a number of initiatives: controlling spending and reducing taxes, jobs and economic development, infrastructure improvement, and welfare reform. They would all be represented in the budget. I also began by asking my cabinet secretaries to submit a budget for their departments that was 95 percent or less of what the agency had spent the year before. It got them thinking about priorities right from the start. Once I made the final spending decisions, I would give each secretary the opportunity to discuss and challenge points they disagreed with before the final budget was sent to the legislature. If they were intent on spending in one area, I would usually agree, while asking them to find cuts elsewhere. I continued this throughout my time as governor. I think it advanced an expectation that they were going to be involved in governing. If there was a meeting in my office that affected their agency, they were there. They would represent me at events around the state that dealt with issues involving their agencies. The cabinet secretaries knew what our message was, because they were involved. We listened to them.

In August 1987—just a few weeks after I signed my first budget into law—I took my entire cabinet up to the University of Wisconsin–Superior and operated state government from there for a week. We called it "moving state government," and it was such a smashing success that we repeated it—in different parts of the state—every subsequent summer. Governors in other states quickly copied the idea.

We would arrive on a Sunday night and generally play a softball game, the governor's staff against people from the town. Afterward we would all have brats, pizzas, and beer. I think in all the years we moved state government, our team won only one of those softball games. The town loved it, loved our being there and the attention it brought them. In Superior that first year, my cabinet secretaries and I stayed in a UW–Superior dormitory. The governor's office was set up for the week in the chancellor's office. I had picked Superior because during my campaign against Tony, I had visited Douglas County and heard repeatedly from residents that "no one" in state government cared about them or even knew they existed. They were too far north. I told them that if I got elected, I would find a way to let folks know about Douglas County. Moving state government there for a week accomplished that. (I didn't carry Douglas County in that first election against Tony—it had generally been a Democratic county—but I carried it in my next three runs for governor.)

Another thing the week accomplished, of course, was building cohesion among the cabinet members. They got to know each other, increasing the chances they would work well collectively.

The 1987–89 budget I signed prior to our trip to Superior had generated considerable controversy earlier that summer. I knew the legislature was likely to pounce on whatever budget I sent them. Both houses, assembly and senate, had Democratic majorities. Many of those legislators were still angry to the point of denial that I had won and Earl had lost. Even those who had begun to grudgingly accept the idea of Tommy Thompson as governor figured me for one term, no more. They didn't want to work with me. If I sent them a budget with spending and tax cuts—and, worst of all, changes to welfare, which they considered their exclusive domain—they would riddle it with amendments and changes and send it back.

Way back on November 13—not ten days after I was elected governor—a Democratic assemblyman, Richard Shoemaker, was quoted by the Associated Press saying, "I don't want to say Tommy Thompson's budget is going to be dead on arrival when it hits the Legislature, but it is."

On that score—giving the Democrats in the legislature a budget they could fume about—I didn't disappoint.

My budget called for simplifying the state income tax and reducing the rate; it included a phasing out of the inheritance tax, a retention of the 60 percent exclusion of taxes on capital gains income, and an increase in state aid for local education, tied to spending controls on schools, which would lead to property tax cuts.

Those were significant measures, but the headline grabber, without question, was my welfare reform initiative. Compared with what was to come over the next decade in Wisconsin—by 1996, we would eliminate welfare altogether in the state—my first 1987 budget proposals, which included a cut in cash payments (with the savings then used for education and job training, to help the recipients eventually get off welfare), might not seem all that revolutionary. But they caused a stir, a big stir—both the cut in cash benefits and the requirement that teenagers stay in school or see a reduction in the benefits paid to their families.

It was never going to be easy, but I had no doubt about the necessity for change. The system was irretrievably broken. There were two fundamental flaws in the welfare system as it existed. First, it discouraged individuals from becoming self-sufficient. Second, even if a desire for self-sufficiency existed, there was no component to help people achieve it. Consequently, the number of people on welfare just kept increasing. In Wisconsin the numbers by 1986 were particularly alarming, with three hundred thousand people—6 percent of the state's population—on the rolls as of April. Even some Democrats recognized the problem. That month, April 1986, when I was just beginning my official run for governor, Wisconsin enacted a work-welfare program called Work Experience and Job Training, which included a requirement that clients take unpaid public-sector jobs if they couldn't find work in the private sector. That shift—and what I consistently heard while traveling the state campaigning—convinced me that the time was at hand to push for meaningful change.

Where better than Wisconsin? Our state had become a welfare magnet, which may be a cliché, but phrases become clichés for a reason. There were stories in the press by reporters who followed people who came up here from Chicago, got a welfare check, cashed it, and were back home in time for dinner. I heard anecdotally—I never saw it—about a sign in an Illinois bus station that detailed exactly how you could get a round-trip bus ticket to Wisconsin, get and cash a welfare check, and be back home the same day.

Some of what I heard campaigning might surprise people. While it was often working people who expressed the sentiment that "people receiving welfare should have to work," I heard, too, from welfare recipients who knew that in the end, it was a losing proposition. I remember especially a young woman in Milwaukee who grabbed my arm at a campaign stop and said, "Please do something about welfare. It's killing us." She said she had two kids and wanted a future for them that did not include welfare. She knew that otherwise it was self-perpetuating, with no end in sight.

The situation had always been complicated by politics. In broad terms, when the shortcomings of welfare were discussed, Republicans responded by saying, in effect, just cut everybody loose. Go find yourself a job, and quit complaining. Democrats called that heartless and responded—although, as I've noted, this was beginning to change by 1986—by simply throwing more money at the programs.

In my first term as governor, we took a different path.

Our plan was to cut the cash benefit, but then channel that money—in the end, we invested even more than we saved in cuts—into programs and services designed to get people off of welfare and keep them off.

What services am I talking about? I think we had a pretty good idea of the kind of things we needed to provide to help people transition from welfare to work, but eventually I arranged to have a series of luncheons at the Executive Residence with mothers who were on welfare. Each time, it was just me and a few of the welfare mothers, eating lunch and talking. My staff wasn't in the room, and neither were the welfare caseworkers. The women were initially reluctant to talk to me. Some weren't even sure why they were there. But we broke the ice, and in the end it was productive. I told them how I had grown up in Elroy, in a family that while not exactly poor, was anything but rich.

I know it isn't easy, I said. But if you're willing to work, I can help you.

They talked about having to look after their kids, not having an education to attain a meaningful job, and losing their health insurance if they did find work.

I told them, essentially, that if they went to work, we would help them get all those things: childcare, education, health insurance, and more. It was a meaningful back-and-forth dialogue. Each hurdle they brought up, I answered. I wanted to convince them we were committed to helping.

Implementing that help wouldn't be easy, because most of those proposals required getting waivers from the US Department of Health and Human Services, which administered welfare on the federal level. The federal welfare bureaucracy was massive. To its credit, it was also making an effort at reform. In February 1987, just weeks after I took office, I attended a meeting of the National Governors Association in Washington, D.C., at which the association asked us to endorse a huge, $1 billion work-based welfare program that would be run largely by the federal government.

I was the only governor to vote against it. I felt that what we were proposing in our first budget in Wisconsin put us out front. Relying on the feds would only slow us down. In the end, Washington gave us most of the waivers we requested, because getting people off welfare and keeping them there saved the federal government money. Our deal called for some of the money it saved to come back to Wisconsin, allowing us to fund still more initiatives. Over time I received waivers from the administrations of Ronald Reagan, George H. W. Bush, and Bill Clinton. I'm confident no other governor can make that claim. (Let me state here, briefly, that welfare-to-work succeeded in Wisconsin. In 1990, by the end of my first term as governor, sixty-nine thousand people had left the welfare rolls.)

A second welfare proposal in that first budget proved even more controversial than the cut in the cash benefit. The plan grew out of an extended conversation I had with John Tries on one of our long drives during my run for governor. As I recall, we were in Douglas County, between Ashland and Superior. I put down my papers and we started kicking around some thoughts about what worked and what didn't in the system from John's perspective, and he said that if his experience as a Milwaukee cop had taught him anything, it was that once kids dropped out of school, the chances they would wind up in trouble expanded exponentially. It was largely if not entirely a big city problem. I mentioned that in Elroy, dropping out of school just was not an option, our parents would not have it. But in Milwaukee, by 1986, more than half of a high school freshman class would not graduate. The dropout rate was highest among black males.

It seemed possible that a number of those families were receiving welfare benefits. It dawned on me that if keeping kids in school meant they would stay out of jail, as John maintained—along with just increasing their overall chances of becoming successful adults—maybe the smart thing to do would be to require welfare recipients to keep their teenage kids enrolled in school. If the kids dropped out, the benefits, administered through Aid to Families with Dependent Children (AFDC), would be reduced. Before John and I made it to our next stop, I had settled on a name for the proposal: Learnfare.

Learnfare was controversial. How could I hold parents responsible for what their kids did? Tim Cullen, my DHSS secretary, never really bought into Learnfare. Legislative Democrats called it cruel, even racist. I knew there would be pushback, because we were trying something that had never been tried before. There is always going to be resistance to change. Even among members of my own team, Cullen and others, I was encouraged to soften the Learnfare proposal, limiting its scope to teen mothers who dropped out of school. But Betty Jo Nelsen, the skillful assembly minority leader, encouraged me to keep the broader outline, and in the end, I did. The fact was, males were dropping out at a far higher rate than females.

I would like to note here that while Learnfare had a rocky rollout—we overreached by implementing it statewide from the outset, overwhelming some local welfare offices with the changes—it eventually found its footing. School attendance improved. A *Racine Journal Times* article about Learnfare quoted a mother on AFDC as telling her son that "if he cuts school I won't be able to buy him clothes." She said the boy made a point of getting to class, and his grades improved.

What I remember most is being in my office at the capitol late one evening, going through some mail by myself, and coming across a letter that I can quote to this day. It was from a young woman who said that she was fourteen years old and pregnant when I began Learnfare. At the time she thought I was the most evil person in the world. But she did go back to school, so she could get her full welfare payment. She began to apply herself, and her grades improved. Before too long she was getting As. I choked up as I continued reading. She wrote, "Now I'm about to graduate from high school. I'm going to go to college, and law school, and run for public office."

You can handle a lot of criticism when you have a letter like that in your pocket.

Back in 1987 the legislature was not impressed by either Learnfare or my proposal to cut welfare cash benefits, or much of anything else in my budget for that matter. They put forth numerous amendments and changes, eliminating tax cuts and increasing spending. With welfare, they changed my 5 percent cut in the cash benefit to 1 percent, and they changed Learnfare so that only teen mothers were required to stay in school to receive full benefits.

Let me be clear about this. The budget the legislature sent back to me in 1987 was a bad budget. It had spending and tax increases, the very things I had pledged would not be in a budget if I was elected. For reasons I mentioned earlier—mainly their continuing anger over my upset victory the previous November—the Democrats were determined to reestablish their supposed might by taking my proposals and shoving them down my throat.

I, on the other hand, felt compelled to remind them there was a new governor in town.

We had a month to take that budget—an 893-page document—and decide what I should veto before signing it into law. In July the press carried several stories that speculated about what I might veto. On July 23, I told the *Wisconsin State Journal*, "I don't intend to be a timid governor."

By then—just a week or so before I would sign the budget—a number of things had been happening, some more or less in the open, others behind the scenes. I dedicated two conference rooms adjacent to my capitol office for meetings between my staff and members of the public, groups and individuals, who wanted to weigh in on the budget. I attended when I could. In the last two weeks of July I met with 250 separate delegations. We also went over the more than six thousand letters we had received concerning the budget. I wasn't going to be accused of not listening.

But in the meantime, I asked Jim Klauser and his budget analysts in the Department of Administration to identify every single change the legislature had made to my budget. It was a large assignment. Something like 125 of the amendments had actually started as separate bills, but that didn't stop the Democrats from attaching them willy-nilly to the budget bill. I asked Klauser's budget staff for briefings on all the changes, along with recommendations on which ones should be vetoed. That's where the process became still more complicated. In Wisconsin, the governor had extraordinary power and latitude when it came to vetoes. I didn't have to veto something outright, or let it pass. I had the option to exercise a partial veto, striking numbers, or words—even a single letter—from a line in the proposed budget. I would tell the budget analysts what I was hoping to accomplish with a particular passage, generally attempting to change it back to how we had it originally. They would try to make it happen, slicing and dicing the language. As Klauser said, many years later, "They were really happy in the budget shop when they could make a new word."

Through just this kind of use of the partial veto, I was able to eliminate $33 million in new spending, as well as a number of tax increases the Democrats had added to the budget. With welfare, I restored my original 5 percent cut in the cash benefit and also the expanded definition of Learnfare—every teenager, not just teen mothers, would be required to attend school or see their families' benefits reduced. We had some arguments internally about those. Tim thought we should go with the legislature's version. It was also, right up to the end, looking like it might be a moot point: we needed the federal waivers to include welfare reform in the signed budget. We got the waivers just in time, and I restored the original provisions to the bill. I was going to take heat either way. Better to make a statement that we were serious about changing the welfare mindset.

The night of July 30—I would sign the budget at a capitol ceremony the following day—our team met at the mansion in Maple Bluff to finalize the vetoes. We worked downstairs, in the space my staff called the action room. There were two sets of documents. All the changes had to be signed or initialed.

When my vetoes were counted, they added up to 290, by far the most ever by a Wisconsin governor and a figure that brought howls of outrage from

Democrats when I signed the budget the next day. Senator Chuck Chvala spoke for many, I suppose, when he called it "appalling."

But the truth is, governors of both parties had consistently utilized the partial veto. In that regard, it was truly nonpartisan. Tony Earl was the first to strike individual letters to make up new words, although those vetoes were overridden by the legislature. A decade earlier, Pat Lucey struck a digit, changing the figure $25 million to $5 million.

A *Wisconsin State Journal* political reporter, Tom Still, had the smart idea of tracking down Lucey on the day I signed my first budget to get his perspective on the vetoes. Lucey said that when he ran up a total of more than sixty vetoes, legislators accused him of "overdoing" it. Told my number was close to three hundred, Lucey said, "That's remarkable." But then he said this: "More power to him if he thinks it's justified. Anything a governor can do to improve that document from his or her point of view is perfectly legitimate."

I will admit now that I may have gone a little far with my "letter" vetoes, which came to be called Vanna White vetoes, after the woman who uncovered the letters on the game show *Wheel of Fortune*. But that first year I felt like I had to make our views clear and accentuate them by demonstrating we knew where the power resides in Wisconsin state government. We mixed in a little humor. A Republican assemblyman, Cloyd Porter, from Burlington, got a lumberyard in his district to make a five-foot-long pencil that he brought to a press conference, along with a shorter pencil that he said showed how much I'd been using the first one.

It would be wrong to leave the impression that the final power, in regard to the budget in Wisconsin, belongs to the governor. The legislature can override any of the governor's vetoes. It isn't easy—it requires a two-thirds vote of both houses to do it—but it can be done.

Early on, I told the Republican caucuses in both the senate and assembly that if we were going to get anything done—if I was going to be able to run the government—I needed their full support. Even if they disagreed with me on a particular veto, I needed them to stick with me. It worked. In all my years as governor, I never had a veto overridden.

The welfare reform component of my first budget brought a splash of national publicity, and that in turn earned Sue Ann and me an invitation that summer to visit Vice President George H. W. Bush at the Bush summer home on the ocean in Kennebunkport, Maine. It began a relationship that grew into a treasured friendship.

The vice president invited several Republican governors that day, all of whom were planning to support him when he ran for president in 1988. He wanted to hear from us in the areas in which we had expertise—in my case, welfare—and he wanted to sound us out on when and how he should announce his candidacy. He wanted the governors to act almost like support staff, and essentially run his campaign. He wanted us to be active. That day in Kennebunkport we sat around his study—there were staffers taking notes—and he asked what we were doing in our states that we thought might work on the federal level. I spoke about welfare reform.

They were preparing a lobster boil for us after the meeting. But before we ate, the vice president—I think he might have been testing us a little bit—asked if we wanted to go for a boat ride. It was going to be chilly out on the open water, and not everyone did. I said I'd go. The vice president grinned and handed me a Chicago Cubs jacket to wear.

"I like the Cubs," I said. "Good," the vice president said. "So do I."

But before we left the house, George's wife, Barbara, took me aside and said, "Watch him. When he gets behind the wheel of the boat, he can get a little wild."

I laughed, but she wasn't kidding. It was a fairly long walk down some cement steps to get to the boat. There were actually two boats, one for Secret Service agents and one for the vice president and a few governors, including me. The vice president put on a commodore's hat, and it was as if that hat turned him from Dr. Jekyll to Mr. Hyde. He fired up the twin engines, swung the boat around, and started maneuvering at high speed between these giant granite rocks that jutted out of the water in the inlet. He had probably done it often enough that he could do it with his eyes closed, but for a first-time passenger, it was, well, *exhilarating* would be one word for it. There are others.

When we reached open water he really let the throttle loose and we were practically flying. Barbara was right. He went for maybe twenty minutes at breakneck speed, loving every moment of it, including the fact that we were unsettled. When he was ready to dock, he brought the boat in at very high speed, cutting the engines only at the last minute. We drifted to a stop right at the dock. He absolutely knew what he was doing. He grinned back at us and said, "Did you enjoy the ride?"

He was such a nice guy, really a wonderful man, but he had a competitive streak. When he lost the 1992 election to Bill Clinton, he invited some of his favorite governors to Camp David, right around Christmas. Tom Ridge was there, John Ashcroft, as well as Sue Ann and I. At that point George had only a few weeks left as president.

A year or two earlier I had stayed in the Lincoln Bedroom at the White House. The president invited me to town for the Alfalfa Party, put on by the Alfalfa Club, a venerable Washington, D.C., organization that exists only to hold an annual banquet, in late January, during which a mock presidential nomination is made. George H. W. Bush is one of very few men to have been a member of the club while actually serving as the real president.

By the time Sue Ann and I received the invitation to Camp David in late 1992, the president and I were good friends. He wanted us to experience Camp David, and it was a beautiful place, with walking trails, scenic natural spaces, volleyball and basketball courts, and a horseshoe pit. Along with the governors, he had invited the country singer Amy Grant, who performed a song for the governors, and the husband and wife actors Bruce Willis and Demi Moore. It was a Christmas party, and it was fun, though earlier that afternoon we had played sports and the president's competitive side came out. He was an athlete and very aggressive. He liked nothing more than spiking the volleyball and guarding up close and in your face playing basketball. He didn't want to lose. The governors were a lot younger but he didn't give an inch; he was right in there pushing and shoving. It was a fun day, with a special man.

I also have Bush—Bush 41—to thank for putting me on the board of directors of Amtrak. After he was elected president he nominated me, and my confirmation hearing in the Senate was in April 1990. Amtrak became a passion of mine, probably because I had loved trains since I was a kid in Elroy. Bush couldn't have done anything nicer for me—but then, he always said I was one of his favorite governors.

I've mentioned before that my boyhood home of Elroy was a railroad hub and a turnaround point on the Minneapolis-to-Chicago line. The freight trains went back and forth on Second Street, and I lived just a couple blocks over on Academy Street. I'd go over there, sometimes with a friend, and we'd hop a freight. No one ever knew. I was about twelve years old and lucky I didn't get killed, when I look back on it. We'd hop on in the railroad yard and stay on until they got up to about fifteen miles an hour or so, just out of town, and then hop off. You kind of hit the ground rolling and it wasn't too bad.

Some famous people came through Elroy on the train when I was growing up. Most of them I only heard about. Before I was born, the former king Edward of England was on a train through Elroy, just a month or so after he abdicated his throne so he could marry the American socialite Wallis Simpson. Calvin Coolidge went through once or twice on his way up north to go fishing.

In 1948 Harry Truman was campaigning for president, on a train through Wisconsin from Minneapolis, and he stopped in Elroy and gave a speech. I was six years old. In my memory, my father and I were the only ones who went down to see him. But I've since learned that nearly all the parents took their children to see the president. Somehow my dad got close to the caboose. He put me on his shoulders and Truman spoke for about five minutes.

A few years later, Richard Nixon came through. He was either vice president or campaigning for that office. I didn't see him, but I found the story one day when I was doing some research on Elroy history. Nixon and his wife, Pat, had signed some menus and were handing them out to people off the back of the train. In the story I read, a young kid reached out, and Nixon, trying to be nice, took the kid under his arms and lifted him up onto the train. Just at that moment, the train began to leave. Nixon was holding the kid and you can imagine them both looking back wide-eyed at the boy's father as the train begins to pick up speed and pull away. They got the train stopped after about a hundred yards, and Nixon was able to return the boy to his father.

I actually had two terms on the Amtrak board. Bush appointed me first. I cycled off the board in the mid-1990s, but then, in 1998, I got a phone call from President Bill Clinton, with whom I was friendly. As I noted earlier, Bill served as a mentor for me with the National Governors Association when I was first elected governor. It was an interesting phone call. Clinton explained that he had a problem. He wanted to appoint Michael Dukakis, the former governor of Massachusetts and a former Democratic nominee for president (he lost to my friend George H. W. Bush in 1988), as chairman of Amtrak. Since some Amtrak board seats were subject to Senate approval, Clinton felt it would help Dukakis if a Republican was nominated at the same time.

"I know you love railroads," Clinton said, "and I understand that under President Bush you did a great job on the Amtrak board. I would like to appoint you again."

"I will consider it, Mr. President," I said.

I think he called on a Wednesday. He said he would call back in two days, which he did. I don't think he was prepared for what I said that Friday.

"I'll take it, Mr. President," I said. "On one condition."

"What's that, Tommy?" Clinton said.

Well, I loved Amtrak. But I had been on the board. What I really wanted was to be chairman.

"I will take it if you make me chairman," I said.

He said, "I can't do that! I'm a Democrat. I promised Mike Dukakis he could be chairman."

"Make him vice chairman," I said.

Clinton said, "I won't do that. I can't do that. No. I'll make you vice chairman."

"I am chairman," I said, "or I won't do it."

"I can't do it," he said.

"Well, that's fine," I said. "Good-bye."

A few days later, the following Monday I believe it was, Clinton called back. "You can be chairman," he said.

I can only assume he talked to Dukakis, and Mike wanted to be on the board bad enough that he didn't mind not being chairman. He wound up as vice chairman. The funny thing was, before that series of phone calls, Dukakis and I didn't get along. On the Amtrak board, after we were both confirmed, we became very good friends. Mike and I helped make Amtrak's high-speed train, the Acela Express, a reality.

We were both onboard the Acela on its maiden voyage from Washington, D.C., to New York City in January 2000. There was a christening ceremony before we left Washington, and I broke a bottle of California champagne on the train's tapered nose. I spoke and said the train's debut was a truly defining moment for this generation of Americans. We got to New York City two minutes ahead of schedule and set an Amtrak speed record, hitting 135 miles per hour at one point in New Jersey. I spoke again when we arrived at Penn Station. A crowd had gathered and I shouted, "We deliver!"

It's not hard for me to get excited about trains. Eight months earlier, in April 1999, the National Association of Railroad Passengers (NARP) presented me with the George Falcon Golden Spike Award at its annual reception at the Columbus Club in Union Station. NARP president John R. Martin presented the award and said, "We particularly appreciate Governor Thompson's effective, persuasive, and tireless efforts in carrying to Congress the message that passenger rail enjoys broad, bipartisan support."

As much as I appreciated receiving that award, something that I will truly never forget happened some two and a half years later, when I was no longer governor of Wisconsin and no longer on the Amtrak board.

I had resigned as governor to join George W. Bush's cabinet as secretary of health and human services in early 2001, and then that May I resigned as chairman of Amtrak, though I did so reluctantly. I had been getting pressure from the White House to resign because only one cabinet member is allowed to be on the Amtrak board, and the White House, naturally enough I suppose, wanted the new secretary of transportation, Norman Mineta, to have the spot. It made sense, but you'll recall I had talked with then president-elect Bush and his staff about the transportation secretary job. He wanted me at HHS. As a consequence, I had to leave the Amtrak board.

That may have been part of why I found it so rewarding that fall—it was November 1, 2001—when there was a ceremony, again at Washington's Union Station, in which a locomotive was named for me. George Warrington, the Amtrak CEO and president, made it happen. He appreciated what I had done for the organization. When I spoke that day, at the ceremony, it was from the heart.

"In politics," I said, "you get a lot of awards and citations. But to have an engine named for me is something that touches me very deeply. I have a model of the 'Governor Tommy Thompson' on my desk at the Department of Health and Human Services, and every time I see it, I'm reminded of why I love Amtrak and why I'm so passionate about America's railways."

I went on to try to communicate something of what hearing the trains from my bed on Academy Street had meant to me (though I left out the part about having jumped some freights): "There's something haunting about the sound of a train in the night. As a boy, it fired my imagination and inspired a sense of wonderful mystery. Thinking of where a train might be going, of what I could see as I traveled, of what I would find at the end of the line—all those things created within me a passion for rail travel that has never diminished."

I invoked history—mentioning that one of my heroes, Abraham Lincoln, was a champion of the railroad—and I talked about the future and the importance of making Amtrak a success.

I said that day at Union Station that getting a train engine named for me was one of the greatest honors of my life, and I meant it.

6

Eighteen months after I signed my first budget as governor in the summer of 1987, I gave a speech that highlighted just how well things had worked out once the initial controversy over my vetoes had passed.

It was my annual State of the State address, on January 25, 1989. There is always a lot of cheerleading in a speech like that, but I never minded being accused of being a cheerleader for the state of Wisconsin. We had a lot to cheer about at that point, in part, I believe, because the Democrats came to realize they were going to have to work with me. No matter who is governor, legislators want things for their districts. My door was open, and I made a sincere effort to work with both Democrats and Republicans. Democrats started coming and cutting individual deals with me. Joe Andrea, a Democratic senator from Kenosha, was in my office weekly when the legislature was in session. He showed up every Tuesday. If Chuck Chvala or someone else in Democratic leadership turned him down on something, he would say, "OK, I'll talk to the governor." Andrea may have been in my office nearly as often as he was in his own, and he brought other Democrats. We would horse-trade.

I had especially spirited negotiations with Marty Beil, executive director of the Wisconsin State Employees Union, a division of the American Federation of State, County and Municipal Employees. Marty was a giant of a man, both physically and in his personality.

When we did labor contracts, he eventually met with Jim Klauser. They would bargain and argue and nearly always end a half percentage point apart. At that point, Marty would insist on coming to see me, and Jim would bring him over. Marty wouldn't have known—well, maybe he suspected—but Jim and I had already talked, and had ascertained how far we could go. Jim would actually set funds aside, knowing that in the end I would be able to put forth a little extra and make Marty happy.

Marty—who died in October 2015, just four months after retiring—loved the give-and-take. He would come in yelling and pounding his fist, and then we would sit down and cut the deal. Once you got past the bluster, Marty was fair. The other thing talking to Marty did was give us insight into what was happening in the various departments. What was *really* going on. His people knew what was working and what wasn't. When I talked to cabinet secretaries, inevitably they would say that everything was running smoothly. I got another perspective from Marty.

Marty Beil wasn't alone in appreciating the fact that I would personally meet with him. Getting to see the governor means something to people. It was an implicit goodwill gesture that didn't cost me anything but time, and often helped to accomplish things. When you are working with people with whom you may have fundamental disagreements—but who are in the same business you are in—you find a way to work together, to have a meeting of the minds, in search of the best outcomes.

I referenced that kind of collaboration early in my 1989 State of the State speech. I quoted Alice E. Smith, a prominent Wisconsin historian and author, who noted of the people of the state: "Through the years they have sustained a remarkably cohesive society, despite the unusual diversity of their cultural and economic interests. They have taken pride in the stability of their institutions, even as they have made Wisconsin a laboratory to test the new and untried. They have built well, for the future as well as for the present."

By 1989 the Wisconsin economy had recovered from its dismal performance during the first half of that decade. In those years, the relationship between government and private business had deteriorated to the point that some Wisconsin business groups got together and took out an ad in the *Wall Street Journal* warning companies that the state was no place to do business. The statistics bore them out. Wisconsin lost 23 percent of its manufacturing jobs between 1979 and 1983. The state's economic growth rate was one-half the national average. In job creation outside of farming, it ranked fortieth.

By January 1989 we had turned that around. With a mix of programs and promotion, we had worked hard to transform Wisconsin's antibusiness image, and the results spoke to our success. We had added two hundred thousand jobs since I took office. Unemployment in December 1988 was 3.8 percent, the lowest in nearly two decades. New construction totaled $4.6 billion in 1988.

Part of it was changing perceptions. To help the many residents in Wisconsin who ran small businesses like motels and restaurants—particularly in the north—I increased our tourism funding by 300 percent in my first budget. On the other end of the scale, I invited Roger Smith, the chairman of General Motors, to lunch at the Executive Residence. Smith told me he'd never been invited to the governor's residence in Michigan. I listened to him. He later issued a quote that I used in my 1989 State of the State speech: "Wisconsin is one of the best places in the country to do business. If all the states were like Wisconsin, it would be better for the country."

If any single change could be said to summarize how we tried to bring collaboration and common sense to state government, it may have been the Office of Business Advocacy that I established in the Department of Development (DOD). Its mission was to assist business people who were having trouble dealing with one or another state agency. Often, that was the Department of Natural Resources (DNR), which, fair or not, had by the time I was elected governor developed a reputation as being staunchly antibusiness. The sides had become polarized. You were either a businessman or an environmentalist; no one could be both.

I rejected that scenario. Clearly I was probusiness. But I also considered myself if not an environmentalist, then someone with a deep appreciation for Wisconsin's natural resources. When I was kid growing up in Elroy without a lot of money, the state's waters and woods were my playground. After my first inaugural address in 1987, a reporter wrote, "Thompson surprised observers at the noon ceremony in the capitol rotunda by highlighting his commitment to preserving the state's natural resources." It shouldn't have surprised anyone. I hunted and fished as a kid, and I taught my own kids to snow-ski and water-ski. As governor, I was out at the opening of deer season, and I generally got a deer. I was even more committed to the opening of fishing season, which was celebrated every year with the Governor's Fishing Opener, an event sponsored by Wisconsin Indian Head Country and launched in 1965 by Governor Warren Knowles to promote tourism in the northwest part of the state.

Warren always joined me at the opener, to which I would also invite cabinet members, friends, and legislators. We'd make a weekend of it, going up north on a Friday afternoon. It was fun, a big party. We made bets about catching the most fish. One year, Chuck Thompson, from my cabinet, put some kind of oil on the fishing lures of Pete Helland, the DNR board chairman, so Pete wouldn't catch any fish. It was turnabout because Pete was always pulling things like that. Most of the time, Jerry Baumbach, my security man and close friend, was responsible for making sure everyone had a working beer, including—first and foremost—himself. One year we made the mistake of assigning Mark Bugher, who served as cabinet secretary of two different departments, to bring the beer. It seemed to make sense: Mark is married to Kate Leinenkugel, of the great Wisconsin beer family. I don't remember how much beer he eventually brought, maybe a couple of six-packs, but it was paltry enough to elicit howls of disbelief and outrage among the thirsty fishermen and women. We still kid Mark about that.

On a more serious note, during my first term we established, together with the legislature, a fund that would purchase and protect environmentally sensitive land. It started when a representative of the Nature Conservancy contacted me and broached the idea. I think he was a bit surprised when my reaction was positive. While the legislature wanted a $500 million endowment, we settled on a $250 million Stewardship Fund, which in its first decade financed more than 1,400 land purchases, including the two largest in Wisconsin history—twelve thousand acres of the Turtle-Flambeau Flowage and the sixty-nine-hundred-acre Chippewa Flowage. I personally got involved in the discussions. By the end of my time as governor, we had acquired more land for conservation than any administration before or since.

You can see why I refused to accept that being probusiness and proenvironment were mutually exclusive.

The purpose of the new Office of Business Advocacy was to assist businesses that had problems dealing with state government. Often, because things had become so polarized, the problem was with the DNR. Right from the start, its toll-free telephone number began averaging 250 calls a month. My thinking in establishing the office was that a state employee who calls the DNR to have a conversation *on behalf* of a businessperson is going to be better received than the businessperson calling him- or herself. It's common sense. They're both state employees. The perceived business-environment antagonism is set aside. Because the people in the business advocacy office were also much better versed in state rules and regulations than a business owner could possibly be, they could make a better case for whatever was hoped to be accomplished. Things would move faster, and presumably both sides would be happier.

I don't mean to suggest that any of this is easy. I'm not sure my DOD secretary, Bruno Mauer, ever really adjusted to running a bureaucracy, which, no way around it, is the definition of a state agency. Bruno was a businessman who had spent his whole life fighting government. I liked him, and overall in his relatively brief tenure he accomplished what I hoped for: He put a new face on business in the state. He set the tone that Wisconsin was open for business.

Another of my appointments—one I announced with considerable fanfare during my 1989 State of the State speech—lasted only three hours.

Drug and alcohol abuse was an issue in Wisconsin, as it was across the country, and in 1988 I hosted a conference in Madison that drew five hundred people to consider ways to combat the problem. Together with Attorney General Don Hanaway and schools superintendent Bert Grover, I established the Alliance for a Drug-Free Wisconsin. The coordinator of the alliance would be responsible for bringing together students, teachers, parents, police, social workers, and others in a comprehensive effort to educate about ways to prevent drug abuse in Wisconsin. I think it was Jerry Whitburn, then Klauser's deputy at the Department of Administration—and soon to join my cabinet as a secretary himself—who came up with a high-profile choice for alliance coordinator. It was so high profile that it had to be kept secret. Jerry liked keeping things under wraps anyway. His suggestion—which I acted on—for the drug alliance coordinator, a title that was quickly shortened to "drug czar" once we announced it, was Tedd O'Connell, a longtime reporter and anchorman at WISC-TV in Madison. I should note that Jerry said recently that he doesn't recall advancing Tedd for the position. In any case, keeping it secret was our undoing. If more people on my staff had known about it, someone would have spoken up, and we would have avoided a significant embarrassment.

It was near the end of my State of the State speech that I introduced Tedd O'Connell, who was at the capitol that day. I still remember seeing Tedd in the balcony, above me to the left. He stood and waved when I introduced him.

Within minutes of finishing my speech we began to hear people buzzing and asking if we had done due diligence in researching Tedd's background. The worst thing on the record was that Tedd had been busted for drunk driving, although it had happened eleven years earlier. But it also turned out that he had a considerable reputation around Madison as someone who enjoyed a party, and all the things that went on at parties in the 1970s and 1980s. Everyone knew what that meant. It was not the background you would look for in a drug czar. The lesson was clear: a governor, or any leader, needs to fully vet appointments long before they're announced.

Tedd said later he had started getting phone calls from reporters almost immediately. So did my office. It was clear the appointment was not going to stand. To Tedd's credit, he did the right thing, and he did it quickly. Three hours after the original announcement, I received a letter from Tedd: "While I looked forward to joining your administration in the new position, I regret that for personal reasons I must decline."

We moved on, not letting that unfortunate start curtail our antidrug efforts. In the same speech in which I introduced Tedd, I announced an aggressive new proposal to create drug-free school zones in Wisconsin. It called for a mandatory three-year prison sentence for anyone convicted of selling drugs near a school or school bus. When the *Milwaukee Journal* did a poll a few weeks later, asking state residents what they thought of the idea, 92 percent were in favor.

The newspaper also polled on what it called another "major new initiative" that I referenced in the speech: school choice. The *Journal* noted that my proposal would allow parents in most parts of the state to send their kids to public schools outside their own district if they chose to do so. In central city Milwaukee the parents could choose nonreligious private schools. In each case, state tax dollars would, in effect, follow the students. It gave parents a choice in their children's education. The *Journal* poll showed state residents to be slightly in favor of the proposal. By January 1989 the proposal, or at least the idea of school choice in Wisconsin—and especially Milwaukee—was anything but new. It had been on my radar since we introduced Learnfare in my first budget and discovered that on any given day Milwaukee couldn't tell us which students were in school and which weren't.

I mentioned earlier the dismal graduation rate of students in the Milwaukee Public Schools system at the time I took office. Half the incoming freshmen would not graduate from high school. The statistics for minorities were even worse. Far too many black males dropped out of high school before graduating. In talking with Klauser and others I trusted, it was clear we needed to try something, and maybe something radical, to change those numbers. Otherwise, we would be building more prisons. When an underclass begins to see its situation as permanent, people lose hope and get angry. With the opportunity for a good education, there is reason for hope. We needed to do something. At least, we needed to try.

By 1987, my first year in office as governor, attempts to end segregation in Milwaukee's public schools with busing had been going on for a decade. But almost nobody liked busing kids out of their own neighborhoods—it was largely black kids being bused—and it was doing little or nothing to improve test scores or graduation rates. I remember having a discussion with a black religious leader from Milwaukee, Sedgwick Daniels, as well as others, who said busing was essentially just telling black parents where their kids should go to school. They said black parents needed to be more involved. At the same time— and more vocally—a state representative named Annette "Polly" Williams, with whom I had served in the state assembly, was insisting that busing had failed. Williams was black; her district included central city Milwaukee. Her liberal Democrat bona fides were unassailable. She had chaired Jesse Jackson's presidential campaign in Wisconsin.

Polly Williams pointed out what she said were several flaws in forced busing, including the fundamental one: some 90 percent of the kids being bused were black. She also resisted the idea that desegregation was inherently a good thing. Williams said she didn't know why a black child needed to be sitting next to a white child to learn well.

Williams's first attempt to end busing was a 1987 legislative amendment that narrowly failed in the assembly. It would have required parental consent to bus a child. After it failed, Williams brought forward another idea. She suggested carving out a nearly all-black school district in the Milwaukee central city. It would be called the North Division district (it included North Division High School) and would be 97 percent black. Williams—and she was not alone—felt that a black school district under black authority couldn't help but improve the education of black kids. Parents would be free to choose schools for their children, adding a parental control component to the plan.

Before Williams and her supporters took the idea to the legislature (where it ultimately failed), they met with me in my office. I told them I understood what they were trying to do, but said I didn't agree with their plan. (Klauser and I had kicked around an idea—we eventually discarded it—of trying to split the Milwaukee Public Schools system, which then had around one hundred thousand kids, into four separate and more manageable districts, each with its own board and more localized control. I still think the idea has considerable merit.) Back in late 1987, when I met with Williams about her black district plan, I expressed my doubts about the wisdom and viability of creating a segregated district. I don't recall mentioning this to her, but I was also leery of the state funding that would be required for a district that wouldn't have much of a property tax base. We had been shoveling money into Milwaukee Public Schools for years, and I was convinced it had done little good other than empower an education bureaucracy run by powerful—and, to my mind, arrogant—teachers' unions that resisted all change. To say that, of course, is to be labeled "antiteacher" or even "antieducation." I didn't believe I was antiteacher. My parents were teachers. My wife was a teacher. But I also like to think I have enough common sense to know that when something isn't working, it's worth trying something else, even if it might be controversial.

My recollection is that one of the people who came to my office that day in late 1987 with Polly Williams was Howard Fuller, then the dean of general education at Milwaukee Area Technical College. A few years later, Fuller would become superintendent of Milwaukee Public Schools. At one point in our discussion of the potential North Division district, I recall Fuller saying that there were already some good schools in those predominantly low-income neighborhoods, but the schools were private.

At which point, I said, "Well, if those schools are doing such a good job, and they're located in the neighborhoods where many of the children live, why not let the children attend those schools?"

There was a stunned silence. As people grasped the meaning of what I said—and I had said it off the top of my head, without an ideological agenda in mind—someone voiced the notion that if such a plan were to become reality, it would somehow be the end of public schools. It's an argument that continued to be raised whenever the idea of what came to be called school choice was discussed, and it's an argument I did not and do not buy. Instead, the opposition—and the real argument—was political. Throughout the discussions, and they went on for years, the number of students who would be part of any choice program was tiny in comparison to the vast public school enrollment. I felt that many Democrats, along with the teachers' unions, had a proprietary interest in public education. Even a small change had to be resisted by every available means. If the change might actually benefit black kids in poor neighborhoods, well, that was acceptable collateral damage. What mattered was keeping control of public education.

Of course, little of that came up during that early meeting. As time went on, it became clear that Williams, for her part, was by no means wed to the status quo. It was her frustration with forced busing and how the system was failing black kids that had brought her to my office in the first place. Still, she was not excited about the choice option I raised that day. She had her own plan—the separate black school district—and she intended to push for it.

I went ahead and included school choice in the budget I submitted in January 1988. Some on my staff had argued against it, feeling it had little chance to pass the legislature, and that raising it as an issue would allow critics to portray me as a far-right-winger. I didn't care. What I thought about were things like talking to the Milwaukee Metropolitan Association of Commerce and learning that the city's businesses were having an increasingly hard time finding young workers with any kind of job skills. It went straight to the terrible high school dropout rates. If I could change that for one thousand students, I had to try. One thousand was the number I put in the budget—those one thousand low-income Milwaukee children would be allowed to attend any school of their choice—public, private, or parochial—with the state paying the private school tuition up to the level of state aid currently being provided to Milwaukee Public Schools, about $2,400 per student.

That first attempt at school choice never even made it to the floor of the legislature for a vote. The proposal died in committee. It was ridiculed by everyone from the Madison-based Freedom from Religion Foundation—for the religious schools component—to Superintendent Grover. The teachers union, predictably, had a collective heart attack, calling school choice an assault on public education. Black leaders in Milwaukee were not vocal against my plan, but neither had they championed it. As my team—notably education adviser Tom Fonfara—began to regroup on the issue, I knew that had to change.

On January 9, 1989, I was invited to a White House Workshop on Choice in Education hosted by President Ronald Reagan and President-Elect George H. W. Bush. I was allowed to bring one guest, and I invited Polly Williams, who accepted. I don't think the conference entirely converted her on the issue of school choice, but it helped. Black leaders from around the country attended, many of whom thought choice was in their constituents' best interest.

I put school choice into my budget again later that month. It was a two-pronged approach, which I referenced earlier in regard to a *Milwaukee Journal* poll a few weeks later that said a slight majority in Wisconsin favored the idea. My plan called in effect for public school choice statewide; that is, parents could send their kids to public schools outside their immediate district. In central city Milwaukee, low-income families could send their children to nonsectarian private schools. I didn't like taking the religious schools out of the plan—in many poor neighborhoods, they were easily the best schools—but I felt it gave choice a more realistic shot at passing. I wanted to win this time.

I didn't. Once again, in April, the legislature's Joint Finance Committee removed school choice—both proposals—from the budget. The statewide initiative had received criticism we hadn't considered—local school districts were worried their best high school athletes might be lured into competing against them. As for the Milwaukee private school plan, even without the religious school component, it drew considerable fire. We were abandoning public schools! Both Milwaukee daily papers editorialized against it. But significantly, the largest black-owned newspaper in the state, the *Milwaukee Community Journal*, supported the Milwaukee private school plan.

Polly Williams, too, perhaps in part due to her attendance at the Washington conference earlier in the year, was warming up to parental choice as an alternative to her original hope for a black school district. While Joint Finance had removed my proposal from the budget, there was still the opportunity to introduce the Milwaukee component as separate legislation. It wouldn't have stood a chance if a Republican representative introduced it, but if Williams did, it might. My recollection—and this has never really been publicized—is that Betty Jo Nelsen, the Republican minority leader in the assembly, worked hand in hand with Polly crafting the legislation. The language was pretty close to mine in the budget bill, though it called for more than one thousand students to be eligible. Religious schools were not part of it. Betty Jo was also responsible for making sure her entire Republican caucus voted for the bill. History has settled on Polly Williams as the one who made school choice happen. Fair enough, but Betty Jo Nelsen had a significant role, too.

Williams introduced the Parental Choice Options bill in October 1989. It was still controversial; all the old arguments against it were resurrected. But Williams had rallied her constituents. When the bill was voted on in the assembly on March 13, 1990, the assembly chambers were filled with low-income families from Milwaukee who recognized the value of being able to select the schools their children would attend. The bill passed the assembly easily.

The senate, however, was another matter. Like the assembly, it had a Democratic majority, where the bill had no obvious champion like Polly Williams. There was also time pressure. The legislature was scheduled to adjourn at the end of March and not convene again until after the November elections. A Democratic leader, Bob Jauch, announced that the choice bill passed by the assembly would not get a senate hearing before adjournment. It looked like another defeat, except that Gary George, the senate's only African American, had begun to change his mind on parental choice, and George still had an opportunity to save it by including it as an amendment in the omnibus budget bill that had yet to be voted on.

Multiple forces were at work. George was a power in the capitol; indeed, as cochair of Joint Finance, he had twice removed school choice from my budget. Along with other Democrats in the capitol, he was hearing a constant drumbeat from the teachers union, the Wisconsin Education Association Council (WEAC), and others, about the supposed evils of parental choice. But by spring 1990 George was also starting to hear what some in Milwaukee's black community were saying. The bill was important to them. It would be good for black families.

While the pressure on George to kill parental choice was still intense, there was a feisty aspect to his personality that took him against the grain on occasion. Add to that the constituent and black leadership voices he was hearing from in Milwaukee, and, well, the unexpected happened. On March 19, six days after parental choice passed the assembly, George used his power as cochair of Joint Finance to include it as an amendment to the budget bill.

Two days later, the full senate and assembly passed the bill, with choice included, and I signed it. There were immediate legal challenges; Grover and WEAC argued it was unconstitutional. The national press weighed in. The prominent African American syndicated columnist William Raspberry wrote a column in support of the Milwaukee plan. William F. Buckley, the well-known conservative columnist and author, wrote a piece criticizing both sides on the issue. Buckley zinged it for being too timid and restrictive, while also attacking its opponents, what he called the education establishment, for their opposition to what he felt was an unprovocative program.

I never talked to Bill Buckley about school choice, but I recall a long conversation one night in Madison during which he surprised me by taking me to task for my use of the partial veto. I believe Buckley was in town to raise funds for the *Badger Herald*, the student paper that had been founded as a conservative alternative to the *Daily Cardinal* on the Madison campus. He really felt strongly that crossing out a letter or a digit in a budget bill was wrong.

"Nobody should have that kind of power, Tommy," he said.

I argued back about why I felt it was important, but he wasn't swayed. That conversation with Buckley did get me thinking. We had always congratulated ourselves on how clever we were when we utilized the partial veto. I eventually came to believe that Buckley was right and I was wrong. It's why I supported a constitutional amendment in Wisconsin that in 2009 put some limits on the governor's partial-veto power.

Back in spring 1990, the legal challenges brought against the parental choice program were unsuccessful. There were still more lawsuits in 1995, when I signed an expansion of parental choice that included neighborhood-based religious schools. Ultimately, those challenges failed as well. In June 1998 the Wisconsin Supreme Court ruled that Milwaukee could spend taxpayer money to send students to religious schools. The *New York Times* ended its lengthy article on that court decision with a quote from me: "Religious values aren't our problem. Drop-out rates and low test scores are."

By the time that article appeared, I had been working for parental choice for more than a decade. It was one of the hardest fights, and most satisfying accomplishments, of my time as governor.

At around the same time the parental choice issue was being debated in Milwaukee, another, much different controversy was raging in northern Wisconsin. It was a conflict that some people told me I would have been smart to stay out of, but that's not my style. I didn't choose sides, but I got involved, as governor in a leadership capacity, and tried to solve the problem. It was messy, but in the end I feel we succeeded. Nobody got killed, and that was a real possibility given the heightened tension and tempers at the time. The issue was Indian spearfishing. These years later it is often referred to as the walleye wars.

The battle was fought for years in federal courthouses in Wisconsin and Chicago, beginning in the 1970s. The legal arguments were complex, but they essentially came down to interpretations of treaties signed by the Ojibwe bands of northern Wisconsin and the United States back in the nineteenth century. The tribes believed the treaties gave them the right to off-reservation fishing without government restriction. The government disagreed and appealed when the Indians prevailed in court in the early rounds. The issue went back and forth between the district and appeals courts (the US Supreme Court declined to get involved), and in August 1987, during my first year as governor, US Judge Barbara Crabb in Madison ruled that six Ojibwe tribal governments had largely unrestricted off-reservation hunting and fishing rights, as long as they didn't decimate the state's natural resources.

Crabb's ruling meant that the spring of 1988 would likely bring a showdown, because of course it wasn't just government lawyers who opposed unrestricted fishing by the tribes. Many citizens of northern Wisconsin feared that if the Ojibwe used modern technology to spearfish in lakes when licensed Wisconsin residents could not, it would destroy the fish population and the tourism industry along with it.

All told, it was a volatile situation, serious enough that I ordered the state Division of Emergency Management to organize a treaty rights task force and to have police and state patrol officers in riot gear present when protests to the spearfishing—which were generally well publicized—were to occur. I visited the area often myself during three successive spring fishing seasons. I would meet with the protest leaders, one in particular named Dean Crist, who owned a pizza restaurant and said the Indians were guilty of "economic terrorism." I would go from a meeting with Crist to a meeting with Tom Maulson, head of the Lac de Flambeau tribe, whose boat had been rammed by protesters he referred to as *crazies*. I was trying to calm things down. I think Crist began to at least have some grudging respect for what I was trying to do. I basically told him, "The law's the law," and I would see that it was upheld. Maulson was a big guy who wore a red baseball cap that said Walleye Warrior. I tried to impress on Maulson that in the long run, his side needed tourism, too. What I was doing was promoting compromise. I thought it might be possible for the tribes to work with DNR wardens and come up with quotas that would apply to both sides, and that's what happened. It took some time and some close calls—there were more than two hundred arrests of protesters that first spring of 1988—but finally I think leadership on both sides realized they had to find some kind of common ground.

I remember literally smoking the peace pipe one day with a group of leaders of the various tribes. We met at a cabin in the woods that belonged to Trig Solberg, a civic-minded friend of mine who owned several grocery stores up north. We sat and passed the peace pipe, and I remember that someone in the circle had a terrible cough, the result of a cold or something worse, and we were all smoking the same pipe. It was not a happy moment. But I smoked it, and I survived.

I'm pleased to say northern Wisconsin survived those contentious springs, too. In the end, there were fistfights, but nobody got killed. In May 1990 Judge Crabb agreed with the quotas compromise and the controversy was significantly diffused. I certainly don't mean to suggest everyone was happy; they weren't. I think Maulson hated the deal, and Crist and the protest crowd weren't too pleased, either. It was a hardship. Some lakes had a one-walleye limit. But I think a majority of people understood some kind of compromise was the right thing, and maybe the only thing that made sense. Tourism stayed strong. For my part, it was a proud moment in 1996 when a fish hatchery in Spooner in northern Wisconsin was extensively renovated and renamed the Governor Tommy G. Thompson Fish Hatchery. In most years that hatchery produces more than half the muskellunge and walleye stocked around the state.

While all this was happening in the first half of 1990—the passage of parental choice, the spearfishing compromise, and more—I was facing a campaign for reelection as governor. Dating back to my earliest assembly races, I've always tried to campaign as if I was behind. My likely opponent this time was assembly Speaker Tom Loftus, who had held that post for eight years, longer than anyone in state history. I respected Tom and still do—we're good friends—but longevity in the legislature as a Dane County liberal was anything but an automatic springboard to statewide success. Loftus knew he had an uphill climb in front of him; he couldn't help but know. In the first week of 1990 the Sunday *Milwaukee Journal*, which still commanded a big circulation across Wisconsin, had this banner headline: "Thompson Starts Year Strong." The story began, "Tommy Thompson enters the 1990 election year as a popular governor with broad support. Most Wisconsinites continue to give him good marks in office. Few dislike him. And people know him much better than his likely Democratic challenger, Assembly Speaker Tom Loftus." The newspaper had taken a statewide poll and the numbers were astonishingly positive for me: 72 percent of those polled rated my performance as governor either good or excellent.

Later that same month, after my State of the State speech, the *Milwaukee Journal* ran an editorial headlined "Why Governor Will Be Tough to Beat." The paper's editorial board clearly didn't embrace all my policy initiatives, but it had come to respect my political savvy: "For a small town politician who has been chronically underestimated," the editorial noted, "this one could give lessons to the big city bosses."

In June of that year I received a handwritten note from former governor Lee Dreyfus, who almost sounded as if he missed public life. "Gov. Tommy," Lee wrote, "You're the first Republican Gov. to go for reelection since 1968 so it should be fun. I'd have gone on if it was still two years but four more would have put Joyce into the hospital." I've noted earlier that it was consideration for Joyce that led Lee not to run for a second term in 1982. In his note to me, under the date, Lee wrote, "Gods! I'm 64 today! Codger Power."

I've never been a big believer in polls, and I kept insisting to people that the race was close. Once Loftus had secured the Democratic nomination, I agreed to two debates, the same number Tony Earl had given me four years earlier. Scott Jensen, my chief of staff since July 1989—he had come from the assembly Republican caucus—and Bill McCoshen, a young policy guy in our administration, had moved over to the campaign, and Jensen got tabbed to portray Loftus in a mock debate that was part of my preparation. Except that with everything else that was going on, I didn't prepare properly. Jensen—as Tom Loftus—pretty much kicked my butt in that mock debate. At one point I got mad enough that I accidentally broke off a piece of the podium I was standing behind. Jensen claims to still have it. After that, I calmed down, did my homework, turned the tables on Jensen in the next prep debate, and, I think, used my record to make it very tough sledding for Loftus in our actual debates. The fact is, the state was in great shape. The economy was booming—unemployment in September 1990 was 3.8 percent, the lowest for that month in two decades—and we had new highways, a terrific expansion of state parkland purchases, welfare reform, and tax cuts. What was Loftus going to run on? In our first debate, at Carroll College, he tried to suggest I might leave the state for a cabinet position with George H. W. Bush.

Tom said, "It is unlikely President Bush will appoint me. But Governor, ambassador to Norway is what I've always cherished."

Funny, Tom Loftus actually became United States ambassador to Norway, under another president, Bill Clinton. In late 1991, when Samuel Skinner resigned as secretary of transportation, the Bush administration asked if I wanted to be considered for the job. But I was early in my second term as governor, enjoying it immensely, and had no desire to leave. Andrew Card, later chief of staff to George W. Bush, was named secretary of transportation.

Loftus and I had a second debate in October, again without any real fire-works. When Election Day came, November 6, I won reelection resoundingly, with 58 percent of the vote. I carried sixty-six of seventy-two counties, including Milwaukee County, which no Republican governor had won since 1946.

Winning never gets old, I thought that night. We had accomplished a great deal since I'd last stood on the stage at the Concourse Hotel in Madison, sur-rounded by my family—Sue Ann, Kelli, Tommi, and Jason were there with me again in 1990—yet I felt we were just getting started.

One initiative that had its roots early in my first term and carried over through much of the next decade was the effort to save and celebrate Frank Lloyd Wright's legacy in Wisconsin.

It began with a trade mission to Japan in 1987 and a speech I gave to a large group of businesspeople in Tokyo. I was doing one of the things I think I do best—selling Wisconsin as a great place to do business—but for whatever reason, I wasn't connecting. In fact, I was afraid I was putting people to sleep. (I was told later the closed eyes in my audience were instead an expression of concentration.)

In any case, the audience finally came alive when I mentioned Wright—his 1923 Imperial Hotel, of course, was a Japanese landmark—and pointed out that the great architect's Taliesin home is only forty miles or so from where I lived and worked in Madison. Suddenly people were engaged, and that stayed with me. Wright's impact worldwide had not diminished in the nearly thirty years since his death.

Not long after I returned from Japan, Nick and Carol Muller gave me a heads-up about some serious problems at Taliesin. Nick was director of the Wisconsin Historical Society, and Carol was director of the Executive Residence and a friend of Sue Ann. They were big Wright supporters—Nick would eventually leave the historical society to become executive director of the Frank Lloyd Wright Foundation.

Nick and Carol told me at the time—it was late 1987 or early 1988—that the

Wright Foundation was struggling financially and Taliesin was in considerable disrepair. Could the state do something?

By coincidence, around the same time, Marshall Erdman came to see me. Erdman was a vastly successful builder of medical clinics nationwide who got his start building Wright's Unitarian Meeting House in Madison. He revered the architect and shared a bit of his flair. Where Wright had his cape and cane, Erdman often wore shorts and a bow tie.

Erdman began to tell me a story similar to the Mullers'—that Taliesin was in imminent danger—but then he interrupted himself and harrumphed that he didn't know why he was bothering.

"I've approached other governors over the years—Democrats who were good friends of mine—and they all turned me down," Erdman said.

He looked at me as if to say, "I suppose you will too."

I surprised him instead: "We're going to help." I'd already discussed it with Jim Klauser, who was enthusiastic.

In June 1988 I announced the Governor's Commission on Taliesin, charged with figuring out how to save this national treasure and how much it would cost. I made Erdman the chairman, and among the twenty-eight members were Sue Ann, Klauser, and Nick Muller.

The most significant recommendation from the commission was the creation of the nonprofit Taliesin Preservation, Inc. (TPI) to oversee the restoration. In 1993 the state of Wisconsin gave TPI $8 million in the form of a loan from the Wisconsin Housing and Economic Development Authority. One of the first restoration projects involved Wright's "Romeo and Juliet" windmill tower. TPI also purchased the Wright-designed Spring Green Restaurant and turned it into a visitors' center. Taliesin still has challenges, but I'm glad we acted when we did to help preserve this important legacy.

Around the time we were assisting at Taliesin, Klauser and I were approached about helping the City of Madison build the Frank Lloyd Wright–inspired convention center that is now known as Monona Terrace. Proponents had been laboring mightily for decades to get it built on the shore of Lake Monona just down from the capitol, and opponents had been equally tenacious and inventive—lawsuits, referenda—in keeping it from happening. By 1990 it looked like Monona Terrace might finally get built, but they needed state money.

The account in a book on the battle to build Monona Terrace recalls a December 1990 meeting between Klauser; Madison mayor Paul Soglin; George Austin, director of Madison's Department of Planning and Development; and George Nelson, the Madison businessman serving as chairman of the Monona Terrace Commission. Nelson was ready to read from a list of twenty-five reasons why the state should get involved in the project.

He didn't have to offer a single reason. We were already onboard. Klauser and I had discussed it over lunch a day or two earlier and agreed it was a good idea. But we didn't want to just give the city the money. Instead, in the meeting with Soglin and the others, Klauser said we would put in $15 million—the final figure was $18 million—to build a parking ramp for the facility. The state would own the ramp and allow state employees and people doing business with the state to use it. The city was thrilled, and understandably so. I think it's fair to say Monona Terrace wouldn't have happened without state participation.

It took until late in my third term as governor—1997—for Monona Terrace to open. I was there for the grand opening in July, on stage with Nelson, Austin, and Soglin, who was no longer mayor. When asked to speak, the occasionally irascible Soglin used the opportunity to take a shot at me over the state's position on revenue sharing with cities. It was the wrong time and place for that, and I just shook my head.

Well, nobody said being governor was going to be easy.

At some point around the middle of my second term, two friends of mine, state legislator Dave Zien and Mark Bugher, secretary of the Department of Revenue, came into my office with something on their minds.

"You're not having any fun," one of them said. I don't remember which, but they were in it together.

"What do you mean?" I said.

"You're working all the time. Fifteen, sixteen hours a day. You need to have some fun."

Bugher and Zien—vastly different individuals—shared a passion for motorcycles. They suggested that I learn to ride a motorcycle, specifically a Harley-Davidson. It would be fun for me, and might also help promote the ninetieth anniversary of the Milwaukee-based Harley-Davidson Motor Company.

Well, I hadn't ridden a motorcycle since my college days in Madison. Back then, I dated a girl who had a Yamaha, and I learned to ride from her. But that was decades earlier. Still, I figured Bugher and Zien might be right. It would be fun, and I was always looking for ways to help promote Wisconsin businesses. Zien brought a motorcycle out to the Executive Residence, I rode it around just long enough to get a learner's permit, and then we rode from Maple Bluff to the capitol, where five others, including Bugher and a few legislators, joined us in a small caravan to Milwaukee and the lakeshore to celebrate the Harley anniversary. This was June 1993. I was nervous, but I did OK. Jerry Baumbach drove ahead of us in a car. It was pretty low key. There really wasn't a great deal of publicity, and Zien and Bugher were right, it was fun.

Two years later, I was remembering how I enjoyed that short Madison-to-Milwaukee ride when it dawned on me that some kind of expanded Harley ride—one with more riders, traversing much of the state—might be both fun and a smart move politically. We settled on a plan for a three-day Governor's Harley Ride that would start in Superior. Along the way we would dedicate a refurbished bridge over the Saint Croix River, between Hudson, Wisconsin, and Minnesota.

We went up to Superior the night before. The first leg of the trip would be Superior to Hudson. I had the idea that I would drive my motorcycle through a ribbon to dedicate the bridge. A couple things happened that made the day—it was August 29, 1995—more interesting than originally planned. For starters, about one hundred people showed up to ride with me—many more than I thought possible—and with them were newspaper reporters and television crews from at least three stations. I couldn't believe the commotion when I got there. I still wasn't exactly confident about my ability to ride a motorcycle. Two years before, someone had started the bike for me. I hadn't really learned to shift gears. Now here I was, in front of a big crowd, about to get on a big motorcycle that I didn't even know how to start.

I motioned to Bugher, who walked over. "Mark," I said, "please get this thing started. The reporters have been asking to talk to me, so I will go do some interviews. You start it, I'll come back, and you can show me how to shift and get me out of the damn driveway."

Mark agreed. I went over to chat with the reporters, and of course the first thing they wanted to know was whether I had a motorcycle license. The press was always trying to trip me up. Fortunately, I had gotten a license shortly after Zien first brought a bike out to the Executive Residence, the year of the Harley anniversary. I produced the license, much to their chagrin.

When I finished with the reporters, I went back to where Bugher was standing, under a canopy, next to the Harley I was going to ride. I was still fretting and not wanting to look like I didn't know what I was doing, which, of course, I really didn't. Bugher had started the bike. He pointed at the gear shift and said, "See that thing? Push it forward. That puts it in first gear."

He went on: "Just make sure you let the clutch out slowly, so you don't kill it."

I got on, and, well, right away I killed the engine. And, of course, I still didn't know how to start it. Zien had walked over by then, and he and Bugher kind of huddled around me, and we got it going again. They gave me a few more tips about getting it moving, and off I went, still uncertain of what I was really doing. We were in a big flat area, a parking lot, and I came out from under the canopy, looking for the driveway, only to be confronted by a large semitruck, parked directly ahead of me, maybe thirty feet away. It was all happening so fast, I knew I was going to hit it. Everyone knew I was going to hit that truck. People were shouting and covering their eyes. I still think the good Lord turned that motorcycle, because I don't believe I did. But I missed the truck. We got on the road, and it took me a couple of hours to feel comfortable. I would double-shift, or shift up when I meant to shift down. But by the time we got to Hudson, I was feeling pretty relaxed on the bike. I gave a speech and rode the motorcycle through the ribbon to christen the new bridge.

Dennis McCann, a talented feature columnist for the *Milwaukee Journal Sentinel*, was on hand, and his story, along with a large photo of me on the bike, ran above the fold on page one the following day.

McCann began his piece: "Under gloomy skies of iron gray but to the sweet sound of heavy metal thunder, Gov. Tommy Thompson led a pack of Hell's Republicans onto the new bridge across the St. Croix River Tuesday, squeezed to a halt near the marching band, revved his borrowed hog once for show and only then dismounted to remove his leather jacket."

McCann's piece, obviously, was somewhat tongue-in-cheek. He went on to write, "Bridge openings will never be the same after this, a stunt of such hot dog proportions that the Oscar Mayer Wienermobile couldn't have done the job better."

Maybe so, but it was *fun*. Once I had the bike figured out, I loved it all—the fresh air, the camaraderie of the riders, the celebration of Wisconsin.

We wound up doing a Harley ride every summer from that point on while I was governor.

They were all enjoyable, but I think the 1998 ride, when we were celebrating Wisconsin's Sesquicentennial, was the most memorable. We rode to Washington, D.C., and Harley-Davidson gave me a leather motorcycle jacket to present to each governor in the four state capitals we stopped at along the way.

We had 250 in our group. We went through Illinois first. In Springfield, Governor Jim Edgar declined our offer to take a ride, but he accepted a jacket. The governor of Indiana, Frank O'Bannon, a Democrat and gracious older gentleman, wouldn't ride either, but he loved the jacket.

After seeing the Indiana governor, we met with Tony George, who operated the Indianapolis Motor Speedway, home of the famed Indy 500 race. We gave him a Harley jacket, and someone asked, "Would you consider letting Governor Thompson ride his motorcycle on the Speedway?"

I don't know whether it was because we'd given him a jacket, but he agreed to let us on the Speedway. It was a big deal. He said we couldn't go fast, he didn't want any accidents—he said twenty-five miles per hour was it—and we could go around only once. Still, it's one of the fun memories of my life. I led 250 Wisconsin motorcycle riders around the Indy 500 course. Zien and Bugher were there, and Mary Panzer, who was in the state senate. Everyone had a ball. I swore it felt like two hundred thousand people were cheering me on as I approached the finish line.

Outside Columbus, Ohio, we visited the American Motorcycle Association headquarters and museum, and the secretary of state, Bob Taft, gave me a denim vest decorated with AMA patches. The trip concluded with a motorcycle parade on Pennsylvania Avenue in Washington, D.C.

The next year we spent five days traveling around Lake Superior, this time with nearly three hundred riders. It was a beautiful trip. My last ride as governor, in 2000, was out to South Dakota, another scenic trip. I usually managed to get some work done on the rides, and this time, in an open-air arena in the shadow of Mount Rushmore, I held a hearing, attended by people from all over the country, on the Republican platform for that year's national convention in Philadelphia (I was chairman of the platform committee).

I still have my Harley, though I don't ride it much anymore. What good times we had. If I have any bad feeling at all about those rides, it's because of something that happened at the end of the first one, in 1995, the ride that started with me almost crashing into a truck and then busting through the ribbon to open the new bridge at Hudson.

During that trip, I gave a speech in Neillsville in support of a new Milwaukee Brewers stadium, a deal I had been working on with the legislature, Milwaukee mayor John Norquist, and Brewers owner Bud Selig since my first term as governor.

One component of all those negotiations on how to fund the new stadium—which I will get to in more detail momentarily—was a 0.1 percent sales tax to be levied in the five counties that surrounded the proposed new stadium location, adjacent to the old facility, County Stadium, west of downtown Milwaukee.

It had been a tiring trip on the bike, starting up in Superior. I spoke in favor of the new stadium wherever we stopped, but then, in Neillsville, I made a mistake that I deeply regret to this day. In trying to explain why the stadium deal made sense for the entire state, I told the crowd that day that by supporting it they could "stick it" to Milwaukee, because it was only those five Milwaukee-area counties that would be paying the additional tax.

Somehow that phrase—"stick it to 'em"—just slipped out. What I was trying to say was that it was a good deal, your legislators up here should vote for it, because you will get the benefit of the new stadium and not have to pay for it. I should have never said "stick it" to Milwaukee. I suffered for that, as I suppose I should have. Sometimes you just screw up. It slipped out. I apologized to the press the next day, and when the trip ended, at the Harley-Davidson headquarters in Milwaukee, I apologized again, accepting a piece of cake from Mayor Norquist. On the cake was written, "Stick it to 'em." I took a bite and said, "Today I'm eating those words."

Two decades later, I still have a bad taste in my mouth about that. The truth is, I have a bad taste about the whole stadium deal—Miller Park opened in 2001—which to me in hindsight seems pretty much a fiasco, or at the very least, a series of profound misunderstandings. I have always said my word is my bond, and I like to deal with people who operate the same way, people who are straightforward.

It began at some point in the late 1980s, during my first term as governor. My recollection is that the first time I spoke with Bud Selig about the Brewers was in 1987 or 1988 in the governor's office. He came over with my friend Mike Grebe, an esteemed Milwaukee lawyer and nationally prominent Republican, who was on the Brewers board. What came out of that meeting, as I recall, was their ironclad belief that they needed a new stadium. I don't remember any specifics being discussed. They said several times, "We're not threatening to move," but they always followed that up by reiterating it was impossible to make the numbers work for them—a small-market team—in an old ballpark like County Stadium. What was that if not a threat to move?

Selig grew up in Milwaukee, and he got on the city's baseball radar in the 1960s, when he was among those fighting—unsuccessfully—to keep the Milwaukee Braves from moving to Atlanta. A few years later he was part of a group that bought the struggling Seattle Pilots and moved them to Milwaukee, where they became the Brewers. Selig had helped salve the wound of the Braves leaving. So he had a fair amount of goodwill built up, especially among baseball fans, by the time we started talking about a new stadium.

A few weeks later I invited Selig and Grebe to the Executive Residence for a working breakfast. Klauser would join us. At that time, Selig began by saying that plans were in the works for a new stadium for the Brewers. His only reason for coming, he said, was to put it on our radar. He—the Brewers—would pay for the stadium themselves.

Selig said, "I am going to build the stadium myself. I will get it built, and we're not going to ask the state, city, or county for anything. We're not asking you for anything. We just want you to stay informed."

As the years passed, I often wished I had a tape of that conversation.

After Selig and Grebe left that day, I looked at Klauser. "Do you believe him?"

"No," Jim said. "But let's let them try."

I don't have a tape of those early conversations, but I do have a newspaper clipping from that general time period, an August 3, 1988, story in the *Milwaukee Journal*. It refers to an interview Norquist gave after meeting with Brewers officials, and it said this: "Norquist told reporters after the hour-long, closed-door meeting that it was fortunate that the Brewers had agreed to pay construction costs for the stadium itself and that the state, city and county must eventually work out details of paying for other costs associated with the new stadium."

Note the phrase: "the Brewers had agreed to pay construction costs for the stadium itself." That's what Norquist took away from his August 1988 meeting with Selig.

Norquist did say the Brewers had indicated that the city, county, and state should chip in for "other costs," which was not what Selig had originally proposed to me. Still, at some point early on, he did say—Selig and Grebe came to Madison several times—that they would need help from the state on things like streets, parking lots, and other infrastructure.

I said, "Is that it?" They said it was. I said, "I think we can do that."

Meanwhile, Norquist had begun to talk about the possibility of building the new stadium in downtown Milwaukee, a proposal Selig was adamantly against.

In hindsight, it seems possible that Selig, at least originally, sincerely thought he could build the stadium without a lot of public money. In 2004 I was interviewed for an excellent *Washington Post* series on a proposed new baseball stadium in Washington, D.C. Selig was baseball commissioner by then, and, according to the *Post*, "holding out for a state-of-the-art publicly financed ballpark. No stadium, no team."

The *Post* articles traced Selig's history with the Brewers and stated that when it was decided County Stadium was outmoded, "Selig told friends that he wanted to be the first owner to finance his own ballpark since Walter O'Malley built Dodger Stadium for $18 million in 1962."

The problem was, by the late 1980s, television revenue in baseball was moving from network broadcasts to local cable deals, which gave big-market teams like the Yankees and Cubs a tremendous financial advantage, and it began to be reflected in the quality of players that teams could put on the field. The small-market Brewers were being left in the dust. They needed other revenue sources—a new stadium with luxury boxes, for instance—but the hard reality was they couldn't afford to build a new stadium. "The bottom line," Norquist told the *Post*, "is the Seligs really couldn't afford to own the team."

You might ask, well, why didn't I just let the Brewers fend for themselves? I've never really talked about this, but the answer in part is that, as the stadium talks moved along, I sought the counsel of Jim Thompson, the governor of Illinois, who had been through the same thing fairly recently in his state. Jerry Reinsdorf, the owner of the Chicago White Sox, had demanded public funding for a stadium. Otherwise, Reinsdorf said, he'd take the White Sox to Florida. In the end, Illinois put $150 million toward a new stadium. I hadn't paid a lot of attention at the time—the White Sox stadium was approved in 1988—but not long after, I talked to Thompson. Clearly the Brewers were on my mind.

"What did you do?" I asked. "And why?"

"Tommy," he said, "you and I are both progressive governors. The truth is, I got very much involved. A modern baseball park cannot be built unless the governor takes the initiative—a leadership role.

"It will be extremely controversial," Jim continued, "and I can assure you you're going to end up with more enemies than friends. But it's the thing to do. As long as we've each been governor, we've talked about leadership opportunities. I'm here to tell you, if you want the Brewers to stay, you've got to build a stadium. They can't do it without you. You will be the key."

I took Jim Thompson's advice to heart. It was always in the back of my mind that if the Brewers left, it would be on me. It's my watch. There was a need for a new stadium, and it wouldn't be built unless I showed leadership.

What became frustrating was trying to get a straight answer out of the team as to exactly what they needed. It was like trying to hit a moving target. As time went by, they kept asking for more. I remember Klauser coming back from one of those meetings and saying, "They're giving me a headache."

In early July 1991 Mayor Norquist came to Madison and we met in my office for more than an hour to discuss the new stadium. At that point we were talking about a state loan to the Brewers in the neighborhood of $35 million, with the city and county kicking in roughly the same, though my recollection is they would receive the naming rights revenue in return. Norquist was still arguing for a downtown site, and it made a lot of sense to me. I went out to see the new stadium in Baltimore, Camden Yards, which is right downtown, and beautiful. I loved it. How great is it that people can leave work and go see a Major League Baseball game? But Selig was dead set against it. Who knows why for sure? He said he didn't think people would want to drive downtown, that parking would be tough.

Selig won that one in the end, as he did most of the other disputes that arose. Early on—just a few months after my 1991 meeting with Norquist—when the amount of public assistance the Brewers were claiming to need was around $70 million, the Milwaukee County Board considered a resolution for an advisory referendum on providing taxpayer money for a stadium. It was voted down, and there was no referendum. Later, when the amount of public money for the project had escalated sharply, there was an attempt to finance it with a sports lottery, a plan that was soundly defeated in an April 1995 statewide referendum. A plan was then developed that would fund it instead with a 0.1 percent sales tax in the counties surrounding the proposed site—Selig's site, near the existing County Stadium. I felt then that there should be a referendum in those five counties, but Selig went ballistic when it was brought up. He implied they'd move the team before putting it to a referendum. Selig had already talked—in the wake of losing the sports lottery referendum—about an offer he had to move the team to Charlotte, North Carolina. The five counties never got a referendum to vote on.

I wound up signing an agreement with Selig for a $250 million ballpark near County Stadium. The Brewers, according to the agreement, would contribute $90 million. The state would pay $160 million, to be financed with that local sales tax.

It was a local tax, but it needed the approval of the legislature before it could be instituted. In late August I took my motorcycle trip and gave speeches in support of the bill, including my unfortunate "stick it to 'em" remark. Many people lobbied hard for the bill. A lot of money was spent in support of it. It passed the assembly, but the vote in the senate was going to be very close. The senate voted on October 5, 1995, but in fact there were three votes, and they went into the following morning, nearly until dawn. I was at the capitol until at least three o'clock. On the first senate vote, the bill lost 16–15. It meant there would be no local sales tax for the stadium. Then there was a request for reconsideration. Another vote was taken, and it lost again, by the same tally. My recollection is I went home at that point.

The *Washington Post*—in its 2004 series on Selig and the proposed new stadium in D.C.—reported that at about four o'clock, with the senate session still not officially gaveled to a close, Selig met with Norquist in the office of assembly Speaker David Prosser. Selig was fuming, and lashed out at Norquist. "You killed baseball in Milwaukee!"

Norquist had hoped to resurrect the downtown site as a compromise, but that wasn't going to happen. While Selig raged, thinking it was over, an extraordinary thing happened. A Republican senator from Racine, George Petak—who wanted the new stadium but felt his county should be exempted from the sales tax, as it was not really close to the stadium site—agreed to change his vote from no to yes. There were a couple of Republican senators with safe seats who could have voted for it but didn't. Petak did, and it cost him dearly. Petak was recalled and, in a special election less than a year later, lost his seat. I respect George, and he's my friend to this day. He was the first Wisconsin legislator to be successfully recalled.

It still wasn't over. There remained the $90 million that the Brewers were responsible for under the memo of understanding I had signed with Selig. They ended up getting $40 million of that by selling the naming rights for the stadium to Miller Brewing Company. That wasn't a double-cross, exactly—there were no documents signed saying they *couldn't* sell the naming rights—yet we had early conversations in which it was suggested the naming rights monies should go toward the public's portion of the stadium bill. Why not? The public was paying for most of it. We knew selling the name could bring a big number. I remember Bud saying he wanted to handle those negotiations himself. They negotiated the $40 million deal with Miller, kept the money, and all of a sudden the Brewers' actual contribution to building their $250 million new stadium was down to $50 million.

Except they didn't have that, either. At the same time the naming rights were being negotiated, we had helped to arrange a $50 million loan to the Brewers through the Wisconsin Housing and Economic Development Authority (WHEDA). In the end, WHEDA couldn't justify giving the Brewers the loan. The team had virtually no collateral. Fritz Ruf, a savvy banker I had appointed to head WHEDA, said this to the *Washington Post* a decade later: "I had lived around here all my life, and I knew the financial position of the Brewers wasn't going to blow anyone's socks off. But the more you got into it, the more it became apparent that the only thing the Brewers were going to be able to give us was a hearty handshake."

The Brewers ended up getting $50 million in low-interest loans from the Metropolitan Milwaukee Association of Commerce, the Milwaukee Economic Development Corporation, and the Bradley Foundation.

In the end, the financing package was almost exactly the opposite of what Bud Selig had said when he first came to Madison to discuss a new stadium: he wanted to build it himself. Instead, it was built mainly with money from everywhere but the team.

I was there for the Miller Park opening, but I wasn't particularly happy, and I was even less happy after what transpired that night. By then—Miller Park opened April 6, 2001—I was secretary of health and human services under George W. Bush. The president and I flew to Milwaukee on *Air Force*

One. He and Selig threw out ceremonial pregame "first pitches," and Robin Yount, the great former Brewers star, was introduced on the field. While Selig and I were no longer friendly, I certainly expected that the contribution of the state and the nearby counties to making the new stadium a reality would be acknowledged. I had led a long, hard, costly—in terms of both money and political capital—fight to make it happen. But there was no acknowledgment on the field that night. I felt it was a slight to the citizens of Wisconsin whose tax dollars had built the stadium.

In December 1997—a year after construction started on Miller Park—my brother Ed was involved in a controversy that generated its own set of newspaper headlines around the state. Eddie's supper club in Tomah, the Tee Pee, was raided, and he was charged with having illegal poker machines on the property. His refusal to plead guilty to a charge less than a felony resulted in prolonged publicity that I could have done without. Nevertheless, I have nothing but love in my heart for my late brother Ed, who died in 2011. I'm not alone in that, either. To this day, it's rare for a week to go by without someone stopping me and saying, "God, I miss Ed." He had the kind of spirit and engaging personality that people really respond to.

There was a sibling rivalry—I was the older brother—but there was no question we loved each other dearly. I was proud of the way he turned his life around in the early 1990s, when he gave up drinking and smoking after becoming far too proficient at both. Before buying the supper club, Ed had been a boxer, a poker player, a snowplow driver, and a prison guard. He wasn't really interested in government or politics—that came later—and I think that was because I had succeeded in that arena. Ed needed to look elsewhere.

It was in the early 1990s, after he had beat liquor and cigarettes, that he bought the Tee Pee. He was a good restaurant and bar man, but really, Eddie should have lived 150 years ago and been a cowboy. Or maybe an actor. He loved the spotlight. In fact, he did act, successfully, in numerous plays in the Tomah area. He was a good actor and generally played the lead. And he had his own show on local cable access TV.

By 1997 Ed was making the Tee Pee hum—I loved stopping there—and he had given back to the area by providing free turkey dinners on Thanksgiving to anyone who asked. The number grew to one thousand, some at the restaurant, some delivered by Ed and a crew of his friends.

It was shortly after Thanksgiving 1997 that the Tee Pee was raided. It was one of forty-three taverns that were hit the same night. It was a serious business, because the illegal poker machine charge was a felony, and a conviction meant the owner would lose the liquor license. Forty-two of the forty-three tavern owners agreed to plead guilty in exchange for reducing the charge to a misdemeanor. The only holdout was my brother. He felt that because Native Americans were allowed to have casinos—where they could also sell food and drink—he should be allowed to have video gambling machines. He was adamant about it, and he was a fighter.

A few weeks earlier, I had been at a dinner in Madison hosted by the Wisconsin Chiropractic Association, seated next to someone who introduced himself as Steve Hurley. I knew the name. Hurley was a prominent criminal defense attorney in Madison. We had a really good time talking that night. He was obviously bright and knew how the world worked, but his manner belied that. He didn't call attention to himself. He listened more than he spoke, and he had a good sense of humor, too. When the dinner was over, he said, "Governor, call me if you need me. And you will."

When Ed got in trouble with the supper club, I phoned Hurley. It was pretty late at night. He had given me his home number. "Steve?" I said. "It's Tommy. I didn't think I'd be needing you so soon."

Hurley and I became friends during the time he defended my brother. We were both trying to convince Ed to listen to reason and take the plea deal. He refused. I called Hurley at least once a week in the months leading up to Ed's trial. I kept telling him he had to get Eddie to accept the deal. I was sincerely worried about my brother, of course, but I was also sick and tired of all the newspaper stories about Tommy Thompson's rogue brother and the felony charge.

At one point, Hurley said, "He won't budge, Governor." He then related a recent conversation he'd had with Ed.

"Dammit," Ed had said, "if you go fifty miles in one direction from the supper club, there's a casino. Go fifty miles in the other direction, there's a casino. On Saturday night those casinos sell prime rib, all you can eat, for $9.99. I can't buy it for that off the truck. If a casino can have a restaurant, a restaurant can have a casino."

Hurley was worried, too. He genuinely liked Ed, but what kind of defense could he mount? It looked hopeless. The existence of the poker machines had been recorded on videotape.

The trial was scheduled for December 1998, a full year after the bust. Ed was out on bail, of course. Hurley had explained to me that criminal defense attorneys worry about bail, because if you're charged with a felony and violate the terms of the bail, that in itself is another felony. Prosecutors pile on conditions of bail thinking people will screw up and that will give them leverage on the first charge. But Hurley said he wasn't worried about Eddie violating his bail conditions. Eddie didn't drink. He wouldn't do anything stupid. He was done with all that.

One day—Hurley told me later—a pretrial conference with Eddie, his lawyer, the prosecutor, and the judge was set for early afternoon. The judge was allowing Hurley to appear by telephone, rather than drive up from Madison.

At twelve thirty—a half hour before the scheduled conference—Ed called Hurley in Madison.

"I'm bleeding," Eddie said.

"Eddie!" Hurley said. "What happened?"

"I got in a fight with Daisy," Ed said. "He stabbed me. He didn't mean to."

I heard later from Ed what had happened. One of his good friends was the butcher in Tomah, Dave Peth, but everyone called him Daisy. Ed bought all the meat for the Tee Pee from Daisy. On the morning in question, however, Daisy had gone to the Tee Pee to drop off some meat. When he opened the refrigerator, Daisy saw a package of steaks from another meat distributor. The guy had just left them for Ed, to try for no charge. Daisy was furious and stalked out. Ed heard about it a little while later and went to the butcher shop to explain. Before he could, Daisy started yelling at him, and Eddie yelled back. They scuffled. Daisy had been cutting meat. During the struggle he stuck the knife in Eddie. A few minutes later Eddie called Hurley in Madison.

"You have to go to the hospital," Hurley said.

Instead, my brother went home, used duct tape to slow the bleeding, put on a fresh shirt, and went to the pretrial conference to meet the judge. Amazingly, it went pretty well. Back home, Eddie removed the duct tape and stitched himself up.

Did I mention my brother Eddie was tough?

Eventually, word got out that something had happened, and the police showed up to talk to Eddie. He didn't want any trouble for Daisy, so he said he'd cut himself boning a steak, something like that.

The stabbing episode eventually faded away, but there was still the felony gambling charge to deal with. The Monroe County district attorney who organized the raid, John Matousek, was prosecuting the case, but by December 1998 Matousek was a lame duck, having lost his bid for reelection. Eddie had helped slate a young lawyer to oppose Matousek, and the voters—signaling how they felt about the gambling raids—tossed Matousek out in a landslide.

During jury selection for the trial, it was clear most potential jurors had the same mindset. Eddie was very well liked. He would deliver Thanksgiving dinners, dozens and dozens of them, free of charge to people in need. Hurley told me that one potential juror, when he was being questioned by the judge, said, "Why are you picking on Eddie?" Another, asked if he could be fair, said, "No, I could never convict Eddie."

It became apparent that seating an impartial jury was going to be difficult, if not impossible. During a recess, Matousek approached Hurley and said, "It occurs to me I might not win this case." The two lawyers eventually reached a deal that said if Ed paid back the cost of the raid, which was under a thousand dollars, all charges would be dropped.

Ed became something of a celebrity. He promoted a bill in the legislature that dropped the penalty on video poker machines to a small fine. It passed, and I signed it. Next Eddie ran for mayor of Tomah and won big. He joined the Libertarian Party, and after I resigned as governor to join George W. Bush's cabinet, Ed decided to run for governor. He didn't consult me first, which didn't surprise me. We would talk after he'd made a decision. Part of the brother rivalry thing, I guess. He wasn't going to ask my permission. He didn't like Scott McCallum—my successor—and McCallum didn't think much of Ed. It put me in an embarrassing situation. Reporters called me in Washington, asking who I was supporting. I didn't make an endorsement. In the end, Jim Doyle, a Democrat, was elected governor in 2002. .

Ed dabbled in politics after that—he lost a state senate race and won again for mayor of Tomah—but in 2010 he was diagnosed with pancreatic cancer. It's a terrible cancer. Ed died in October 2011. He was sixty-six. I was devastated, but I managed to release a statement that day recalling Ed's "infectious candor and spirit."

I went on: "His life was defined by an intense affection for his friends, neighbors, and those who may have fallen on hard times. Ed ran for public office because he believed government had forgotten about working people, and in many ways, he was right."

Of course, a statement can only convey so much. These years later, I still miss Eddie every day.

Pancreatic cancer also took the life of my other brother, Arthur, less than two years after Ed's death. It's a terrible cancer, and since losing my brothers I have worked hard to raise money for pancreatic cancer research. It should be no surprise that some of the most promising work being done is happening in Wisconsin, at UW–Madison, at the Veterans Hospital in Madison, and the UW Carbone Cancer Center. I have also invested in two private sector companies that show great promise in developing treatments for cancer—helping find a cure has been one of my passions since leaving government.

My sister, Juliann, and I are involved in an investigative study at the Mayo Clinic for people who have lost close relatives to pancreatic cancer. I go up to Mayo every six months for a test. They are looking for genetic clues to this horrible disease. I'm glad to be involved and salute Dr. Suresh Chari at Mayo, an esteemed scientist and researcher of pancreatic cancer.

We lost our mother, Julia, to cancer, too—ovarian cancer. She died April 11, 1984. My brother Ed and I were in the room with her when she passed away. My mother was beloved in the Elroy area. After retiring from teaching in 1973 she gave tirelessly to Saint Patrick's Parish, taking Holy Communion to the sick in their homes and helping prepare children for their First Communion.

My mother was always doing things for others. When she built an extra room on her house in 1980, people said it was so she could hold more parish meetings there. She enjoyed giving friends rides to the grocery store or appointments. My mother drove a big red Cadillac and she knew only one speed—fast. People in Elroy didn't mind. They called it her red taxi.

wanted to run for president in 1996. In the end, I didn't, which I now feel was a mistake. My gut feeling was to run, and I should have listened to my gut. It was my time. I was on top of my game.

I had won reelection in November 1994 to a third term as governor, beating Democrat Chuck Chvala by an overwhelming margin.

If this sounds like hubris, so be it, but I really do feel like our '94 campaign may have been the best political race ever run in the state of Wisconsin. We'd set it up perfectly. Jim Klauser and I had a theory that you really win the election in the third year of the previous term. In those twelve months we would make sure the Republican base was happy. Conservative issues were addressed. Organizational matters, on the county level, were taken care of. It allowed us to go into the fourth year of the term—election year—free to campaign hard, travel around the state, and see how many independent and Democrat votes we could get. Klauser and I took it personally that we couldn't somehow figure out a way to get *all* the votes.

Against Chvala we had a terrific young campaign manager, Bill McCoshen, and we did almost as well toward getting all the votes as anyone in Wisconsin ever has. Chvala, a Dane County liberal, had an uphill fight against me. He didn't raise much money. We had plenty of money. We'd lined up endorsements from city officials, sheriffs, and district attorneys on both sides of the aisle. I attended 167 campaign events between June and November. In the end, I won with 67 percent of the vote to Chvala's 31 percent. It was the largest winning percentage in a governor's race since John Blaine, a Republican, won in 1922 with 76 percent of the vote. I carried seventy-one of seventy-two counties, losing only Menominee, by just twenty-two votes. I won Dane County and I won the city of Milwaukee, unusual for a Republican, with 59 percent of the vote.

It was the kind of performance that gets you noticed nationally, and together with the press I'd received across the country for my welfare and school choice initiatives, I found my name being mentioned as a potential candidate for the '96 Republican presidential nomination.

I had traveled to New Hampshire and Iowa and been well received, but I let some time pass—I wasn't fully committed—in part because my family didn't really want me to run, and neither did my inner circle of friends and advisers. I finally waited too long to be able to raise enough money to really give myself a fair chance. It was personally disappointing. I can remember a Saturday meeting at the old Country Inn, off I-94 in Pewaukee. It was one of the places Republicans met in those days, convenient for people from both Milwaukee and Madison. This meeting included people from my administration like Jim Klauser, Chuck Thompson, and Gerald Whitburn, as well as Milwaukee Republican leaders like Mike Grebe and John MacIver. I said I wanted to run for president. The younger people in my administration and those who had worked on the '94 gubernatorial campaign had encouraged me to run. But the reaction from the veterans that day in Pewaukee was lukewarm at best. I didn't get the support I thought I would. Even Klauser wasn't in favor. I think Whitburn, who was completely negative about the idea, may have persuaded him. Everyone talked about how well things were going in Wisconsin. Someone said, "It's not your time, Tommy." Well, it was my time. I think some of them were tired. It doesn't get any harder than running for president. I'd been asking people for twelve-hour days, and they could see a future—a presidential run—that would mean fourteen- and sixteen-hour days. I suppose they felt like my friend and security guy Jerry Baumbach, who one day raised a white flag and said, "You don't stop, Tommy."

I actually had to talk Klauser into staying in the administration through 1996. He had a tough job. They all did. I was working so hard and had so many ideas, yet they were the ones who had to flesh them out and make them work. Putting together budgets and that kind of thing never bothered me. I always had the enthusiasm and the ability to get up every day and keep going. It was a fantastic rush, but then it was easier for me, where I was, on the front lines—being the one who's always talking—than to be behind the scenes, doing the work without the applause, so to speak. It was natural that they were slowing down.

I announced I wouldn't run for president at the state Republican convention in Appleton in June 1995. Right away, people began touting me as a possible pick for vice president. I didn't discourage it. Bob Dole had come to Wisconsin while I was still considering running for president, asking me not to run and instead to support him. Later, once it became clear Dole would get the nomination, we talked about the vice presidency. He led me to think he was going to ask me. I filled out a lot of paperwork, and the FBI did a thorough background check. I remember national reporters camping out at the Edgewater Hotel in Madison, waiting to interview me when the announcement came. It never did. Dole picked Jack Kemp, who had been in Congress and George H. W. Bush's cabinet. He had also played quarterback for the Buffalo Bills. When Dole called to tell me, I don't think he even mentioned Kemp by name. He said, "We're going to go with the quarterback."

I was disappointed, but it didn't last long. I was too busy. We had unfinished business in Wisconsin, and in 1995 I'd become chairman of the National Governors Association (NGA). My hope was to get the NGA more involved in national policy decisions than it had been in the past, and we set up a policy arm for the organization that is retained today. I had five other governors working with me in the mid-1990s—Democrats Bob Miller (Nevada), Lawton Chiles (Florida), and Roy Romer (Colorado), and Republicans John Engler (Michigan) and Mike Leavitt (Utah)—and we turned the NGA into a force to be reckoned with. We helped resolve the 1996 budget impasse between President Bill Clinton and the Republican-controlled Congress. And we put together a package of welfare reform proposals that was endorsed unanimously by the entire NGA—including eighteen Democrats—that I took to Capitol Hill and a hearing before Florida representative Clay Shaw's Ways and Means Subcommittee on Human Resources, which was examining the issue on the federal level.

We'd been making strides in Wisconsin toward not just reforming welfare but ending it altogether, at least in the way it was generally understood. The idea that it might actually be possible to end welfare dated to the fall of 1993, and it originated in an unlikely place—the Democrat-controlled state assembly.

As I later came to understand it, the genesis was a backyard picnic that September hosted by Milwaukee mayor John Norquist. A Milwaukee assemblyman, Antonio Riley, who had a great many constituents on welfare and felt it was a self-perpetuating cycle in serious need of reform, had a conversation with Norquist's chief of staff, who had studied the issue, too, and encouraged Riley to come up with a fresh idea. He did. Riley drafted a bill that would repeal Aid to Families with Dependent Children by 1999. Instead, people would be given minimum wage jobs.

Wally Kunicki, the Speaker of the assembly, embraced the bill. In some versions of the story, Kunicki cooked up the idea himself. My guess is he saw it as a way to put me in a box. I suspect Kunicki felt I would have to veto such a drastic bill, and that would give him and his colleagues license to portray themselves as more reform minded than me. Wisconsin Democrats, certainly including Kunicki, who at that point was considering running against me for governor in 1994, were upset with all the national attention I'd been getting with my welfare reform initiatives. The Democrats were territorial about welfare. They fumed when the *New York Times* and *Wall Street Journal* came to Wisconsin to interview me about it.

Late one night during the budget debates, the bill passed both the assembly and senate. Jim Klauser and I had gone home, but Jerry Whitburn, my head of Health and Social Services, was there, and he showed up early the next morning for breakfast at the Executive Residence. "You won't believe what they did last night," he said.

Whitburn was beside himself, muttering that the bill was an outrage and I had to veto it.

"Of course you're not going to sign this, Tommy," Whitburn said.

I looked at him, and said, "Jerry, why not?"

Klauser was at the table, and said, "Why wouldn't he sign it?"

I said, "Absolutely I will sign it."

"It's irresponsible!" Whitburn insisted. "Everyone will make fun of you."

"I don't think so," I said. "They know I'm all for welfare reform. It puts us in a position where we can rewrite the law."

What I had going for me was a team of people who over the past eight years had implemented welfare policy changes, seen what worked and didn't, in the process becoming as expert a group on the issue as existed anywhere. We also enlisted the Hudson Institute, an Indianapolis-based think tank, which lent us a full-time employee, Andy Bush, who spent a year in Wisconsin helping my team—led by Jean Rogers—develop a legitimate alternative to welfare. Whitburn, despite his initial reluctance, got onboard, and shortly before he left the state—Massachusetts governor William Weld hired him in 1995 to run that state's welfare program—Whitburn gave me a name for our new initiative. It had been suggested by Jim Malone in Health and Social Services—Wisconsin Works, or W-2.

The core component of W-2 was moving people into private sector jobs as quickly as possible, and that would not be cheap, not if we were going to help in the transition by paying, as we had before, for childcare, health insurance, and transportation. Fortunately, because of the success of our earlier reforms, the welfare rolls were significantly reduced by the mid-1990s, and our new plan used those savings for childcare and other expenditures, while asking participants for a copay once they began earning money. Bottom line, W-2 was a jobs program, not a welfare program, and indeed the goal was for it to end AFDC in Wisconsin once and for all. Many of the jobs would be subsidized at first, but there would be a limit on the length of the subsidy and incentives to move up—we established a tier system, a grouping of jobs based on skills—and eventually out.

I signed W-2 into law on April 25, 1996. Unfortunately, it was largely symbolic, because we still required waivers from the federal government in order to proceed, and they were not immediately forthcoming.

A strange dynamic was at work in 1996 when it came to welfare. As we were making news in Wisconsin with the success of our reform initiatives, there was a move afoot for welfare reform on the national level. Clinton, a savvy politician if there ever was one, knew which way the wind was blowing, and it was in the direction of major reform. Clinton had been talking about welfare reform for several years. At the same time, many Democrats recoiled at the idea of radical changes to the so-called safety net. Clinton was in a tough spot. He'd vetoed a welfare reform bill in January—his second such veto—calling it too harsh. Meanwhile, his eventual opponent for reelection in the fall, Republican senator Bob Dole, began doing whatever he could to outflank the president on welfare reform.

I was in the middle of all of it because, by 1996, I was pretty much the poster boy for welfare reform. Our successes in Wisconsin and the attendant publicity had seen to that. Frankly, I was much more interested in being left alone by the feds to implement W-2 and follow up our early successes in Wisconsin. In a perfect world, as I saw it, the states would be given responsibility for welfare—getting people off welfare and into jobs—while the federal government would become largely responsible for Medicaid, the health-care program for low-income families and individuals. I helped the Republican congressional leadership develop legislation to that end, to be introduced in March 1996.

As I noted earlier, a month before, in early February 1996, the NGA, which included eighteen Democrats, met in Washington, D.C., and endorsed a similar welfare/Medicaid package. Congressional Republicans were happily surprised by that, I think. Why would eighteen Democratic governors go along? Because Medicaid was crippling state budgets, no matter which party controlled the governorship in any given state.

Of course, Democratic governors were one thing, congressional Democrats another. On February 20, I testified about the welfare proposals in front of the House Ways and Means Subcommittee on Human Resources. Tom Carper, Delaware's Democratic governor, testified too. John Engler was supposed to be there, but his plane was diverted due to bad weather, and he missed the hearing.

It was an interesting day. Shaw opened the proceedings with a statement that essentially threw down a gauntlet to his Democratic colleagues, saying only "extreme liberals" could possibly object to the bipartisan reforms we governors were proposing. Next, Michigan Democrat Sandy Levin launched into an attack on Shaw, criticizing him for stooping to overtly partisan opening remarks. Levin then presented an overtly partisan opening of his own, attacking our proposals.

When I got to speak, I think I surprised some people—and probably irritated some conservatives—by saying this was not a proposal that would save a lot of money, at least not initially. I said it could not be done on the cheap, that moving people from welfare to work required a significant investment up front. Money would be saved on the back end, of course, because people would be working, but those savings would take some time to be realized.

I nevertheless took some hits from congressional Democrats. A representative from Catholic Charities had testified that our plan meant turning our backs on poor families and children.

A California Democrat, Pete Stark, asked me directly, "What do you say to the Catholic Church, Governor?"

I answered, "I say the Catholic Church is wrong, just like you are wrong."

At another point, speaking to the congressional Democrats, I said, "Governors are just as concerned with children as you are. We will not allow children to go without protection, without food, without sustenance."

The Medicaid proposals were the most controversial part of the package. In mid-March, Engler, myself, Newt Gingrich, and other Republican leaders had a press conference to announce that we had, in discussion with leading Democratic governors, come up with a compromise bipartisan agreement on funding Medicaid. In my recollection—and granting this is being written at a distance of two decades—we had. The Democratic gubernatorial leadership—Lawton Chiles, Roy Romer, and Robert Miller—had agreed to our proposal. But in the aftermath of that March 14 press conference, they backed away from it. I think they did so because they received tremendous pressure from Democrats in Washington. Gingrich's involvement didn't help. Congressional Democrats had been having a war—no less a word will do—with Newt Gingrich, and now here were Democratic governors falling in line with him on an issue of great national importance?

Eventually, the Medicaid component would be separated from the welfare reform bill that was being debated in 1996. John Kasich, an Ohio representative at the time, told me during his presidential run two decades later that he was involved behind the scenes in getting them unattached. It's doubtful there would have been a national welfare bill if Medicaid had been included.

It still wasn't a done deal, regardless. Again, I found myself involved, at least peripherally. I signed our W-2 welfare reform bill on April 25, 1996, in a ceremony at the Brenner Tank Company in Fond du Lac. Brenner had been involved in our Work Not Welfare program, a kind of prototype for W-2. By signing the new bill at their plant, I hoped to encourage other businesses to do the same thing.

Signing that bill was a big deal, and I said so. "This is the biggest change in social policy in Wisconsin, and this country, in sixty years," I said.

The *New York Times* reported on the signing and quoted a scholar at the American Enterprise Institute: "Whether it works or not, this is the most revolutionary thing we've seen on welfare."

Of course, as I've noted, we still needed waivers from Washington, D.C., to actually implement it.

Clinton, by this time, had proved adept at paying lip service to our efforts at welfare reform in Wisconsin, while stringing us along and not following through when we needed waivers from his administration for implementation.

That scenario repeated itself less than a month after I signed W-2. On May 18, Clinton used his weekly radio address to the nation to embrace W-2.

The president said: "Wisconsin submitted to me for approval the outlines of a sweeping welfare reform plan, one of the boldest yet attempted in America, and I'm encouraged by what I've seen so far."

Clinton's timing was a little suspect, in that Bob Dole was just days away from a Wisconsin visit in which he planned to announce his support for W-2.

Major media outlets gave Clinton's address significant play. The *New York Times* story was headlined, "Clinton Endorses the Most Radical of Welfare Trials." The *Wall Street Journal*, in the lead to its story, played up the timing angle: "President Clinton, trying once again to preempt Robert Dole and the GOP on a welfare-system overhaul, embraced a radical initiative developed by Wisconsin's conservative governor, Tommy G. Thompson."

It didn't take long for some Clinton aides to begin assuring reporters that the administration wasn't really ready to "embrace" W-2. There were problems with some of the waiver requests, they said. The waiver package as a whole was more complex than any other they'd received.

From where I stood, it seemed pretty clear Clinton wanted to be perceived as a welfare reformer without ever having to pull the trigger.

That, coupled with a deep well of frustration owing to our having to go on bended knee to Washington in the first place to institute our reforms, led me to ask a couple of Republican Wisconsin congressmen, Scott Klug and Mark Neumann, to introduce a bill in the House that would grant our waivers (though it would also need to pass the Senate, a much less likely proposition). Speaker Gingrich brought the bill to the floor, and it passed. Some House Republicans, including Clay Shaw, were furious with Gingrich, feeling he brought our waivers to the floor solely to embarrass Clinton, with whom Shaw and others were trying to work out a deal on the national welfare bill. It's important to remember that at this point, early June, Medicaid was still in play as part of the reform package nationally. House Republican staffers who had been working behind the scenes for months on the national bill were fearful it could all fall apart. On the floor, John Tanner, a Democrat from Tennessee, said of the bill granting our waivers, "If we are going to spend time on the floor discussing welfare, we ought to be discussing a national welfare bill."

In the end, the Wisconsin waivers bill passed the House. It never made it to the Senate. It didn't have to. I don't know if all the handwringing over our waivers was a catalyst, but the dominoes began to fall. The House Republicans peeled Medicaid off the welfare legislation, and in August 1996 Clinton signed the bill, called the Personal Responsibility and Work Opportunity Reconciliation Act. In the years since, he has referred to it as the most significant legislation of his presidency. In Wisconsin, it authorized us to do most of what we had been asking for with the waivers.

At the time, the federal bill was highly controversial, especially among Democrats. Health and human services secretary Donna Shalala, who, of course, had significant Wisconsin ties—she'd been chancellor at UW–Madison prior to joining the Clinton administration—was among those who had fought, mostly behind the scenes, against welfare reform. Two prominent officials in her department—Peter Edelman and Mary Jo Bane—actually quit in protest within a month of Clinton signing the bill.

The hard feelings among those who remained are worth noting. They may well have caused a delay in our initiating a program in Wisconsin that in the years since its inception has been widely praised by both Republicans and Democrats: BadgerCare.

One waiver that we still needed to secure, even after the passage of the national welfare reform bill, was related to health care. What we wanted was a more sophisticated version of an idea I had been nursing ever since my earliest days in the Wisconsin legislature in the 1960s. The idea was to help working families get health insurance, and it came out of a discussion I remember to this day with a few members of the Joint Finance Committee, the majority of whom were highly conservative Republicans.

We were talking about the legal system, and that if you were indigent, the government by law had to provide you with a competent attorney. But what if you were poor, yet not quite poor enough to qualify for a government-appointed lawyer? You were out of luck.

"Let me get this straight," said Ken Merkel, an assemblyman from the Milwaukee area. "If you're really poor, you can get a good lawyer to defend you. If you're wealthy, you can get an even better lawyer. But if you're just getting by, not dirt poor but certainly not wealthy, you can't expect any help?"

Everyone agreed that pretty well summed it up.

Merkel jokingly said, "Then you end up having to hire somebody like Shabaz!"

He even pointed across the table at John Shabaz.

For some reason, that exchange always stayed with me.

Fast forward thirty years. Inside my administration, we were discussing health care and the way it was structured: if you were really poor, the government would come in and take care of you; if you had money, you could buy health insurance and get good doctors; but if you were working but just getting by, you often had to go without. I saw it happening in my hometown area— Juneau, Adams, and Marquette counties—small businesspeople and farmers who worked very hard, seven days a week in some cases, yet couldn't afford health insurance. They were out there naked, so to speak. It reminded me of what Merkel had said about lawyers, and that wasn't right.

I got my team together and I said, "You know what I really want to do? I want to help that small businessman on Main Street, Wisconsin. Maybe he's making $18,000 or $20,000 a year, paying his bills, but he can't afford health insurance. There's got to be a way for these hard-working people to get health insurance."

I remember saying to Joe Leean, my health and family services secretary, "Let's come up with a plan for these people who are going naked as far as health insurance."

Less than a year after Clinton signed the welfare reform bill, Congress passed legislation that included the State Children's Health Insurance Program, known as SCHIP. The $40 billion program was aimed at insuring children in low-income households.

Our idea, called BadgerCare and advanced around the time SCHIP passed in August 1997, was to utilize the funds to insure low-income *families*— the working parents, as well as their children. We estimated we could provide health insurance to some fifty thousand currently uninsured children and adults, families earning below 185 percent of the federal poverty level.

I believed in the plan for reasons of simple fairness, as I've noted. Hard-working people who need a little help to afford health insurance should be able to get it. But research was also beginning to show that the best way to make sure kids had health insurance was to get the whole family insured.

The Wisconsin legislature approved the BadgerCare plan in September 1997. That month, we submitted an informal concept paper to the Health Care Financing Administration (HCFA), now known as the Centers for Medicare and Medicaid Services and part of HHS. It outlined the waiver we needed to include parents in our BadgerCare plan. Leean told me his initial discussions with HCFA officials regarding the proposal were positive. By December we were far enough along that I stated publicly we had an agreement that would allow the launching of BadgerCare in summer 1998.

The *Capital Times* in Madison ran a story on December 17, 1997, with the following headline: "BadgerCare Wins Federal OK, Will Start July 1."

It didn't happen. July 1, 1998, came and went, discussions continued, and then in August, our waiver to include parents in BadgerCare was denied. I was frustrated and angry. Leean called that day, August 19, his most disappointing day in fourteen years of state government service. Were politics involved? I suppose my answer would be, When are politics *not* involved? It's possible Secretary Shalala was still smarting over the welfare reform bill from two years earlier, and she was also hearing from legislative Democrats in Wisconsin that they certainly weren't in any hurry to see my administration get a lot of favorable publicity for yet another bold social services initiative. The official reason for denying the waiver was that they were leery of setting a precedent of allowing funds targeted for children to be used for parents too. Well, if that was the issue, why string us along for months? Any way you look at it, they misled us.

Negotiations continued, and I believe it became clear that a vast majority of people on both sides of the aisle felt BadgerCare was a smart, innovative idea that would help a great many Wisconsin residents. We were winning the public relations battle. On January 22, 1999, HCFA did approve our plan, providing us a waiver. But even then, they couldn't quite give us what we wanted. This gets complicated, but the waiver we were granted was actually from a different provision of the Social Security Act—Title XIX—rather than a waiver from Title XXI, as we had requested. The difference is that Title XIX is an entitlement, which could have caused us some budget headaches. It was a compromise we agreed to in the end, but we kept working for the Title XXI waiver— even getting Democratic Representative David Obey to send Shalala a letter in support—and finally, in January 2001, that waiver was granted.

The state should be very proud of BadgerCare. One year in, the program had enrolled more than seventy-two thousand participants. States across the country looked on it as a model. My political opposite, Democrat Mike Dukakis in Massachusetts, called it one of the best health-care ideas he'd ever seen.

What of the worries that including the parents might shortchange the children?

Consider that in 2013, fourteen years after the debut of BadgerCare, the federal government awarded Wisconsin a bonus of $13.9 million for the state's success in improving children's access to health care—through the BadgerCare program.

9

In the late 1990s I accepted an invitation from Kirk Fordice to come to Mississippi and speak. Fordice became his state's first Republican governor in a century when he was elected in 1992. We got along well. I suppose I was flattered that he spoke highly of a number of my initiatives in Wisconsin and tried to install some of them in his state.

I stayed overnight at the Governor's Mansion in Jackson, which is the second oldest—to Virginia—governor's residence in the country.

I noticed that most of the work around the residence—cooking, cleaning, serving, yard work—was being performed by prisoners, inmates at state correctional institutions.

I mentioned it to Kirk, and he said, "Getting the prisoners involved has really worked well."

I thought, "That is a great idea. Why don't we do it?"

When I returned to Wisconsin, I began talking about it, originally just to see how people would feel. I didn't imagine there would be any significant opposition. As it turned out, just about everyone was opposed.

The staff at the Executive Residence never said anything to my face. But they were calling Sue Ann, who was in Elroy with our kids, and members of the State Capitol and Executive Residence Board.

"Governor Thompson wants to have prisoners out to the mansion!"

My legal counsel, Stewart Simonson, was adamantly opposed to the idea. Stew was imagining all the ways that something might go wrong. That's what lawyers do. But I told him I was serious, I wanted this to happen.

Still, nothing did. Stew later admitted he had been "slow rolling" the proposal. Finally, I called him in and said, "Stewart, I really want to do this."

He grimaced, but said he would get started. "Work it out with Mike," I said, referencing Michael Sullivan, secretary of the Department of Corrections.

It turned out the Corrections folks also didn't like it. What if the prisoners proved a danger to the mansion employees? Use prisoners who aren't dangerous, I said. What will the other prisoners think when they hear about it? Maybe they can aspire to be one of those picked, I said. Everything they threw out, I answered.

I recall Joe Dodge, the chef at the mansion, who was a burly six foot three and towered over everybody, telling me he was worried. I said, "Don't worry, Joe. I'll protect you."

Everybody was just up in arms, but finally they realized that I was serious, and it was going to happen. Mike Sullivan talked to June Gengler, superintendent at the Thompson Correctional Center, a low-security facility between Deerfield and Cambridge. It wasn't named for me, but rather for the Forger Thompson Farm, which dated to the 1840s. Gengler agreed to provide some well-behaved prisoners.

It was summer, and rather than take an actual vacation, I would sometimes head back to the mansion around noon and work from there, or just take a little time for myself. Immediately prior to our launching the prisoner program, Stew came out to see me, told me it was set to go, and cautioned me that it was serious business. He didn't want me fraternizing with the prisoners.

"No horsing around," Stew said.

"Of course not," I said.

We started with just a couple of guys, and there were strict ground rules, like they couldn't come in the house. But the prisoners were courteous and hard working, and eventually the staff at the Executive Residence really started to like them. We increased the number to four and let them help in the house, and Joe taught them to cook. It was what I wanted to see happen.

One day that summer I went home early, around lunchtime, and the four guys were out working on the lawn. It was hot. I chatted with them—there was no way I wasn't going to talk to them—and at one point I said, "Do any of you know how to water-ski?" It just popped out of my mouth.

Well, they hardly knew how to swim, never mind water-ski.

I ended up asking my kids—Kelli, Tommi, and Jason—to take the prisoners out on the lake. We got swimsuits and life preservers, and out they went onto Lake Mendota. Everyone had a great time, except that at one point one of the prisoners fell while on skis and sprained his ankle.

His injury wasn't serious, but it came back to haunt us. The prisoners thanked me profusely when it was time for them to return to the correctional center later that afternoon. Once they were back, of course, word of what transpired got around. Before long it reached Gengler, and I heard later that she called in the prisoner, who was still limping from his lake adventure, and they had a conversation.

The next day, Stew got a call from Sullivan. "You need to call June Gengler," he said.

Stew made the call.

"What kind of operation are you running over there?" Gengler said.

"Mediocre, most days," was Stew's wry response.

"I can believe that," Gengler said. "One of my prisoners came back from the Governor's Mansion with a severely sprained ankle. He said he went out water-skiing with the governor."

After their conversation, Stew learned I'd gone home for lunch at the mansion and drove out to talk to me. He found me in the kitchen.

"How are things working out with the inmates?" Stew said.

"Everything's fine," I said. There was a detail working outside as we spoke.

Stew's face, however, was getting red. I could tell he was trying to control himself.

"What happened the other day?"

"I don't know," I said. "Did something happen?"

"June Gengler told me you took them water-skiing and one guy got hurt!"

"What?" I said. "Stew, come on. Of course not."

But I knew he knew, and he knew I knew he knew. I'm sure I had some kind of sheepish grin on my face.

"What if it gets in the press?" Stew said. "We're trying to pass truth in sentencing!"

Stew eventually calmed down. "Never again," he said. "Going forward, no funny business."

"Agreed," I said.

At which point Joe Dodge came into the kitchen and retrieved a cake and ice cream to take outside—it was one of the prisoner's birthdays.

I relate this story in part as a way for me to begin discussing the evolution of my thinking on incarceration, and the politically expedient way so many people running for elective office declare themselves in favor of being "tough on crime." I said it myself, as governor in the 1990s, and I backed it up by vastly increasing the number of prison beds in Wisconsin, building a "supermax" prison for the worst offenders, and signing tough truth-in-sentencing legislation.

I can't walk away from those decisions. I was involved. I will suggest that part of it was the tenor of the times and a matter of giving the state's citizens what they wanted. At the end of the 1980s, the infamous "Willie" Horton political advertisement in the Bush-Dukakis presidential campaign had an out-sized impact on the criminal justice system nationally. Horton was a prisoner who committed a heinous crime while on a "weekend furlough" program that Massachusetts had instituted. Some people believe the TV ad cost Dukakis the election.

At the same time, we'd had some prominent cases in Wisconsin in which judges gave lenient sentences and the offenders committed serious crimes once they got out. The parole and probation system was under fire; we were seeing a lot of recidivism. So, we got "tough on crime." I didn't have a problem then— or now—seeing tough sentences handed out to violent criminals, but our ap-proach in the 1990s, like the trend nationally, was much more sweeping. Looking back, I wish we had approached it differently.

I started thinking seriously about prisons during my first years in the as-sembly. You may remember I authored a bill called the Youthful Offender Act. My idea was to give young people who committed crimes a second chance by putting them in an institution where they could receive counseling and voca-tional training. They would have to meet certain criteria to qualify. Obviously, violent, vicious offenders would not. But I thought about myself—I was pretty wild growing up. I had friends who were even more wild and could have been put away. You do strange things when you have a belly full of beer.

My plan for a different kind of institution for young people got scuttled when Pat Lucey was elected governor in 1970 and made a point of saying he thought a prison in Adams County—it was already nearly completed—was a terrible idea. The state later sold the facility to the federal government.

I was disappointed and angry, and never really forgot about it. What I saw in my law practice, when I was home from the legislature, was a reminder that there had to be a better way to do it. The area where I grew up is anything but wealthy—certainly my family wasn't—and once I started practicing law, I represented a lot of poor people. I liked them and I could identify with them. I'd get a young kid who might have thrown a rock through a window, and a judge would put him in a juvenile institution for six months. It really rankled me.

A life can be ruined with a stroke of a pen. When I was practicing law I represented an eighteen-year-old kid who had been going steady with a sixteen-year-old girl and the kid wound up charged with statutory rape. There was no reason for that young man to go to jail. He was sentenced to six months. The girl was in court begging not to send him away. They wanted to get married, and subsequently they did. But he spent six months in jail. The kid who threw a rock through a window in Elroy was sent to reform school and was just a mess when he got out. That kind of "justice" has always really bothered me.

It did to some extent while I was governor, even as we were building more prisons. I took pardon applications very seriously. I would take the files and actually read them all the way through. I granted 148 pardons during my time as governor. Pardons are always difficult calls, but who said being governor was going to be easy?

The legal counsel in the governor's office would generally discourage me from granting pardons. When Stew Simonson came into my office with the requests, I used to say, "All right, Pontius, what do you have?"

Stew was doing his job, protecting me from a Willie Horton kind of nightmare. But that's why I gave a lot of time to each request. Right before I left office, I was given a large number of pardon requests. I granted 12 and turned down 143. I was criticized for granting a pardon on a drug conviction to the son of a state senator, but in that instance the sentencing judge had sent me a letter in support of the pardon.

In recent years, my thinking has evolved to the extent I've come full circle, back to my original idea a half century ago, for the youthful-offenders facility in Adams County. It's been shaped in part by discussions I've had with friends like Steve Hurley, the Madison criminal defense attorney, and Nick Chiarkas, who spent more than two decades as Wisconsin's Public Defender.

They got me thinking more ambitiously about reform and rehabilitation, in part because of the sorry state of prisons today.

In my view, we need to turn these prisons into education and training centers. It wouldn't be cheap, but like welfare reform, it would pay for itself in the end, with the added benefit of being the right thing to do. I would have experts go in and interview the prison population and determine which inmates would make good candidates for learning and apprenticeship programs.

Not everybody would be eligible. Don't misunderstand me. A significant number of individuals belong in prison, period. But others—maybe as many as half—could be reclaimed and become useful members of society. They're going to get out and we're not doing enough in the meantime to prepare them.

I have made a point of talking to people and pushing hard on the idea that at least one of our prisons should be turned into a vocational school. Inmates in the program would be educated about drugs and alcohol and regularly screened; there would be strict rules of conduct and zero tolerance for violations. The training would be for occupations that are in demand, making securing jobs on the outside easier.

I would get chambers of commerce around the state and groups like Wisconsin Manufacturers and Commerce to buy in, helping offset the expense. I envision it being organized more like a college. Prisoners would have to sign an agreement that they would pay back a portion of the cost of their training, just as in higher education. It would be the equivalent of a state loan while they're incarcerated. We're giving you substance abuse treatment and educating you. You're going to get a job, and you owe society to pay back the cost of some of that.

I actually thought I had a chance to get some version of this program passed in Wisconsin in 2015. I'd talked to many people, including some in the Walker administration and the legislature, and received positive feedback, but it didn't happen.

I still think it's a great idea. We could make it into something other states could follow, and we could begin reducing the prison populations nationally. I believe we should think about—this may be too radical for some—putting a kind of "get out of jail" card as a carrot at the end. In other words, if you successfully complete the program—it would mean a commitment of several years—and if you have a job waiting, you will be released from prison even if you haven't completed your entire sentence.

We need to do something. The prison system as it exists is broken. Prisoners sit there and vegetate and get attacked and brutalized. If they could get a real education, showing progress along the way, with a real hope of getting out at the end, I think that could have a profound impact on our prisons. They wouldn't be the dangerous places they are today. Everyone would know that this was a meaningful second chance. If they screw it up, they're done. I think the majority of prisoners would buy into it. It could change the whole prison society. It's probably my biggest goal right now. I need to find some champions for it among elected officials.

If I am not particularly proud of the prison construction that occurred in Wisconsin in the 1990s, there was another highly ambitious project from that time that I look back on with unabashed delight: the renovation and restoration of the Wisconsin State Capitol.

During my two decades in the assembly, I had seen the capitol, one of the most beautiful statehouses in the country, both fall into disrepair and suffer architecturally at the hands of growing legislative staffs, which knocked out walls and otherwise redecorated without regard to the history and integrity of the building.

It wasn't just the legislators. In the 1960s, the gorgeous cherry wood in the governor's conference room was painted green. That kind of thing happened through the 1970s and into the 1980s. Office walls were painted on a whim. The building wasn't air conditioned, causing many people to get window units, so from the outside the capitol started looking like a cheap motel.

Air conditioning the capitol was the impetus for the renovation, which had been discussed since Democratic senator Fred Risser, as head of the Building Commission, broached the idea back in 1979. When I became governor, we met in my office and talked about the need for air conditioning and the various ways the capitol had suffered, physically, in the past few decades. Fred and I agreed a bipartisan effort to renovate the capitol was both necessary and possible.

In my first year as governor, 1987, we rededicated the capitol—it was part of the state's celebration of the bicentennial of the US Constitution—and also got a Capitol Master Plan approved. I knew we would have to take it in increments, or the expense would appear overwhelming. In 1988 the Assembly Chamber was renovated, as a kind of test run. Actually, restored might be a better word. I felt we should try to go back to the original intentions for the capitol when it was built. We eventually dug up the old plans, and J. P. Cullen and Sons from Janesville did a fantastic job. I remember seeing artists and carpenters on hands and knees with toothbrushes, cleaning and polishing wood. It was an amazing effort.

Restoration of the north wing of the capitol began in 1990 and was finished in 1992. It looked fabulous. As each wing was restored—the west wing was next, then the south—it just looked better and better. It was a wonderful group effort. The east wing—where the governor's office resides—was last, in 1999. We moved into temporary quarters in the south wing, and the attorney general's office and the supreme court actually relocated to other nearby buildings.

The east wing wasn't completed until November 2001, after I had left the governor's office for Washington, D.C. I am pleased to say the wood in the governor's conference room was restored. The entire capitol project took a dozen years, and its success can be judged by the fact that in the year of its completion, 2001, the Wisconsin State Capitol was designated a National Historic Landmark.

A small but important part of the project involved regilding, with twenty-four-karat gold leaf, the statue of a woman that stands atop the capitol dome. I've always called her Miss Forward, as many people do, because her right arm is thrust forward, to symbolize the state motto: Forward. The sculptor was Daniel Chester French (he also created the Abraham Lincoln statue at the Lincoln Memorial in Washington), and her official name is Wisconsin.

The regilding of *Wisconsin* was taking place in the fall of 1990. On Election Day that year, 1990—my race against Tom Loftus—I got it in my head driving in to work at the capitol that I wanted to climb up and touch the top of the statue, or at least the ball she's holding in her left hand. My security guy, Jerry Baumbach, was aghast, and so was Dean Stensberg, a trusted aide who over the years became like a son to me. Eventually we gathered eight or nine people up on the lantern observation deck, where the general public is not allowed. It was windy. There was scaffolding that enabled the workers to reach the top portions of the statue.

I liked few things better than kidding Jerry, so I told him he had to climb up with me.

"You have to protect me," I said.

"I'll protect you from down here," Jerry said. "I'm not going up there."

The workers, who had been surprised to see us, were there and in position to make sure I didn't tumble from the scaffolding. Still, it was a little daunting. The statue was huge! She stands fifteen feet five inches and weighs three tons. I'd always assumed she had a crown on her head, but when you get a close look at it, it's a badger. The ball in her left hand is in fact a globe, with an eagle perched on it. I climbed up and touched the globe. Then I looked down. It's a long way to the ground. I managed to get myself down, and I walked around exhilarated the rest of the day. We never really told anybody, but I related the story in a Facebook post on the one hundredth anniversary of the capitol in 2017.

I've noted before that it's interesting what one remembers best from a long and varied career filled with highs and lows. Certainly one of the highs for me in the 1990s came in June 1998, when the Wisconsin Supreme Court ruled 4–2 that our school choice program could include religious schools. I mentioned this briefly earlier but want to elaborate. It had been a long, hard fight. Two years before, the high court deadlocked 3–3, sending it back to the lower courts. Unsurprisingly, the June 1998 decision in our favor was appealed, and most people expected the United States Supreme Court to hear the case, but that November the highest court in the land decided against accepting it, so the state court ruling stood. We'd won.

What I remember best is a visit to Messmer Catholic High School in Milwaukee on the first day of classes that fall. The Wisconsin Supreme Court ruling in June had triggered an enrollment surge at Messmer. It had 366 students to start the school year—a 20 percent increase from 1997—and another 30 on a waiting list, the first in the school's history.

The principal of Messmer was a man I greatly admired, Brother Bob Smith. He came to Messmer in 1986, to teach theology, and within a year had been asked to be principal. He was an impressive guy who got impressive results. Messmer was in an unprosperous, largely black neighborhood on the city's north side and drew most of its students from the neighborhood. Brother Bob saw to it that Messmer had a graduation rate of 98 percent—double the citywide average—with 85 percent of those graduates going on to college.

At my visit to Messmer, on September 1, 1998, I wanted to salute the school's achievement as well as the supreme court ruling that would, to my mind, make the Messmer story possible all over Milwaukee.

Bob Smith introduced me to a packed auditorium.

I thanked him and began, "Welcome to a new era of education in Milwaukee."

All of a sudden I felt a hand on my arm. It was Brother Bob.

"Excuse me, Governor," he said, and gently moved me to the side of the podium so he could speak.

Brother Bob pointed into the audience and said, "Young man in the seventh row, on the right side."

There was silence in the auditorium. It was the first day of class, and this kid had obviously been chatting up the girl next to him. Maybe he was asking about her summer, or trying to make a date. Either way, it didn't fly with Brother Bob.

"At Messmer," he said, "when we have a speaker, we all pay attention."

Brother Bob startled me so much that when I took back the podium, I forgot what I was going to say. I managed this: "Instead of busing our kids all over town to a public school that just doesn't measure up, we're going to give parents the chance to send their kids to a school right down the street. And if that school is private, so be it."

Two months later, by refusing the case, the US Supreme Court affirmed that opportunity. When I think about it now, I think about Brother Bob Smith, who retired in 2012. He knew how to get the job done.

A proud postscript for me came in fall 2016, when I received Right Wisconsin's inaugural Ronald Reagan Award for a lifetime of service to the conservative cause. The presenter was Brother Bob, who was on stage but handed off the presenter duties to a student, Edgar Sanchez, who attended choice schools and went on to UW–Madison to study journalism.

Sue Ann and me with our granddaughter Sophie at the Executive Residence. (Thompson family)

Eight Wisconsin governors. *Standing, left to right*: Gaylord Nelson; me; Patrick Lucey; Lee Dreyfus. *Seated, left to right*: John Reynolds, Tony Earl, Warren Knowles, Martin Schreiber. (Department of Special Collections and University Archives, Marquette University Libraries)

President Bill Clinton and I got along well. Bill was my mentor in the National Governors Association when I was first elected, and he later appointed me chairman of the Amtrak board. (Thompson family)

Vice President Dick Cheney swearing me in as secretary of the Department of Health and Human Services in the Oval Office as President Bush and my son and daughters look on. (Thompson family)

Aboard *Air Force One* with President George W. Bush and Alex Azar. Alex worked for me at health and human services and in 2017 became secretary under President Donald Trump. (Thompson family)

At Ground Zero on September 13, 2001, a day I will never forget. (Kevin Keane)

In the operations center that we built at the Department of Health and Human Services after 9/11. (Thompson family)

On a medical diplomacy trip to Africa as secretary of the Department of Health and Human Services. (Thompson family)

My farm outside Elroy is one of the great joys of my life. (Thompson family)

At my daughter Tommi's wedding to Brian Duffy in California in October 2004. *Back row, from left*: Ellie Iglar, Kelli Thompson, Chris Iglar, Tommi Thompson, Brian Duffy, Jason Thompson, Notesong Srisopark Thompson. *Seated*: Sophie Iglar, Sue Ann, and me. (Townsend Photography)

The four Thompson siblings: me, Art, Juliann, and Ed. (Thompson family)

With the best kids a father could ask for: Kelli, Jason, and Tommi. (Thompson family)

My wonderful grandchildren at our farm outside Elroy. *Left to right*: Sophie Iglar, Ellie Iglar, Jason Thompson, Hayden Duffy, Eily Duffy, Maggie Iglar, Sabrene Thompson, Juliana Thompson, and Teddy Duffy. (Thompson family)

A portrait taken when I joined the Akin Gump law firm after leaving government service. (Akin Gump)

10

The hardest speech I ever gave as governor was my last one.

I detailed at the beginning of this narrative how difficult the decision was for me to leave Wisconsin for Washington, D.C., in 2001 to join George W. Bush's cabinet as secretary of health and human services. I changed my mind a dozen times—more than that, actually—and in the process drove my friends and family a little crazy. I wanted the opinions of the people I loved and trusted. I called the same people night after night. I think deep down I knew that it was time to move on. Even before Bush was elected president, I had announced I wouldn't run for governor again in 2002. Throughout the election year of 2000, I was asked, by reporters and others, what I would do when I was no longer governor.

In September of 2000 the *Capital Times* ran a long story headlined, "Gossip Sizzles on Thompson's Future."

The reporter, Matt Pommer, interviewed several people about what they thought I might do. Nobody knew for certain, for the very good reason that I didn't know myself.

If Bush won, of course, a cabinet post was in play, but more than once when my future was brought up, I said I was considering the private sector. The challenge of running a company appealed to me. It was also true that just because I said I wasn't intending to run again in 2002, that wasn't written in stone, particularly if Jim Doyle, the Democratic attorney general in Wisconsin, decided to run for governor. Doyle and I were far apart politically, and I would have enjoyed running against him.

179

Still, change was in the air. Sue Ann retired from teaching in 1999, and that year our first grandchild, Sophie, was born. Less happily, I lost much of the hearing in my right ear on the trip to the 2000 Rose Bowl. My doctor told me it's called sudden hearing loss, and mine may have been caused by a virus I picked up on the plane. It usually affects one ear, not two, and it's more common than most people realize. If you are seen immediately, there is a steroid that can counteract the effect. I waited nine days, and it was too late. The treatment didn't help. I've now lost about 85 percent of my hearing in my right ear, without a hearing aid. Even with the aid, it isn't good. I tell people my Republican ear is gone, but my Democrat ear still works.

My victory over Ed Garvey in November 1998—my fourth win running for governor—was decisive and satisfying, but I sensed in my team a little less elation, a feeling that we had done it all before, which we had, three times. I didn't fret about it and stayed busy, which has never been a problem for me. I was cochairman, with Jim Klauser and John MacIver, of Bush's campaign in Wisconsin. He came to the state often to campaign, and I got to know him a little bit better. We'd moved past a serious argument we'd had in the mid-1990s, when I was head of the National Governors Association, and Bush was one of a few new governors who belittled the organization and talked about walking away from it. That was after I'd gone down to Texas and helped him raise money for his race against Ann Richards—a race nobody thought he would win.

So, there had been some friction, but once I decided not to run for president in 2000—I had considered it briefly—and George H. W. Bush called to ask me to support George W., we warmed up a bit. I remember one fundraiser in particular in Milwaukee in July 1999 where I watched Bush work the room and came away impressed. Once he set his mind on something, he was relentless in pursuit of it.

As I've related, he set his mind on me as a potential cabinet appointee, perhaps in part as a result of the night a few days before the election, at the state fairgrounds in West Allis, when I had helped him get past a press ambush about his drunk-driving arrest more than two decades earlier.

It was just a few days after Bush was officially declared the winner that he called and said he wanted me to come to Washington to be part of the cabinet. It set off an agonizing two weeks for me. In the end, it was on the trip to Mexico with my family over Christmas when I made my final decision: I would resign the governorship. The president was asking for my help. As much as I loved Wisconsin and loved being governor, it was time for a new challenge.

After calling Bush to tell him I would be his HHS secretary, I flew to Washington for the official announcement on Friday morning, December 29.

Bush was extremely gracious in his remarks about me that morning, saying, "I know this man very well. I know his record. I know his ability to lead. Tommy has been a creative, conservative, compassionate governor of Wisconsin."

And this: "Welfare reform began in Wisconsin and has been duplicated in other states. He's a leader and an innovator. He's also been a champion of education reform and for opportunity for disadvantaged Americans. He will bring creativity and conviction to Washington."

When I was asked about the issues I expected to be on my radar at HHS, I said, "Welfare reform, health-care reform, long-term care for seniors, greater opportunities for the disabled, helping the poor find work and helping the working poor find rewards in their efforts, biotechnology, and scientific research. I am absolutely passionate about these issues."

Right after that press conference, I called Russ Feingold, the Democratic US senator from Wisconsin, whom I respected, and asked if he would introduce me at my Senate confirmation hearing later in January. Russ said he would be happy to, adding that he didn't think I would have a problem being confirmed.

If I'd had any doubt that actually leaving the governor's office was going to be an emotional experience, it disappeared later that same day, when I returned to Wisconsin after my appointment was announced. That evening I addressed a gathering of about one hundred people in the conference room just outside the governor's office. There were members of my staff, friends, and reporters who realized this had been a historic day.

I looked around the room and I knew it wasn't going to be long before I was fighting back tears. It doesn't matter how hard I try not to, whenever I talk about myself or my family, I start crying. I wish it didn't happen, but there's no stopping it.

"I love you," I said at the outset. "How do I leave?"

I talked a bit about my reasoning—reiterating that when the president calls, it's one's duty to serve—but pretty soon I was sniffling into a handkerchief. "Even in the closest of families," I said, "we find a time when we must move on.

We need to go forward. It's a new beginning for myself, my family, and our great state."

I left the room without taking questions. I just couldn't handle it.

Over the next several weeks, I answered plenty of questions, not just from the press. The FBI needed to talk to me too. A background check was required prior to my being confirmed at HHS. Most of it was just filling out forms—a lot of forms—but the FBI sent agents up to Elroy to ask around about me, and then one Sunday morning two agents came to interview me in my office at the capitol.

I asked Steve Hurley, the Madison attorney who had done such good work for my brother Ed and who had become a trusted friend, to sit in on the interview.

"Is there something you're worried about?" Hurley asked.

"No," I said. "But it's the FBI."

They were there several hours. Most of it was routine—"Have you ever been in trouble with the law?"—but at one point the lead FBI agent pulled out a stack of papers that must have been eight or ten inches thick. He explained that they were the relevant pages from every lawsuit in which I had been named a defendant while serving as governor. It's routine for any plaintiff suing a state agency to also name the governor as a defendant, so there were dozens—no, scores—of suits.

The agent said, "We have to ask about each of them. It's OK for you to say you don't remember." He had told Hurley earlier he expected me to answer that I did not recall most of them.

What the agent didn't understand was that, as with pardon requests, I took the lawsuits seriously and, at the very least, gave them a thorough reading. Consequently, I remembered them all and was able to answer their questions.

I don't know who was more surprised—the FBI or my friend Hurley.

My HHS confirmation hearings—I would appear in Washington before two Senate committees—were scheduled for January 18 and 19, good timing in a way, because Bush would be inaugurated as president the following day, January 20. There were big parties scheduled for the nights of both the nineteenth and twentieth.

I didn't realize that I was expected to assume my new position the following Monday. My plan was to go back to Wisconsin, finish preparing my last budget, and deliver my last State of the State address on January 31. I would resign as governor the next day, then come out to Washington and take the helm at HHS.

That's the way it happened, but things got a little interesting. There was some tension with both the White House and the incoming McCallum administration in Wisconsin over my staying in Wisconsin a couple of extra weeks.

On January 18 I testified before the Senate Finance Committee in Washington. Feingold was good to his word and introduced me, but I also had introductions from the other Wisconsin senator, Herb Kohl, as well as Bob Dole and Donna Shalala, whom I would succeed at HHS. I think the committee had to be impressed. In my opening statement, I talked among other things about the need to modernize Medicare, including figuring out how to make prescription drugs more affordable for seniors.

The next day I testified in front of the Senate Committee on Health, Education, Labor and Pensions. The headline of that testimony came late in the day when New York senator Hillary Clinton asked me if I would take any action to undo the FDA's approval of RU-486, the so-called abortion pill.

"I don't intend to roll back anything unless it's proven to be unsafe," I said. (We took no action on it in my time at HHS.)

There was a party in my honor that night, inauguration eve, at the B. Smith restaurant at Union Station, an elegant venue with a cathedral ceiling and chandeliers. It was great fun, if a bit of a blur in my memory. Six hundred people were there, many of them friends who had come out from Wisconsin, and they all wanted a handshake or a hug. There were prominent Republicans and some celebrities too. It was, after all, inauguration weekend. A newspaper story the next day about the party said Oprah Winfrey had stopped by.

When I made some brief remarks, it was to say that it was all a bit much for a boy from Elroy. There was loud applause when I said our goal now was to make America as good and strong as Wisconsin.

My recollection is that it was at lunch the previous day, Thursday, when we learned that even though I wouldn't be sworn in as secretary until early February—after I gave my last State of the State speech as governor—our team would be taking over at HHS on Monday, the first weekday after Bush's inauguration.

Bob Wood, my chief of staff, and I had lunch that Thursday in Washington with Ed Sontag, whom I'd asked in early January to come out to Washington to help with the transition.

Ed said, "I trust you guys understand that we take over on Monday. We're in charge."

We didn't know.

I looked at Wood and said, "I'm going home, Bob." I had budget work still to do in Wisconsin, and a State of the State speech to give. He knew me well enough to realize what that meant. Bob had already agreed to come to Washington and be my chief of staff at HHS.

"You want me to stay?" he said. It wasn't really a question.

Bob had packed for the weekend. He ended up going shopping for some new clothes, resigning state service, and effectively moving to Washington. I don't know that he was happy about it, but he did a great job in those weeks between the inauguration and my swearing in as secretary. Bob served me well in numerous capacities—he was a great chief of staff—and his willingness to uproot his life during the transition meant a lot to me. I was lucky to have a loyal staff as both governor and secretary. Many are friends to this day, and I am proud of how well they have done in the years since we worked together.

Ed Sontag, too, served me effectively during the transition. Ed was an interesting guy who could be up or down. You never knew from day to day what you were going to get with Ed, but he liked me, and I liked him. It was Bob who brought him into the governor's office in the 1990s. Ed wrote and consulted on education issues. Earlier, he had served as a top official in the Department of Education in Washington, with a particular interest in special education and children with learning disabilities. Ed knew Washington, the way the city and the bureaucracy worked, and didn't.

When Bush appointed me HHS secretary, Ed wrote to Bob, outlining what I could expect when I got to Washington. Bob showed me the letter, which contained a lot of helpful advice. In the letter, Ed also offered to go out to Washington and be our point person.

I thought that was a good idea. Donna Shalala, a friend since her days as the chancellor of the University of Wisconsin–Madison and the outgoing secretary, had generously offered us some office space during the transition. I hired Ed to go out and set up the office. I went out once, before the inauguration, to talk with Secretary Shalala and the people putting the department budget together, but for the most part I was back in Wisconsin.

On the Sunday after the Bush inauguration, I went over with Ed to look at the Humphrey Building, which houses HHS. Bob was probably out buying more underwear. I was flying back to Wisconsin the next day. Since it was Sunday, the building was locked, and Ed had fun pointing out that since I hadn't been officially confirmed, I really needed to ask his permission to enter the building. Then he wanted me to ask permission to get off the elevator at the different floors. When we came to the floor where my office was—which I hadn't yet seen—Ed said, "This is the one floor I'm not sure we should visit." He had a great time at my expense.

Sue Ann and I did a little apartment hunting for me on that Sunday, too, and we both got a little sticker shock. One place was eight hundred square feet and rented for $3,200 a month. We weren't in Elroy anymore. We eventually found an apartment in Alexandria, Virginia.

I flew back to Wisconsin on Monday. The Midwest Express flight was delayed a bit after we were seated—Klauser and I were flying back together—and I ended up walking up and down the aisle of the plane shaking hands and talking to people. I am never great at sitting still, and those were Wisconsin folks on the flight. I bet I knew half of them. I heard later that Klauser made a pretty sage remark to an acquaintance on the plane that morning. Referring to me, he said, "He's ready to join the cabinet, but he's not ready to give up being governor."

I was back in my office in the Wisconsin capitol two days later, on January 24, when the Senate confirmed my HHS appointment in a roll call vote a little before noon. The tally was 100–0. The Senate Finance Committee chairman, Charles Grassley of Iowa, said, "It became so apparent that the qualities that made him a successful governor will also make him very successful as secretary of HHS."

Russ Feingold said, "All of us in Wisconsin are very proud, and it will take some getting used to having a different governor, just because it seems as though Tommy Thompson has been our governor forever."

Exactly a week later, on January 31, I gave my final State of the State address. As I noted at the beginning of this chapter, it was probably the toughest speech I've ever given. I knew it was going to be hard. It was in the Assembly Chamber, where my political career had started thirty-five years earlier.

When I was introduced, the legislators gave me a three-minute standing ovation. I appreciated it, of course, and part of my speech that night was directed right at them. I wanted to tell them what a fantastic job, and fantastic opportunity, they all had. Being a state legislator is a position of trust and responsibility, but also opportunity. I told them if they accepted that, they could accomplish great things.

I told them I realized that all of them believed, deep down, that they should be governor. They probably thought I was going for a laugh, but I told them to keep thinking that way. One day, they *could* be governor. Look at me, I said. How could a poor kid from Elroy, who had nothing, go up the ladder to governor, and then go to Washington, as a cabinet secretary?

I said I wasn't different from any of them. They all had the ability. That's what I wanted to leave them with, along with recognizing what a fantastic ride I'd had, and what a fantastic state Wisconsin is. We are unique, I said. Wisconsin is a very special place. I told them never to forget that, and to keep Wisconsin uppermost in their minds while they were doing their jobs.

I got really choked up only once during the speech, after I had introduced Sue Ann, and I thanked the great people of Wisconsin for being so good to my family over the past fourteen years.

"There has been no greater honor in my life," I said, "and there will never be a greater honor, than to have been elected four times to serve as your governor."

The next day was hard, too. I introduced my longtime lieutenant governor, Scott McCallum, that morning in the capitol rotunda prior to his being sworn in as governor by Chief Justice Shirley Abrahamson. I had signed my letter of resignation in private, prior to the ceremony.

I flew to Washington later that day, and the next morning was sworn in at HHS, where I gave an opening address to the agency's employees. I mentioned a lot of goals and possible initiatives that morning. I talked about patients' rights legislation, about improving child support collections and discouraging smoking, and I said we would be reviewing the federal policy on the use of embryonic stem cells in medical research. Wisconsin was a leader in biotechnology in the 1990s, and the stem cell issue would emerge front and center during the first eight months of the Bush presidency.

That first morning, however, I spent the most time talking about another issue that had become important to me as governor: organ donation. I promised a national campaign to raise awareness of the importance of saving lives by donating organs.

My passion for organ donation came out of a dinner I hosted at the Executive Residence in Wisconsin in August 1993. Any governor—any elected official—is going to find himself or herself at innumerable seated dinners over the years, and many of them are forgettable. But some are memorable, either because important policy decisions came out of them or simply because of who was there. One dinner I will never forget came in the early 1990s, when the National Grocers Association asked me to speak at a convention they were having at the Greenbrier resort in West Virginia. My father was a grocer. It was a big deal for me. I got in a day early and Margaret Thatcher, the former prime minister of the United Kingdom, was speaking that night. I was in the audience and she impressed me. She spoke forty-five minutes without a note. Afterward, she ate with a small group, just two or three tables, and I was lucky enough not just to be included but to be seated directly across from her. At one point, I'm not sure what possessed me, I asked her what she thought about the man who was her successor as prime minister.

"What do you really think about John Major?"

Everybody else at the table basically froze. It was like one of those old E. F. Hutton television commercials, everyone hanging on what was going to be said next.

Mrs. Thatcher finished the bite of food she was eating, put down her fork, looked me square in the eye, and said, "Well, Mr. Governor, you must realize, he's just a little wobbly."

That night was fun. A dinner at the Executive Residence in 1993 had important consequences.

It started when Jim Klauser, my secretary of administration and most valued adviser, asked me to invite the new German ambassador to the United States, Immo Stabreit, to Madison for the weekend. Stabreit had already visited us in a more formal capacity that June. In August he was in Chicago for a meeting, and Klauser—who loves all things German—thought it would be nice for him to come up to Madison again. The ambassador and his wife sampled the farmers' market on the Capitol Square Saturday morning, then went out to see Taliesin in Spring Green. That night we hosted a dinner for him at the mansion. I'd invited a few Madison friends of German heritage, including Hans Sollinger, a prominent transplant surgeon at the University of Wisconsin Hospital and Clinics.

I liked Hans and had him seated at my table, but that evening he was late. It wasn't like him. We held dinner but finally went ahead. I couldn't imagine what had happened—remember, this was before cell phones, so getting word back and forth quickly was more difficult. Finally—I think dessert was being served—Hans walked in the door. When he sat down I could tell he was terribly upset.

"Hans," I said, "what's wrong?"

"Tommy," he said, "the worst thing in the world for a doctor is having the power to heal, but not having the resources to make it happen."

The table, including the German ambassador, was quiet.

I said, "Hans, what happened?"

He said, "A patient who had become a very good friend of mine, and who was waiting for a kidney, died late this afternoon. We could have saved him, but we didn't have a kidney to transplant."

Hans was shaken.

"Is there anything I can do?" I said.

"Yes, Tommy, there is," Hans said. "You can help me publicize the need for organs."

It lit a fire in me, and we made organ donation a priority in Wisconsin. Before the year was out, we had launched, in association with the UW Health Organ Procurement Organization, the Governor's Gift of Life Medal to honor donor families. That program continues today. We produced public service television spots and got legislation requiring instruction about organ donation in driver's ed classes.

The bill that brought that requirement became known as Kelly's law when I signed it on May 9, 2000. The previous December, Kelly Nachreiner, a sixteen-year-old Sauk City high school girl, was fatally injured in an automobile accident. It turned out that four weeks earlier, she had been at the DMV getting her learner's permit when the question of organ donation arose. Kelly didn't hesitate. "Why wouldn't I?" she said. She couldn't have known that just a month later, her decision would help save three people's lives.

Kelly's bill was drafted, debated, and signed in just four months. Kelly's mother, Mary Nachreiner, who remains an organ donation activist, brought the idea of the bill to me and I signed it at Sauk Prairie Memorial Hospital.

We moved quickly once I was at HHS, too, starting with that speech my very first day. By April 2001 HHS had launched a Gift of Life Donation Initiative.

One component of that was Workplace Partnership for Life, which brought to-gether employers and employees—one thousand partners in the first year—to reduce the organ shortage.

I brought a valued Madison friend, Camille Haney, who knows how to get things done, to Washington to serve as my point person at HHS on organ donation. In October 2001 we announced new grants totaling $3.3 million to a dozen organizations, part of a three-year, $10 million project studying ways to increase family consent for donation and encourage individuals to both declare their intention to donate and share it with family members.

In April 2002, on the one-year anniversary of our Gift of Life Initiative, I had a press conference in which I introduced Chris Klug, a snowboarder who won a bronze medal for the United States at the Salt Lake City Winter Olympics eighteen months after receiving a liver transplant. I was also able to note that our efforts over the previous year had resulted in a 7 percent increase in organ donations in the United States.

Of course, not everything went so smoothly in my first months at HHS. The truth is, I struggled for a time with the role of secretary. For fourteen years as governor, I had been the boss, and now, even though I was a cabinet secretary, I wasn't the boss. Whether something got done wasn't necessarily up to me. That was a hard lesson to learn.

Over the years I've told a story that I want to share here because there's a lot of truth in it. When I was governor, sometimes I woke up in the middle of the night with a new idea. At seven the next morning, when I got out of bed, I would call someone on my staff and relay the idea. By noon, it would be either accomplished or on its way to being done.

When I went to Washington, especially early on, if I got an idea in the middle of the night, I would go to the office and find myself looking for buy-in from sixty-nine thousand employees, most all of whom had seen HHS secretaries come and go. They reasoned that since the job is temporary, there's no need to listen to a secretary. If you do get buy-in from your employees, then the idea had to pass muster with Supergod. You didn't realize there is a Supergod? Neither did I, until I went to Washington and ran into the Office of Management and Budget (OMB). They turn everyone down, four out of five times, just to show who's boss. If you somehow get your idea past OMB, then it goes to the super-intelligentsia of our society—a young college kid who has never had a job, worked on a campaign and got put in a White House staff position, and doesn't believe that anything important can come out of a secretary's mind. On the slim chance you get your idea past the superintelligentsia, it goes to the president. If the president buys in, it goes to Congress, and if Congress ever passes it—well, by then it's usually time for you to retire.

That's why nothing much gets done in Washington.

All kidding aside, that's a reasonable description of what someone like me was facing. I also learned early I needed to be careful when giving voice to an idea that might not be in line with the White House's thinking. In late February, just a few weeks after I was sworn in as secretary, a *Wall Street Journal* reporter asked me whether I thought the Food and Drug Administration (FDA) should oversee tobacco products, which the Supreme Court had ruled would need an act of Congress to happen.

I said I thought it would be the right thing to do—but the president had yet to take a position on the issue, and I heard about it. I heard about it again the next week, when in an appearance at the National Institutes of Health (NIH) with reporters present, I expressed my support for embryonic stem cell research. It was a sensitive issue for Bush, and one that we would discuss in depth in the months ahead, but I had jumped the gun.

Another thing I struggled with was the sheer enormity of HHS. Nearly seventy thousand employees, three hundred programs, headquarters in ten different regions around the country, and a $423 billion budget that's second only to the Department of Defense. I would submit that HHS touches every American's life at some time during any given day: the medicine they take, the food they eat, the health care they receive, the elderly programs, and the welfare programs—all those things come through HHS. It is gargantuan. Anything nobody else wants is dumped into HHS.

I remember saying, in a conversation early that first spring with Bob Wood, "How can we get a handle on this?"

I believe that by that time I had begun to win over the HHS employees in the Humphrey Building. There was trepidation about me after their eight years of a Democratic administration. But I think they respected how I rolled up my sleeves, worked long hours, and got around to talk to them and solicit their thoughts.

In my conversation with Bob, I broached the idea that I would travel to every agency in the department—from the Health Care Financing Administration (HCFA) in Baltimore to the Centers for Disease Control (CDC) in Atlanta—and spend a week working there and learning about the agency.

In a way it was like my idea in Wisconsin of taking state government on the road, after the people in Douglas County had told me they never saw the governor.

I went to the offices of the US Food and Drug Administration—not that far away, in Silver Spring, Maryland—and became the commissioner for a week. I sat in the commissioner's chair and had the people in the FDA report to me. They had never seen a secretary before. It was a big deal. Then I went down to Atlanta and spent a week as the CDC administrator.

The agency that posed the biggest challenge was HCFA, in Baltimore, the agency responsible for administering Medicaid and Medicare. There were stories in the press saying that HCFA—an acronym with the ugly pronunciation *Hic-Fuh*—had supplanted the Internal Revenue Service as the most hated agency in federal government.

An important first step toward changing that perception was getting Bush to appoint my choice for a new HCFA administrator. I wanted Tom Scully, who had worked for President George H. W. Bush and then become a hospital lobbyist. He knew the way things worked in Washington, and he knew a great deal about HCFA. But others were being touted for the job. The House Ways and Means Committee chairman, Bill Thomas, wanted Bobby Jindal—later governor of Louisiana and presidential candidate—who had worked for Thomas on a Medicare commission. Bush's brother Jeb was pushing Ruben King-Shaw, who had served Jeb as director of the Florida Agency for Health Care Administration.

I was pleased when, in May, the president appointed Scully, though we wound up also hiring Jindal and King-Shaw, who did a good job for us at HHS.

I asked Scully to gather as many of his employees as he could into the auditorium at the offices in Baltimore, because I had something to tell them. It was a Friday afternoon, and notice may have been a little short, but around four hundred HCFA employees showed up.

Remember, the American public *hated* these people, and it really wasn't their fault. HCFA had started as a small agency and then grown, and then grown some more, without an accompanying expansion of bookkeeping and computer expertise.

In my talk that day, I leveled with them.

"Nobody likes you," I said. "The Democrats don't like you, the Republicans don't like you, the Baptists don't like you, the Catholics don't like you, the atheists don't like you, and the Communists don't like you."

I told them that when I was governor, I sued HCFA. The agency was completely unresponsive. The average time for a member of Congress to get a response to an inquiry—a member of Congress!—was 110 days.

"You're unresponsive and autocratic," I said.

But I told them I was going to spend a week working with them in their offices, and I was going to give them the tools to do their jobs right. Scully would help, too. We would begin with one major, fundamental change.

"How can anyone really like something called Hic-Fuh?" I said. "The first thing we're going to do is change the name."

Scully set up an in-house Rename-the-Agency contest. I kind of liked MAMA, for Medicare and Medicaid Administration. In the end, after sifting through some eight hundred suggestions, we settled on the Centers for Medicare and Medicaid Services, whose acronym we shortened to CMS. It proved to be a great success. I think it really did change people's attitudes toward the agency, and of course that was also helped by CMS meeting higher performance standards. I'd told them I wanted the response time on inquiries reduced to fifteen days. We didn't quite make it, but by the time I left, it was down to twenty days.

Along with traveling to the various agencies and divisions within HHS, I found myself visiting Alaska three years running, after an interesting conversation with Ted Stevens, Alaska's senior senator. I think Stevens may have been a little miffed because as part of our new "One Department" initiative at HHS—which had a goal of enabling our various operating divisions to work more closely together—we had also tried to reduce the department's travel budget, and some may have seen that as potentially harmful to faraway Alaska.

When I spoke with Stevens, he said, "We can either get along nicely, or you can have trouble with me. And I can be a sonofabitch."

"How do I get along?" I said.

"Well," Stevens said, "do something for Alaska."

"What if we came to Alaska?" I said.

"Nobody's ever done that," Stevens said, meaning, I presume, that no HHS secretary had visited.

"Why don't I bring my team up?" I said, and Stevens replied, "I'll join you."

We were eventually able to do a lot of good things for the people of Alaska, especially native Alaskans, with whom Stevens was close.

We often had to fly into the villages, because there were no roads. It could be scary at times, but it was always beautiful, the scenery absolutely gorgeous.

Our first Alaska visit was in early August 2002. Stevens was good to his word and accompanied us. We had a news conference in Fairbanks in which I announced more than a dozen federal grants for Alaska, including $10 million for health care; more than $7 million to help children, including building three Head Start facilities; and nearly $4 million for substance-abuse prevention and treatment.

I said, "Alaska has not been given the proper attention from the federal government. Every year for as long as I am secretary, I will bring people up here to learn and find out from the people of Alaska how we can do a better job."

We had some fun, too. In August 2003 our itinerary included Nome, a coastal city of some thirty-five hundred. They had a dinner for us and it seemed like the whole community was invited. I had a big traveling group—all my operating division heads were with me. The atmosphere was festive. The mayor, Leo Rasmussen, told us about the annual Midnight Sun Festival around the summer solstice in June—when the sun shines for twenty-two hours—and he mentioned that the celebration includes a Polar Bear Swim, where people jump into the freezing waters of Norton Sound, an inlet of the Bering Sea.

After hearing that, I got it in my head that everyone in our entourage should jump in the sea.

"We'll do it at midnight," I said. It would still be light.

I looked around and I could see my people were hoping they hadn't heard right.

I smiled and said, "It's not a voluntary thing. It's mandatory." I kept smiling. "I'll go first."

Sometimes I just like shaking things up. The other thing was, I knew going into the Bering Sea at midnight in Nome would be a life memory for everyone.

Word spread, and by about eleven thirty a lot of Alaskans had gathered to watch the crazy visitors jump into the frigid water. Some of them ate picnic lunches in the beds of their pickup trucks. A few of my team members had repaired to a local bar, thinking they could get out of jumping in. I had my security guy go get them.

My general counsel, Alex Azar, really didn't want to go in the water.

"You can go in up to your waist," I said.

"Do I have to?"

"Yes."

I dove in first, everybody else followed, and the crowd standing on the shore just roared. It was really something. The next day the mayor gave us all certificates saying we "took the plunge" into the Bering Sea. Mine is with my archive at Marquette University in Milwaukee.

One early trip I took—to Atlanta, to spend a week at the CDC—resulted in a new initiative when I returned to Washington. One of the central things I picked up at CDC was the agency's concern about how Americans were taking care of themselves—actually, how they weren't.

"They're too fat," I was told, "and they smoke too much. Chronic illness is 75 percent of health-care costs. Obesity alone cost the American economy $117 billion in 2000."

I asked what I could do.

"Set an example," they said.

So I came back to HHS and decided to try to make the department healthy, starting with me. I gave up potatoes and sweets, burgers and beer—for the most part—and lost fifteen pounds. I started noticing that there really were a lot of overweight people walking around the Humphrey Building, and a lot of people smoking. I started a program to encourage people to walk the steps rather than take the elevator. We piped music into the stairwells. I began handing out pedometers, with the goal of having people walk ten thousand steps a day. I gave them to all the cabinet secretaries—Don Rumsfeld and his wife began having competitions to see who took more steps—and I gave them out to the ministers of health in many foreign countries in my travels. Each one of them said they would attempt a similar program.

In 2002 we formalized it a bit by launching the Steps to a Healthier US initiative. Part of that program was to see which cities could do the best job of preventative health care. Cities became really competitive, and we had an awards banquet.

Getting healthy and encouraging others was one of the most rewarding things about my time at HHS. I got a little fanatical about it. When I got to the Humphrey Building in the morning, I would police the grounds. I walked around and took cigarettes out of people's mouths. Occasionally I'd forget and do it at other buildings. A couple of times I got slapped. It was worth it.

The HHS employees picked up on my mission pretty quickly. One morning at the Humphrey Building I came around a corner and surprised a man I recognized, someone who had been working for the department for decades. He was smoking a cigarette and when he saw me, his eyes got wide. He quickly took it out of his mouth and stuffed it into his shirt pocket, with predictable results.

The day that gentleman retired, he came in my office to shake my hand and tell me I changed his life.

"How so?" I said.

He smiled. "After that day I set my shirt on fire, I never smoked another cigarette."

11

George W. Bush didn't appear to like cabinet meetings. Consequently, we didn't have that many, maybe one every six weeks or so. In my view, Bush might have benefited by relying more on his cabinet. For the most part, he governed by listening to a select few people he trusted, many of them from Texas. His inner circle included top advisers Karl Rove and Karen Hughes, defense secretary Don Rumsfeld, Vice President Dick Cheney—though Cheney played a lesser role toward the end. In any case, Bush's management style was such that once he set his mind on something, he hardly ever reversed course. He was punctual, didn't like to waste time, and wanted to get to a decision quickly. Meetings were all business, no cell phones allowed. It was a style that worked for him, and he became a very effective president.

It meant there wasn't a lot of back and forth at cabinet meetings. The meetings were held in the West Wing of the White House, in the Cabinet Room, adjacent to the Oval Office. Each cabinet secretary had a special chair, with his or her name and department engraved on a brass plate on the back. Any previous cabinet positions were reflected on separate plates on the back of the chair. It sounds nice, and I suppose it is, except that the chair was the most uncomfortable chair I think I've ever sat in. When you leave the cabinet, you are given the opportunity to buy your chair. The HHS employees bought mine for me. Later I lost track of it, but Jason Denby, who worked for me at the Akin Gump law firm in Washington after I left government service, told me recently the chair is in storage at the firm's office. I appreciate having it—as long as I don't have to sit in it.

At the cabinet meetings the president always sat at the center of the table, with his back to the Rose Garden. The back of the president's chair is two inches taller than everyone else's. The vice president sat directly across from the president. A cabinet secretary's position at the table was determined by how long that department had been a part of the cabinet. HHS was relatively late to the cabinet, so I sat on the same side of the table as the president, but down toward one end. Defense, state, and treasury were close, along with agriculture and the interior. The education secretary was even farther down the table than I was.

It was at a cabinet meeting that first spring—probably in June—when Bush asked me if I would stay afterward.

"I need to address stem cells," the president said. "I want to know more about them."

I nodded.

"I know you are for the research," the president continued, "and I know Karl Rove is against it. I am going to schedule a lunch for the three of us. I want you to come in and I want you and Karl to discuss it."

I wasn't surprised. The issue had come up during my discussions with Bush's team during the transition, before the secretary job had officially been offered to me. In my 1999 State of the State speech, I introduced James Thomson, a UW–Madison developmental biologist whose lab, in 1998, was the first to isolate stem cells from human embryos. His findings were published in *Science* magazine in November 1998, and the following month the Wisconsin Alumni Research Foundation (WARF) received a patent on the discovery. Even in those early days it was being touted as a breakthrough that could revolutionize modern medicine and health care.

But the research was not without controversy. Though the cells Thomson used were left over from fertility clinics—and the donors had signed off on their use in research—some right-to-life people called it immoral, unethical, or both. They were furious with me for introducing Thomson during my State of the State speech, and, as I noted, it was brought up again by the Bush team prior to my appointment.

"I support stem cells," I told them. "If that means I can't get the appointment, so be it."

My passionate support of Thomson and WARF were part of my larger belief that the University of Wisconsin's emergence as a leader in biotechnology and biomedical research was great for both our state and humanity in general. Where are lifesaving advances going to come from, if not great institutions like the University of Wisconsin?

As governor, I tried to forge a partnership that would help the UW System grow while at the same time generating new technologies and businesses to pump up the state's economy. During my time as governor, more than four thousand building projects at a collective cost of nearly $2 billion were initiated at campuses across the state. It was a mix of public and private money. I helped Donna Shalala, before she left the UW–Madison's chancellor job to join the Clinton administration, generate private funds to advance the expansion. Later, I called it the New Wisconsin Idea—a collaboration between academia and the private sector that would benefit both and bring good-paying new jobs to Wisconsin.

I can't understand why any public official wouldn't see the University of Wisconsin System as an ally, especially in a world that is changing faster than ever.

I remember having a discussion at some point in my last term as governor with John Wiley, who would later be UW–Madison chancellor but at the time was provost. John said he wanted me to meet Michael Sussman, a biochemist on campus who was doing some interesting work perfecting gene chips—also called DNA chips—utilized in identifying genetic abnormalities that can eventually lead to new drugs and ways to fight disease.

I said I'd be happy to meet Sussman. During my first term as governor, Chancellor Shalala had approached me about assisting with a new Biotechnology Center on the Madison campus. I agreed to help, and with a mix of federal, state, and private dollars, the center was built on the site of the old Wisconsin High School. It didn't happen overnight; ground wasn't broken until 1993.

By the time Wiley brought Sussman to see me in the late 1990s, the biosciences were exploding on campus, and the center I'd help fund was already inadequate. Sussman sat in my office in the capitol and for two hours talked about DNA and the potential for all this great science to generate medical advances. I liked Sussman, his enthusiasm and genuineness, though we joked later about how he's a Democrat from New York and would never have voted for me prior to meeting me. He said that more brilliant students than ever were interested in studying biology at Wisconsin, but because of space limitations some had to be turned away. He said we weren't losing them to Michigan State—we were losing them to Harvard and Stanford. We're a great university, he said, but we need a new building and more lab space.

He impressed me. Within a few days of the meeting, I called Wiley and promised funding for one of the things we had talked about: five new faculty hires in the area of human genomics (a genome is an organism's complete set of DNA). I toured the existing facilities, learning more about the science all the time. Then, in my January 2000 State of the State speech, I unveiled the $317 million BioStar Initiative, which included an addition to the Biotechnology Center as well as renovations and additional buildings for biology-related departments.

I'm proud of what I was able to do for the University of Wisconsin. It made sense for all kinds of reasons, including economic development. I was always trying to figure out how to help Wisconsin compete with the technology triangle in North Carolina and Silicon Valley. I wanted Wisconsin to be the third pillar out there.

At some point after I left for Washington and HHS, word reached me that Mike Sussman was thinking of leaving UW–Madison. He had a very attractive offer from the University of California, Davis, and was considering it to the point he'd already looked at houses.

I telephoned Mike one night from Washington—he later joked that he'd had a couple of drinks by the time I called—and asked if it was true.

"You're thinking about leaving?"

"Yes," Mike said.

"You can't do it," I said. I talked about all we'd accomplished and all that was still to come.

This was when Mike confessed he was Democrat. "I usually bat for the other team," was the way he put it.

"I suspected it but never held it against you," I said. We laughed. "Now, let's talk about why you're going to stay."

More than a dozen years later, in spring 2016, UW–Madison invited me back and awarded me an honorary degree for meritorious activity "as a dedicated promoter of the Wisconsin Idea and the use of government to enhance the lives of its citizens."

I spoke at the Kohl Center in Madison, and I shared the story of Mike Sussman—he stayed—while just generally touting the assets of this great economic diamond, the University of Wisconsin.

I'm sure all my work on behalf of biomedical research at the University of Wisconsin was somewhere in my mind when I went to the White House in spring 2001 to meet with Bush and Rove to discuss stem cells.

The president had us in to the Oval Office. There's a little room off to the side of the Oval Office, and that's where we sat for lunch. I had a hamburger and the president had a peanut butter and jelly sandwich.

I don't remember what Rove had to eat, but he spoke first, and he was adamant that Bush keep a hard line against allowing the use of federal funds for embryonic stem cell research. He brought up the ethical concerns, but he stressed—and this was not atypical for Rove—the potential political fallout of softening that stance. I must admit I could relate. As I noted earlier, antiabortion groups in Wisconsin were furious with my support of Thomson's research. They are passionate and they are vocal.

But as I have also stated, I believed that in the end, the lifesaving potential of the research should carry the day.

A few weeks before my lunch with Rove and Bush, I'd been visited in Washington by Jere Fluno, a classmate of mine at UW–Madison who went on to a vastly successful career in business. Jere was also a philanthropist. I attended the luncheon in 1997 at the Madison Club when Jere's gift of $3 million to UW–Madison for an executive education facility—now called the Fluno Center—was announced.

Four years later, he was in my office at HHS in Washington to talk to me about his granddaughter, Lauren, who has juvenile diabetes. Jere told me about getting the phone call from his daughter informing him about Lauren's diagnosis. She was two years old. He talked about seeing that tiny girl in that big hospital bed. And he talked about the need for research to find a cure.

"Stem cells give us hope," Jere said.

It was an emotional meeting, and I remembered it at that Oval Office lunch, after Rove had finished and it was my turn to speak. I gave myself a quick, internal pep talk, knowing that the next few minutes might be my only chance to make my case.

"Mr. President," I said, "your mother and father have been great champions in the fight against cancer. They've devoted a tremendous amount of time, money, and effort to that cause. And you've started out your presidency by increasing funding for the National Institutes of Health. I thank you for that. It's the right thing to do, a great use of federal dollars.

"But Mr. President," I continued, "if you come out against embryonic stem cell research, no matter if you double the money for NIH, or anything else, if you turn down embryonic stem cells you're going to be remembered as the president who was antiscience."

The president kept looking at me but didn't say anything, so I went on.

"Every person in your administration has either a member of their family or a close friend who is suffering from a debilitating illness. You had a sister who died young of a terrible illness. Your mother and father did everything they could for that child."

I was referencing the daughter George H. W. and Barbara Bush lost to leukemia before she was four years old.

"Every parent," I told the president, "who has a child with juvenile diabetes, and who has to get up every night, four or five or six times, to check that child's blood, not knowing if that child is going to live or die, those parents are counting on stem cells to come up with a cure. If you, as president, stand in the way of giving those parents the hope and dream of a cure, you're going to be viewed as antiscience and stopping the great progress being made on juvenile diabetes, ALS, Parkinson's—you name it."

"But we don't know that it will work," the president said.

"It's the hope, Mr. President," I said. "The belief. And the dream."

About six weeks later, on August 8, I was called to the White House for an early evening meeting. Kevin Keane, my assistant secretary of public affairs, came with me. Kevin wasn't allowed in the meeting. I remember Karl Rove was there, and the president's chief of staff, Andy Card. The president told me he was going to give a prime-time address—the first of his presidency—the following night to state his position on federal funding of research using human embryonic stem cells. The president had decided to allow federal funds to be used for research on existing stem cell lines—cells derived prior to August 9, 2001. Federal dollars would not be used for any cell lines derived after that date. It was, essentially, a compromise, and while it didn't go as far as I might have hoped, I was pleased that the president at least went halfway. It got the federal funds flowing. I think what I said that day at lunch may have swayed him. The president didn't tell me so, but that's what I believe.

That night I called Carl Gulbrandsen, then managing director of WARF, which held the patent on Thomson's research, to tell him what was coming. Carl was at dinner with his wife, Mary, in Colorado.

I asked Carl, "Can you make these cell lines available?"

"Absolutely," he said. "We'll do everything we can."

By the first week of September, we had signed an agreement with the WiCell Research Institute, a nonprofit subsidiary of WARF, granting NIH scientists access to the cell lines, along with academic researchers, while also respecting WARF's patent and license rights.

There is no question in my mind that my coming from Wisconsin, and personally knowing people like Michael Sussman, Jamie Thomson, and Carl Gulbrandsen, helped us accomplish more in a shorter time frame than would otherwise have been the case. We respected and trusted each other. Carl came to Washington several times during the implementation process and let me know that someone at NIH told him the agency had never moved so quickly on anything. I brought a group of twenty scientists and administrators from NIH to Madison to see where the research was happening and meet the people responsible for it.

I don't mean to suggest any of this was easy. Throughout the debate I was caught in the middle between the strict pro-life contingent and those—like Pennsylvania senator Arlen Specter—who wanted all restrictions on embryonic stem cell research removed.

As a Catholic, I wasn't completely without conflict myself. During this time, I developed a friendship with Cardinal Theodore McCarrick, the archbishop of Washington—a friendship that endured even though we were on different sides of the stem cell issue. One afternoon I asked the cardinal if he'd have lunch with me at the Dubliner, an Irish pub downtown. He agreed and we had a wonderful time. We had corned beef sandwiches and beer, and I think he truly enjoyed all the people who recognized him and came up to say hello. Although the cardinal and I disagreed on the issue, we stayed friends.

A few days before Bush's prime-time speech, I read an article in *USA Today* that profiled Representative Jim Langevin, a pro-life Democrat from Rhode Island who had come out in support of embryonic stem cell research. An accidental gunshot injury had severed his spinal cord and put him in a wheelchair at age sixteen. Stem cell research gave him hope. He told the paper it "has the potential of easing a great deal of pain and suffering. Not only the pain and suffering of the individuals who suffer from these ailments, but that of their families. I know, just from watching what my family had to go through."

That impressed me. I wrote Langevin a letter.

"I would like to congratulate you on your outspoken stand on the stem cell issue," I wrote. "This issue is so important to the future of our nation's health, and with leaders such as yourself, I am sure we will be able to make great advances."

I continued, "After reading your recent article in *USA Today*, regarding your pro-life positioning and your support of stem cell research, I was truly impressed with your personal story. I am sure many people were touched by the article, and it helped put a personal and political face to the subject."

On September 5—the day after we signed the agreement with Carl Gulbrandsen and WARF—both Langevin and I testified in front of Edward Kennedy's Senate Committee on Health, Education, Labor and Pensions. When I was asked about the agreement, I called it groundbreaking. Some senators were worried that the number of cell lines available would be insufficient for the research demand. I said I was confident there would be enough.

More discussions were scheduled and would eventually take place, but all of Washington—all the United States and the world—was rocked by unforeseen events that occurred less than a week after that Senate committee hearing.

12

On the morning of September 11, 2001, I was on my way in to work at the Humphrey Building for a major meeting on flu. We'd invited experts from around the world to discuss preparation and treatment for a disease that at the time killed thirty-six thousand people a year. We worked hard to fight flu—I increased HHS funding for flu from $39 million in 2001 to $283 million in 2005, and developed the nation's first pandemic flu plan—but not that morning. The meeting never happened.

The first I knew that anything was amiss was in the car. My driver said, "Something's going on in New York City."

We turned on the radio. The first plane had just hit. I said, "Get me in."

By the time I reached the Humphrey Building, the TVs were on and we saw the second tower get hit. Stew Simonson, my legal counsel from the governor's office, who was now deputy general counsel for public health, came into my office and soon we were joined by Alex Azar, the general counsel; deputy secretary Claude Allen; and associate counsel for public health Richard Reisberg.

We talked about what we should do. It was hard to get information. We heard nothing from the Federal Emergency Management Agency, maybe because, very quickly, the telephone lines went out. Phone lines all over Washington were overwhelmed. Luckily, at HHS we had a couple of lines—including my personal line, which I used for nongovernment calls—that utilized a different prefix and hadn't collapsed. So at least we could make outgoing calls.

Before ten o'clock, a plane had hit the Pentagon, and the White House had been evacuated (President Bush, you will recall, was in Florida). We weren't sure whether to evacuate HHS or not. The order would have come from the General Services Administration, from whom we heard nothing.

I certainly didn't want to evacuate. Someone on my team—I think it may have been Reisberg—suggested I declare a public health emergency. Under section 319 of the Public Health Service Act, the secretary can declare an emergency, which then allows for "appropriate actions in response to the emergency."

"Let's do it," I said.

They drew up the paperwork and I signed it. Declaring the emergency helped us to get a plane in the air to New York with abundant medical supplies, including, as I recall, one hundred thousand masks and two hundred thousand rubber gloves.

I asked Stew to call NIH in Bethesda as well as the CDC in Atlanta—using one of our few working phones—and tell them to seal their buildings. After all, there was smallpox virus at CDC, and who knew the extent of all that was going on? We just weren't getting any information.

The first official word we received from the White House came from Vice President Dick Cheney, who was underground, under the East Wing, in the Presidential Emergency Operations Center. Cheney wanted me—along with numerous other cabinet secretaries and top government officials—to be evacuated to a secure location, part of a "continuity of government" strategy that may be invoked after catastrophic events. US marshals would escort me to a helicopter that would fly me to Mount Weather, a huge underground government complex built into a mountain west of Washington in Virginia.

I didn't want to go.

We were working hard, mobilizing medical teams and supplies for New York, making the kind of decisions—we wound up evacuating the CDC in Atlanta—that required me to be in my office.

I didn't talk to Cheney directly, but word came back, through my security detail, that I didn't have a choice.

"You're ordered to go."

"I'm not going," I said. I believe this was at about noon.

One of my security officers left the room, came back, and said, "They're telling us the helicopters are going at one o'clock and you're going to be on one—even if they have to put you under arrest."

I said, "Well, then let them arrest me."

I was angry. I was sure some cabinet officers, like Don Rumsfeld and Colin Powell, weren't being forced to leave.

Everyone told me I was crazy. Claude told me I had to leave. Stew and Bob Wood, my chief of staff, were also counseling me to obey the order.

Finally, a little before twelve thirty, two of my top security officers, Jay Hodes and Mike Lonetto, came in and said this was it. I had to be at the staging area in fifteen minutes or I'd be arrested and taken anyway.

I was still upset. "It will take more than the two of you," I said.

Somebody suggested that Jay and Mike step outside for a moment, which they did. Claude, Stew, and Bob pointed out that it would not look good if a cabinet secretary was arrested on the day of the attacks.

They were right, of course. I exhaled and said, "All right. I'll go."

But I asked Mike, my best friend on the security detail, to join me for a moment.

I said, "Michael, I don't know where this Mount Weather is, and I don't know if you know, but you need to find out and after I leave, I want you to drive out there."

He was staring at me.

"I am going to find a way out of there," I said, "and you are going to drive me back."

I knew I could count on Mike.

They had helicopters staged for most of the secretaries down by the Washington Monument. I think the flight took about twenty minutes and then we landed at what is essentially a huge underground city established by President Eisenhower in the event of nuclear war.

Once inside, we had to sign in, and they gave us blankets and assigned us rooms. When I got to mine, I threw the blankets on the bed and asked if I could look around. They said I could. I walked maybe a half mile and found a back entrance. I went out the back door, and there was Mike, in a vehicle. I got in the back seat and said, "Mike, get me to my office." He started driving back to Washington.

That wasn't the last I saw of Mount Weather. Every weekend that fall, through December, they assigned different cabinet secretaries to stay at Mount Weather. I absolutely hated it and more than once found reasons to leave. I'm sure I was the most reluctant and recalcitrant cabinet secretary. It caused a serious falling out between the White House Military Office and me, because I wouldn't follow their orders.

On September 11, Mike got me back to the Humphrey Building sometime before four o'clock. I was glad I went back. My employees were apprehensive. I had tried to talk to them before I left at twelve thirty, but now I had a chance to talk some more—and listen.

Someone said, "Are we going to be open tomorrow?"

"I'm not saying this to put any pressure on you," I said, "and you don't have to come to work. But I'm going to be here tomorrow. I want the Department of Health and Human Services to be open."

It was good I came back from Mount Weather, because early that evening—around six o'clock or so—I got a call telling me that Bush was going to be arriving back in Washington shortly and wanted me at the White House to speak to the press. Kevin rode over with me. It was dusk and the streets of the city were deserted, an eerie sensation.

When I got to the White House I was led to the Roosevelt Room, a conference room in the West Wing across the hall from the Oval Office, where I was eventually joined by transportation secretary Norman Mineta, Attorney General John Ashcroft, and FEMA director Joe Allbaugh. We were watching the news on television when the president walked in. I think it was about seven o'clock. He had a look of grim determination on his face and said he would be addressing the nation—the broadcast was already being set up across the hall in the Oval Office. The president asked us to go to the press room and give the reporters an update on our early response to the terrorist attacks. I remember Ashcroft saying the full force of US law enforcement would be brought to bear on the investigation and that the perpetrators would be caught. I talked about the medical supplies we'd rushed to New York City. A reporter asked me how many body bags we'd shipped. I declined to answer that one. We didn't know the death toll and I certainly didn't want to speculate. A few minutes later, in his address to the nation, Bush gave an indication that the numbers would be horrendous when he said, "Thousands of lives were suddenly ended by evil."

I was back at the Humphrey Building at five o'clock the next morning and stood by the main entrance shaking hands and thanking the HHS employees—more than half—who decided to come to work. I was proud of them. It was another hard day. I asked Stew to go to New York in advance of my plan to go there the following day. He did significant prep work for our visit, then returned to Washington that night. The following morning, September 13, Stew, Kevin, and I took an Amtrak train to New York City. I was the first cabinet secretary to visit after the attack. We went right from Penn Station to the Police

Academy on East Twentieth Street, where Mayor Rudy Giuliani and Governor George Pataki had set up their command headquarters.

Kevin took a photograph of Giuliani and me shaking hands. It was an extraordinary moment, because our eyes locked and neither one of us spoke. I was struck by the look of both pain and determination on the mayor's face. Kevin said later that the moment—with no one speaking—probably lasted thirty seconds, but seemed longer. Then we got to work, talking about what HHS could do to help. I felt I needed to see things firsthand, and the mayor assigned some police officers to accompany us, first to Ground Zero.

I will always remember that day. Driving over from the Police Academy, I was struck by how quiet the city was, the shock still palpable. As we got close to Ground Zero, the stoplights weren't operational, and yet no one was honking horns. Cars took turns, and there was no pushing or shoving by pedestrians. It was everybody coming together in a time of crisis. The closer we got, the thicker the fog of dust and debris became. Firefighters, emergency medical personnel, and construction crews—trying to dig through the rubble—were on the scene. The buildings appeared to still be smoldering.

I took off my jacket and tie, rolled up my sleeves, and put on a mask. I felt like the most immediate good I could do was to walk around and offer encouragement to the men and women who were working, many with little sleep, at the scene. The presence of EMTs indicated there was still hope of finding survivors, and I will never forget that while we were walking we heard someone cry out that a man had been found alive in an automobile near where one of the buildings had collapsed. I was never able to confirm if that was true. I hope so.

Next we went to Saint Vincent's Hospital in Greenwich Village, where many of the injured had been taken. Again, my goal was to buoy up the doctors and nurses who were working so hard and find out from the administrators what more we could do to help. I spoke with patients, too, some in very tough shape. As we walked we saw people holding photographs of loved ones who might have been admitted to the hospital. On a large board were posted photos with numbers to call if anyone had seen these people.

The hardest part of our day came at the Office of Chief Medical Examiner, where we met Dr. Charles Hirsch, an impressive man who himself had been injured when the towers came down. He showed us the receiving area where bags with body parts were being unloaded from ambulances and then taken to be catalogued for identification. It was terribly solemn and I was struck by the dignity with which Hirsch and his staff treated these human remains. People were coming in to the office with hairbrushes and toothbrushes of their missing family members, for possible DNA matches. It was heartbreaking.

We began compiling lists of all that was needed. They wanted more supplies of all kinds, of course, and they needed more pathologists. They needed more dogs to sniff out bodies, and veterinarians to care for the dogs.

I am extremely proud of how HHS responded to the crisis in New York. Our team included rescue workers and public health professionals from CDC and the HHS Commissioned Corps Readiness Force, along with volunteer health and mortuary professionals who were part of our National Disaster Medical System—some two thousand people in all.

We aided over 9,500 rescue workers with injuries ranging from skin irritation to broken bones and heart failure. We assisted the medical examiner's office in processing 15,528 human specimens and identifying 750 victims. Our veterinary teams treated 900 dogs for exhaustion, dehydration, sore paws, and burnt noses.

One important realization that came out of my spending September 13 in New York City was the need for a comprehensive mental health conference to help the brave people who responded to the emergency of 9/11 in New York City, as well as to better prepare the nation's mental health professionals to respond if terrorists struck again.

I called Charlie Curie, the new head of the Substance Abuse and Mental Health Services Administration (SAMHSA), and said I wanted him to organize a conference to be held in New York City.

"Sometime in 2002?" Charlie said.

"No, this year," I said.

Charlie got it done. On November 14, we kicked off a three-day national summit in New York City, "When Terror Strikes: Strengthening the Homeland through Recovery, Resilience and Readiness." Forty-two states and the District of Columbia sent mental health and substance abuse personnel—650 participants in all—to learn about crafting a state action plan for responding to terrorism.

Additionally, first-responders and 9/11 survivors shared their first-person accounts, and psychologists spoke about strategies for coping with the stress and fear that often linger long after a traumatic event.

In my keynote address the first morning, I quoted Churchill, who said, in the early days of World War II, "We shall draw from the heart of suffering itself the means of inspiration and survival."

And I told the professionals assembled in front of me that their help would be needed for years to come.

"Yes," I said, "the psychological consequences of a disaster generally fade with time. People do heal. But we know that the anguish that accompanied September 11 will stay with some people for a long time, sometimes recalled by anniversaries, or a scene on a TV screen, or even renewed by another new attack of terrorism."

It was critical, I said, that everyone realize "mental health support must be an integral part of emergency preparedness and our public health infrastructure."

Well in advance of 9/11 we'd been working at HHS on preparing for another kind of attack: bioterrorism, the deliberate release of viruses, bacteria, and other agents to cause illness or death. Before I made my first trip to the CDC in Atlanta in February 2001, I asked Stew to prepare for me a briefing paper on bioterrorism. In 1999 CDC had established a Bioterrorism Preparedness and Response Program, with Dr. Scott Lillibridge as its founding director.

I made it clear to Lillibridge and others that I recognized the potential catastrophic impact of a bioterrorism attack. We talked about the possibility of creating a position akin to a bioterrorism czar—someone who could coordinate the various federal agencies that would respond to such an emergency.

In July I named Lillibridge—not as any kind of czar, but as my special assistant to the secretary for bioterrorism. He was scheduled to move to Washington in early October, but part of the fallout of the 9/11 attacks was that bioterrorism was suddenly on everyone's minds. Lillibridge came up early, and I charged him with making sure HHS was working in a coordinated and aggressive manner—including reaching out to our state and local partners—on antiterrorism preparedness. We were looking at public health infrastructure, the stockpile of vaccines and antibiotics, food safety, and more.

The threat of further terrorist attacks, including and maybe most especially bioterrorism, had people scared. At HHS we were in the difficult position of counseling the American people to be diligent while also advising them not to panic or live their lives in fear.

On September 30, on the CBS program *60 Minutes* in its segment on bioterrorism, I said I felt we were well prepared to respond to an attack. Our response on 9/11 was part of the reason for my confidence.

On October 3, a few days after that segment aired, I testified on bioterrorism preparedness in front of a Senate appropriations subcommittee. The senators sparred with me on whether we were truly prepared. I agreed with them to the extent that "there is much more that can and should be done." I said they could help by appropriating more funds to prevent and treat biological attacks. They were ready to do that and promised additional funding, in the neighborhood of $1 billion.

The very next day, October 4, the White House received word that a Florida man had been hospitalized and diagnosed with anthrax, a bacterial infection that can occur from natural causes, such as handling animals, but can also be utilized as a weapon in bioterrorism.

The day turned out to be the most controversial of all my time at HHS.

Early that afternoon I got a call informing me that a few hours earlier Bush had learned of the Florida anthrax case and wanted me to address it during press secretary Ari Fleischer's daily briefing. They wanted to get out ahead of the story, which was about to break with a news conference by health officials in Florida.

I asked Lillibridge to come with me. When we got to the White House I was given a sheaf of briefing papers on the case that had been hastily prepared by CDC. The Florida man was a layout editor at a tabloid newspaper in Boca Raton. The gist of the CDC report was that there was no way to immediately know how the man—his name was Bob Stevens—had contracted anthrax. There was nothing to suggest terrorism. A passage in the CDC report said Stevens was an outdoorsman who had drunk from a stream while vacationing in North Carolina a few days earlier. I believe that information came from a journal Stevens kept. But again, nobody knew how he got anthrax. As Fleischer wrote in his memoir, *Taking Heat*, about our going out that afternoon to talk to reporters, "The last word we had before the briefing was this might be an isolated case and there was, at the time, no need for greater concern."

Fleischer introduced Lillibridge and me at the press conference, and I opened with a few remarks.

"Let me, as Ari indicated, just bring you up to date with the information that we have concerning an incident that took place in the state of Florida, and also following up with information that the state of Florida has released within the last hour. The Centers for Disease Control has just confirmed the diagnosis of anthrax in a patient in a Florida hospital."

Then I said, "*Based on what we know at this point*, it appears that this is an isolated case." I have added the italics.

Let me admit right here that this press conference was not my finest hour. I am obviously not a medical doctor, and while I deferred some questions to Lillibridge, I was acting on the president's request to go out and try to calm things down. I tried to do that. Maybe I should have deferred more to the doctor. I did say more than once that we couldn't—at this early stage—be sure what caused the anthrax diagnosis, but maybe I didn't stress that enough. The real lesson I learned was, don't have a press conference when the facts are still so sketchy.

The press, understandably, was preoccupied with the idea it might be terrorism.

Ron Fournier from the Associated Press asked, "Is there any reason to believe that is a result of terrorism?"

"It appears that this is just an isolated case," I replied.

In his book, Fleischer, whose memory of the precise back-and-forth is better than mine, noted that I then added, "There's no evidence of terrorism at this—"

Before I could finish the sentence, presumably saying "at this time" or "at this point," CBS reporter John Roberts, who knew a little about anthrax, cut in with a question about whether the infected man had contact with raw wool, which in rare instances could contain anthrax. I said CDC was currently trying to retrace the man's activities over the past couple of weeks. A minute later, Roberts followed up with another question about wool, this time wondering if the Florida man might have worked around wool products.

I replied, "We don't know that at this point in time. That's entirely possible. We do know that he drank water out of a stream when he was traveling to North Carolina last week. But as far as wool or other things, it's entirely possible. We haven't got all the investigations done and we're doing a tremendous, extensive job of investigating everything."

In other words, nobody knows.

When more anthrax showed up in ensuing weeks, in letters mailed to network news offices in New York and Senate majority leader Tom Daschle's office in Washington, I was savaged in the press. The *Philadelphia Inquirer* said I "theorized" that drinking from a stream had caused Stevens's anthrax. The *Los Angeles Times* said I "suggested" he had contracted it from the stream water.

The drumbeat never really went away. In December, *Time* magazine wrote that I "famously suggested" drinking from a stream caused anthrax.

What I believe I said was that Stevens's time in North Carolina and his drinking from the stream—which was included in the CDC briefing I received prior to the press conference—were among many things that were being looked at early in the investigation.

The criticism was brutal, but I took it. In hindsight, we made a mistake that day by going out to meet reporters with little solid information to share. A decade on, the FBI issued a report that concluded a US biodefense researcher sent the anthrax.

One immediate step we took at HHS endures to this day. In the weeks after 9/11, I decided I needed an on-site operations center—it quickly got labeled the war room—which would help the department coordinate our response to an emergency. At the time, the department's operations center was in Bethesda, which hindered our communications during the chaos on 9/11.

We had the beginnings of a new center—computers, fax machines, and TVs—up and going almost immediately. It was staffed around the clock, in a conference room across from my office. Eventually, when things quieted down a bit, we completely remodeled and upgraded it into a state-of-the-art operations center that connected us to every division in HHS and the health departments in many countries. It had its own ventilation system, in case of chemical attack. I wanted to be able to have face-to-face meetings, so we put in a video-conferencing system and paid for installation of an emergency command center at the headquarters of the World Health Organization. We even used the operations center to encourage the Chinese government to allow epidemiologists into the country during the SARS outbreak and again during the outbreak of H5N1 influenza.

I'm proud of that operations center, which was named for me. I don't know if my name survived during the Obama administration, but I am sure his team was grateful to have it. They no doubt laughed when they saw one aspect of the center. On a large map, one city was far and away most prominently displayed, in letters big enough that anyone would think this place must be the center of the universe.

To me, it is. Elroy, Wisconsin, of course.

In 2002, while the country was still recovering from the 9/11 attacks and the administration was immersed in formulating its response, President Bush said to me, "Tommy, you need to take leadership in getting prescription drug coverage for seniors."

I wasn't surprised. Getting Medicare coverage for prescription drugs had been a major campaign issue in 2000. Bill Clinton had failed to accomplish it in his eight years as president. Bush and his Democratic opponent, Al Gore, both supported the idea, though they had very different ideas about how to realize it. Gore and legislative Democrats saw it basically as an expansion of existing Medicare benefits. No surprise, Bush's plan included incentives for seniors to join private health plans, with Medicare then subsidizing the private providers. Bigger government wasn't part of the Republican agenda.

Bush, as I noted, was preoccupied with the war in Afghanistan—and the coming war in Iraq—so he asked me to work with his health policy analyst, Doug Badger, to come up with a Medicare prescription drug plan. I drew in Tom Scully, my administrator of CMS, and the three of us began meeting, almost weekly, either at the White House, the Humphrey Building, or at CMS out in Maryland.

When I look back, two things stand out about the effort to get the prescription drug benefit: how complex it was and what a tough fight we had to get it done.

In 1999 Clinton had tried and failed. That June he introduced an overhaul of Medicare that was anchored by a drug benefit that for a $24 monthly premium would pay half the costs of prescription drugs up to $2,000 a year. It was exorbitantly expensive and doomed in the House of Representatives, where Republicans in 2000 came up with a plan of their own, which relied heavily on the private insurance market abetted by federal subsidies.

Neither proposal got traction, and while the issue was an important part of the Bush-Gore campaigns in 2000, its immediacy faded—along with just about everything else—in the wake of the 9/11 attacks. After the president handed the issue to Badger and me, we began to develop a plan, even as, in 2002, House Republicans passed (barely) their own bill, which was almost completely marketplace driven. It had no chance in the Democrat-controlled Senate, where in 2002 three different bills—two Democratic proposals and one Republican— were considered and rejected. The primary Democratic proposal, which would have cost $594 billion over ten years, got fifty-two votes but not the sixty that were needed under a budget point of order, which can be invoked during significant-spending debates.

By late 2002—after the midterm elections—and into early 2003, Badger, Scully, and I continued to meet, usually at the White House, now joined on occasion by Stephen Friedman, the former Goldman Sachs chairman who in December 2002 became Bush's top economic adviser. We kept the president advised on our progress. Eventually we decided—after talking with Republicans in Congress—that the best course would be to roll out a broad plan outlining our vision for the Medicare prescription drug coverage, while leaving the details to the intense negotiations in Congress that were sure to come. Our plan—the president announced it in March 2003 as the Framework to Modernize and Improve Medicare—called for prescription drug coverage to be offered to all Medicare patients, though those who joined private plans would have more extensive coverage.

It was our intent to merge a modified free enterprise system, based on competition, with an entrenched government program. We frankly didn't know if it would work, but we wanted the insurance companies to compete. The eventual success of the plan depended on the insurance companies' willingness to do that—to bid for business—which they did, even more than we had hoped. But that's getting a little ahead of the story.

The president's March 2003 announcement began a months-long series of negotiations, often heated, about specifics related to the prescription drug coverage. One piece that was eventually included in the final product was the so-called doughnut hole in the coverage, which meant most beneficiaries would receive nothing from Medicare on prescription expenses between $2,250 and $5,100. It was an effort to keep costs down, and the congressional Democrats didn't like it. They couldn't just take their ball and go home, however—and this applied to Republicans, too, some of whom bristled at any Medicare expansion—because the American public was demanding a prescription drug benefit. Seniors wanted it. That central fact—along with the elections looming in 2004—kept the negotiations going when they might have otherwise fallen apart.

In the end, everyone compromised. Bush agreed in early June to allow equal prescription drug benefits for people who stayed in the traditional fee-for-service Medicare program. Originally, we'd hoped to give those who sought a private plan more extensive coverage, but Senate Democrats were adamantly against that.

Even with the compromises, the legislation nearly derailed numerous times, starting with the separate House and Senate bills that were considered in late June. The Senate bill passed easily enough, 76–21 in the early morning hours of June 27, 2003, though not without some drama when Senator Edward Kennedy objected to an amendment that would have linked prescription drug coverage to income. Kennedy wanted equal benefits for all. Threatening a filibuster, Kennedy told Senate leaders of both parties, "You can have this amendment, or you can have this bill." The amendment was dropped.

There was theater in the House, too, where I spent considerable time and where we knew the vote was going to be very close. Republicans wheeled in some elderly constituents in support of the bill, while some Democrats wore black armbands to show their displeasure with a bill that, they believed, not only didn't go far enough but started Medicare on a slippery slope to privatization.

Vice President Dick Cheney showed up at one point to rally Republican support for the bill. He soon left, but I stayed, helping Speaker of the House Dennis Hastert tally votes and convince the hardline conservatives of the bill's merits. The vote came around two thirty that morning, and only after Hastert had extended the customary fifteen-minute voting period to just under an hour—so we could make sure we had the votes. We did, 216–215. It was that close.

It also wasn't over. The bills had to be unified into one and then voted on again, by both the House and the Senate. Those votes came in November 2003, and if anything, they produced more drama than the votes the previous June.

The House voted first, and again I spent the better part of a few days in the House chamber, encouraging Republicans to support the bill. Bush was traveling—visiting Queen Elizabeth in England—but he stayed in touch by phone, and had Karl Rove calling from Buckingham Palace for updates.

The House began considering the bill on November 21, and the negotiations ran past midnight. Bush had landed back at the White House early that evening and made some calls to legislators. Hastert and I were still engaged in trying to make sure we had the votes to pass the bill. My recollection is that it went to a vote around two o'clock. Roll call votes are usually open for fifteen or twenty minutes. Hastert wound up not closing the roll call on the prescription drug bill because he couldn't be certain we had the votes to pass it. He kept it open for several hours, probably the longest amount of time a vote has ever been open. For a while we were afraid we weren't going to get the votes, but through cajoling and promising and doing whatever we could do, by about four fifteen we felt we were within one vote of passing.

Hastert came up to me and said, "Trent Franks wants to talk to the president. He'll switch his vote to us, but he needs to talk to the president."

Franks was a Republican representative from Arizona. Hastert said Franks wanted assurance from Bush about a federal judge appointment in his district. He wanted a conservative—he didn't have a name, he just wanted to be assured the appointment would go to a true conservative.

Remember, it was four fifteen in the morning. I found a White House congressional liaison who had been helping count votes and said we needed to phone the president.

"He'll be furious," the liaison said.

"It has to happen," I said.

The liaison stepped away for a moment, came back, and said, "OK, call at four thirty."

I did. The president was not happy. I explained the situation, and he said to put Trent Franks on the phone, which I did. They spoke for just a few minutes. When Franks hung up, he turned to me and Hastert and said, "I'll vote for it."

In the end, the bill passed 220–215. I walked out of the House of Representatives feeling good but a little dazed from lack of sleep. The sun was rising. I decided I might as well just go to my office. It was there, in the Humphrey Building, at about nine o'clock, that I got a phone call from the president.

"Two things, Tommy," Bush said.

"Yes, Mr. President."

"You did excellent work," the president said. "Congratulations. But Tommy? Never, ever call me again at four thirty in the morning."

And still it wasn't over. The Senate took up the bill a few days later, and while the numbers looked good for passage—the Republicans had reclaimed the Senate majority in the 2002 elections—the Democrats didn't go down without a fight. Ted Kennedy, calling the bill a first step toward the privatization of Medicare, filibustered against it. A Senate vote of 70–29 ended Kennedy's filibuster. Then Democratic senator Tom Daschle invoked a budget point of order, which would require sixty votes to override before a vote could be taken on the actual Medicare bill. Daschle was furious about Hastert having left the House roll call open for three hours a couple of nights earlier, calling it "the most egregious violation of the rules that I've seen in twenty-five years."

I was in the Senate chamber during the debate, walking around the floor in areas designated for senators only. I remember a Democrat saying, "Tommy, if you want to be in the Senate so bad, why don't you run?"

I didn't really want to be there—I needed to be. It wasn't immediately clear that we had the sixty votes to override Daschle's point of order. We eventually convinced Trent Lott, a Republican who did not like the Medicare drug benefit bill, to vote to end the point of order: he could always vote against the bill itself (which he did). With Lott's vote and a shift by Democrat Ron Wyden, the point of order was overridden 61–39. The bill passed 54–44, on a bipartisan vote.

Bush signed the Medicare Prescription Drug, Improvement, and Modernization Act into law on December 8, 2003. We'd tried to provide choice and let private companies compete with traditional Medicare. Most seniors under the plan would have a monthly premium of about $35 and a $250 deductible, with Medicare paying 75 percent of their drug costs up to $2,250 (when the doughnut hole—no coverage—kicked in) and after $5,100. Higher amounts would be covered by catastrophic coverage. The law took effect in January 2006.

Many Democrats, some Republicans, and numerous pundits predicted doom for the new law—it would be too expensive, it would be this, or it would be that.

In fact, Medicare Part D, as it is most commonly known, has been a tremendous success. The elderly like it, costs have been lower than expected, and we have a competitive model attached to the government Medicare system.

Let me quote a November 2013 column in the *Huffington Post* by Robert B. Blancato, that was headlined, "Why Medicare Part D Worked When Many Said It Wouldn't." Part D was nearing the tenth anniversary of its December 2003 enactment. Blancato, an expert on aging and an advocate for seniors, wrote this: "Part D's success can be measured in a number of ways, most importantly how seniors perceive it. From 2006 to 2013, satisfaction rates among beneficiaries increased from 78 to 90 percent, according to a recent Medicare Today survey. . . . Fiscally speaking, Part D has exceeded expectations. The non-partisan Congressional Budget Office found that total program costs are on track to be $348 billion—or 45 percent—less than initial 10-year projections."

I'm pleased to have played a significant role in making it happen.

At the same time we were working at HHS to get a Medicare prescription drug benefit passed into law, we were also deeply involved in the worldwide effort to fight AIDS.

My knowledge of the disease dated to my first term as governor of Wisconsin, when Doug Nelson, whom I had known since my days in the assembly, was hired as executive director of the Milwaukee AIDS Project, then the state's largest AIDS service organization. Doug came to Madison and talked to me about the dire seriousness of the disease, and the likelihood it would expand in scope. I promised to try to help.

More than a decade later, as I was assembling my team at HHS in the first months of the Bush administration, my colleague Bill Steiger attended a meeting in Rome in which health experts from several G8 countries spoke about the possibility of creating a global fund for health. The spur was the need to combat AIDS. There were a lot of different proposals out there, Bill said, but no one was really taking leadership.

Bill Steiger—son of the eminent Wisconsin congressman of the same name—was my director of the Office of Global Health Affairs at HHS, and he did an excellent job. The idea of a global health fund had been on the table since at least late 1999, primarily at the urging of the World Health Organization (WHO). In August 2000 President Clinton signed a bill that authorized a global trust fund for AIDS patients, but the fund would sit not with WHO but with the World Bank, and no money was appropriated. Soon after, UNICEF suggested it was best equipped to distribute AIDS monies. There was clearly a will for some kind of global fund for health, and discussions had coalesced around

AIDS as the most urgent threat, but as Bill noted, the ideas being floated were short on specifics and lacked a unifying theme. There might be an opportunity for us, Bill said, because the president was looking for a big proposal to announce at his first meeting with the G8 leaders.

Bill spoke with Gary Edson, who was the chief G8 negotiator for the United States under Bush, and he was intrigued enough that Bill proceeded to put a concept paper together—this was March 2001—outlining how a global fund focused on the three biggest killers, AIDS, tuberculosis, and malaria, might best work. It would need both government and nongovernment participation and partnership at every level, rigorous technical review of proposals, independent financial oversight, and intellectual property protection. It would not sit in WHO (a United Nations agency) or the World Bank—but clearly it would need the buy-in of the United Nations to be successful. Gary began to sell the idea within the administration and to the other G8 nations.

To that end, I got a call that spring from Secretary of State Colin Powell, who'd been contacted by United Nations Secretary General Kofi Annan. What did Annan want to talk about? A global health fund. Annan's interest dated to a G8 Summit in Okinawa, Japan, in July 2000, when a massive coordinated effort to fight AIDS was a primary topic of discussion.

He called Powell, who in turn called me and asked if I would meet with Annan. I said certainly. When we met, Annan described his vision of a global fund to fight AIDS. AIDS was his primary interest and concern, but he felt fund-raising would benefit if we included malaria and tuberculosis as beneficiaries of the fund. He wanted the United States to contribute $200 million. I told him I would talk to the president.

It was a Sunday afternoon when Colin Powell and I went to the White House to speak to Bush. That was highly unusual, a Sunday afternoon White House meeting. When Colin and I had pitched the idea at a Principals Committee meeting in the Situation Room a few days earlier, the atmosphere was tense. National security adviser Condoleezza Rice supported our proposal, but treasury secretary Paul O'Neill wanted the fund to focus on clean water. The Office of Management and Budget had just submitted the president's budget and was opposed to an amendment for new spending. The vice president was lukewarm. Edson and the deputy director of OMB ended up in a shouting match after the meeting broke up without a firm recommendation. The president himself would have to make the call.

That Sunday the president was initially skeptical about investing in a multi-lateral fund, because he thought we should do something ourselves, but Powell and Edson were very persuasive. I give them a lot of credit. The president came around. When it was time to find the $200 million for the US contribution, however, I was told half needed to come from HHS, and the State Department matched us.

The announcement of the $200 million contribution to the Global Fund to Fight AIDS, Tuberculosis and Malaria was made May 11, 2001, in the Rose Garden at the White House. Kofi Annan was there, along with President Bush, Colin Powell, myself, and the president of Nigeria, Olusegun Obasanjo.

It was all well received in the press, and the idea caught on, though there was still a lot of hard work to do to establish the details of how the Global Fund would work. More money came in almost immediately. By summer, Britain and Japan were in for $200 million each, France pledged $127 million, and the Bill and Melinda Gates Foundation $100 million.

Bill Steiger—as my representative—attended meetings almost monthly in Brussels and Geneva throughout the rest of 2001, as the Global Fund rules and regulations were being set up. Much of what we had drafted as a concept paper at HHS earlier in the year became reality in the structure and bylaws of the fund. We wanted to minimize the chances a government leader might find a way to misuse the money and needed the organization to be nimbler than the World Bank or United Nations. That was accomplished by incorporating the Global Fund, in January 2002, as a Swiss foundation, a private-public partnership that is essentially a financing organization. It was set up so that the fund's grants are audited by large international accounting firms. It was to be governed by an eighteen-member board of directors: seven from donating countries, one seat each for private foundations and the private sector, seven from implementing countries, and two from nongovernmental organizations.

The first chairman was Dr. Chrispus Kiyonga, a government minister from Uganda. I addressed the first board meeting, which was held in Geneva in late January 2002, on a video link, wishing them well and promising US support. Unfortunately, things didn't go very well for the Global Fund, not that first year. They weren't raising the funds they needed, and it became clear fairly quickly that the chairman, while a nice gentleman, was in over his head. He didn't really know how to run a meeting, and the meetings bordered on chaos. It just wasn't working. I began reaching out to other leaders of the Global

Fund, and in those conversations we discussed the possibility of me taking over as chairman.

There was significant pushback, not against me personally, I don't think, but against the idea that an American would chair the Global Fund. The fear was that the United States was too big and too powerful and might end up using the fund as a tool of its foreign policy.

I said, "I understand your concerns. But I am taking a risk—putting myself out there to be chairman—because it is clear this group needs a strong leader. I can run a meeting. You want to grow this thing? Let me grow it for you."

I spoke with the board members of the donor countries in Europe, trying to allay their concerns, and eventually almost everyone warmed to the idea of me as chairman. I was elected on January 31, 2003, and I feel like we hit the ground running. The fund increased to more than $5 billion during my time as chairman.

One reason the board of the Global Fund accepted me as chairman may have been that by the time we were talking about it, in the second half of 2002, I'd been to the Caribbean and Africa, seen the devastation of AIDS firsthand, and, I believe, played a part in encouraging the president's growing commitment to funding the fight against it.

In April 2002 I led a US delegation to Georgetown, Guyana, for a conference on AIDS with numerous Caribbean health ministers. It was the first visit by a US cabinet member in twenty-five years to Guyana, where AIDS was the leading cause of death in adults ages twenty to forty-five. I signed the Pan-Caribbean Partnership Agreement to fight HIV/AIDS and gave a brief address, in part about the Global Fund. "The United States has been committed to the Global Fund from day one," I said, "ever since President Bush and UN Secretary General Kofi Annan stood together at the White House last May to announce our contribution of $200 million. We have now increased our pledge to $500 million, and we are proposing to spend $1.1 billion in fiscal year 2003 to help fight HIV/AIDS in the developing world."

Also in spring 2002, in my role as HHS secretary, I went to South Africa, taking along Anthony Fauci, director of the National Institute of Allergy and Infectious Diseases (part of NIH). Tony is a personal friend to this day and one of the world's leading experts on AIDS. I also invited Hank McKinnell, the CEO of Pfizer, the maker of a drug, Nevirapine, that can prevent mother-to-child AIDS transmission.

We visited an orphanage run by a Catholic order that housed children ages two to five who were HIV positive. The disease had been transmitted by their mothers, either in pregnancy, at childbirth, or in breast milk. It was a heart-breaking day. I remember picking up a beautiful two-year-old girl who melted in my arms. She just wanted to be held. At one point, I handed Hank a little boy. He was a high-powered CEO, but once he got the boy in his arms, his eyes start to tear up. He couldn't speak. Before we left the orphanage that day, Hank wrote them a large personal check.

What they really needed in South Africa was Nevirapine, and Tony and I had a confounding meeting with Manto Tshabalala-Msimang, the South African minister of health. She would not accept the drug. She told us that eating boiled potatoes with garlic could prevent AIDS. She wouldn't let us distribute Nevirapine in South Africa. It was maddening.

On the flight home, Tony and I talked about the need for the United States to intercede in Africa to try to stem the mother-to-child transmission of AIDS. Not just in South Africa—though clearly minds needed to be changed there—but throughout Sub-Saharan Africa.

Tony and I met with Bush and provided some statistics. At that time, more than two million women carrying the AIDS virus gave birth each year, with 98 percent passing it on to their babies. The president, in June 2002, announced a five-year, $500 million United States-led initiative to prevent mother-to-child transmission of the disease in fourteen countries in Sub-Saharan Africa and the Caribbean.

Privately, the president also told us, "Think bigger." I give him great credit for that. His wife, Laura, was also a strong advocate for the cause. Tony and one of his top deputies, Mark Dybul—who came to work for me to set up the mother-to-child transmission program and later became US Global AIDS coordinator and executive director of the Global Fund—immediately began crafting an expansive plan that, as it turned out, would be unveiled in the president's State of the Union address the following January.

It made what happened at the Fourteenth International AIDS Conference in Barcelona, Spain, highly ironic. That was in July 2002, a month after Bush's $500 million pledge. I was scheduled to speak at the conference. It did not go well. I was interrupted by protesters to where I could hardly be heard by the audience. The protesters were yelling and carrying signs and suggesting the United States was not doing nearly enough for AIDS. Afterward, I spoke to reporters and pointed out how much we were indeed doing—with more to come.

I wonder if anyone who was there that day in Barcelona recalled it, when, on January 28, 2003, President Bush in his State of the Union speech announced the President's Emergency Plan for AIDS Relief (PEPFAR). Drafted by our team at HHS, led by Tony Fauci and Mark Dybul, it called for $15 billion over ten years for global AIDS prevention, treatment, and care in the same fourteen countries covered first by the mother-to-child transmission plan (a fifteenth country, Vietnam, was added later). It became a significant part of the president's legacy, and I feel it is part of mine, too. Certainly my trips to Africa stand out as among the most memorable experiences of my life and career.

A visit in early December 2003 was easily my most ambitious. I led a group of 105 people—leaders in business, government, and health care—on a nearly week-long trip to four African countries, primarily to document the ravages of AIDS and what was needed to combat it. The passengers on the plane—we flew together on a private jet out of Germany—included, to name just a few, my esteemed HHS colleagues Tony Fauci and Julie Gerberding, the director of the CDC; Randall Tobias, Bush's newly announced AIDS "czar"; various drug company executives; officials from WHO, UNAIDS, and the Global Fund; former congressman Ron Dellums; Senator Don Nickles of Oklahoma; and a former US ambassador to the United Nations, Richard Holbrooke, who in that role once initiated a UN Security Council session on AIDS, the first time that august body ever discussed a health issue.

There were a lot of large personalities on that trip. I have said since that they needn't have put fuel in the plane in Germany—the hot air inside could have floated it. Yet in the end, it was well worth the ego jostling and logistical problems of shepherding that many dignitaries around. One thing that made the trip special for me was that my daughter Tommi, who was making a career in women's health, was along.

Our African visit began with a refueling stop in Douala, Cameroon. There was a reception at the airport and what stood out was the heat and humidity. From Cameroon, we went to Zambia to march in a parade to mark World AIDS Day, alongside HIV-positive patients, some of whom PEPFAR had already begun treating. On the second day, we went to Rwanda. The CDC has an office in Kigali, which is home, too, to the Gisozi Genocide Memorial. Holbrooke gave a moving speech at the memorial, condemning the fact that the United

States, among others, stayed on the sidelines in 1994 while the ruling Hutu people slaughtered the Tutsis in staggering numbers.

"The lesson of each genocide is the same," Holbrooke said that day. "The killing really only takes off after the murderers see that the world, and especially the United States, is not going to care or react."

The following morning, some of us were driven about twenty-five miles south to visit a hospital in the farming community of Kabgayi. We had something else in mind, as well. My HHS colleague Bill Steiger, who was along on the trip, had learned that as a courtesy it is proper to bring a gift on such a visit. In collaboration with CDC in Kigali, Bill arranged for us to present a dairy cow that morning. Of course, a cow is very valuable in that rural setting, and this one was a big hit. Word had spread and a large crowd surrounded us when I handed over the reins of the cow to the local bishop and began my brief remarks. I told them the cow was named Elroy, after my hometown back in America. Maybe Elroy heard her name mentioned—yes, Elroy was female—but for whatever reason, she got excited and managed to get loose from the bishop and began wandering through the crowd. Everyone loved it—they were singing and chanting and truly grateful. It got better. It turned out Elroy was pregnant and eventually gave birth to a female calf. A few years later, when my successor as HHS secretary, Mike Leavitt, visited CDC in Kigali, he learned that both cows were alive and well and still much appreciated.

We were supposed to depart Rwanda for Kenya later that day, but we learned that there had been a terror threat against Americans in Nairobi. We didn't know how viable it was, but CNN broadcast the news, and the *East African Standard* newspaper ran a headline, "Nairobi on High Terror Alert."

I met with a few of the leaders of the group and basically said I didn't feel that we needed to change our plans. The meeting was tense. I trusted our security, and the US embassy in Nairobi told us we should still come, but Holbrooke took issue.

"You're right, Tommy," he said. "It doesn't bother me. I'll go with you. But what about the women and young people?"

In the end, we decided that I would take a group to Nairobi, while many in our party would bypass Kenya and go on to Uganda. These years later we still tease my deputy chief of staff, Andy Knapp, who led the group to Uganda. Someone even had baseball caps made up—I've kept mine—that read, "Andy Knapp is *Still* Scared of Kenyan Terrorists."

Of course, nothing terror-related happened in Kenya. In Nairobi there was a reception for us at the residence of the US ambassador, William Mark Bellamy. Kenya's health minister, Charity Ngilu, offered sincere thanks for the Bush administration's commitment to AIDS relief. We talked about the need for health-care infrastructure across Africa.

The emotional core of the trip, for me, came the next day, in Uganda. I wanted everyone in our delegation to visit a family that had been impacted by AIDS. From Kampala, the capital, we rode buses three hours to the eastern Uganda city of Tororo. From there, we split into groups of four and five, each group climbing into a four-wheel-drive vehicle and following a Ugandan health-care worker on a motorcycle who was calling on the poor farms and villages outside Tororo.

The roads were almost nonexistent. The people lived in mud huts. But for more than a year, even before the start of PEPFAR, the CDC had been providing—through a clinic in Tororo, and the workers on motorcycles—lifesaving antiretroviral drugs to HIV-positive people in these rural areas. I only wished the bikes were Harleys (they were Suzukis). We had the drugs with us that day too—in plastic pill cases with each day's allotment clearly marked—and while I knew the drugs were helping people, I was unprepared for the warmth of the reception we received.

My small group—it included my daughter Tommi—first called on a woman in a tiny dwelling who was raising five or six kids by herself. Her name was Rosemary. She told us her husband had died from AIDS and that she was HIV-positive. Her brother had died from the disease as well, and some of the children she was now raising were his. She made sixty dollars a year raising crops on two hectares of land—about five acres. She had a low bed in one of the dwelling's two rooms, while the kids slept on the floor.

By 2002, Rosemary said, she was so ill that a coffin had been built for her. That's when the motorcycles began to arrive with the antiretroviral drugs. They saved her life, she said. I will never forget that woman, how upbeat she was in the face of so much adversity. Rosemary made me cry, which I admit is not all that difficult to do. But she was remarkable.

"I want you to know how much I appreciate the chance to live and raise these children," she said. "I want to thank America."

If that wasn't enough, we next stopped at the small mud home of a carpenter, named Sampson. His wife had died of AIDS two years earlier, and he had buried her outside the hut, as a reminder to their three children about this terrible disease. Sampson was HIV-positive but the antiretroviral drugs were keeping him alive. He, like Rosemary, was just so grateful. He made tea and we sat outside and talked. He said, "Please thank George Bush and the American people for giving me the opportunity to live."

A little later, when all our small groups had returned and we were going to board the buses back to Kampala, I spoke briefly and mentioned how the day had taught me that we were not only saving lives but also promoting a tremendous amount of goodwill for the United States.

"It's medical diplomacy," I said, and I knew I wanted to hang onto the phrase the moment I said it. I subsequently learned that I wasn't the first to call it that; the idea of medical diplomacy had been around for a while. Still, I embraced it, and the more I thought about it and saw it in action, the more passionate I became about medical diplomacy.

I went back to Africa one more time, in November 2004. The ninth meeting of the Global Fund board of directors was being held in Tanzania—the first time for the board in Africa—and it would be my last board meeting as chairman. The meeting was in Arusha and the presidents of Tanzania, Uganda, and Kenya attended. Even Kofi Annan made a brief visit. Clearly it made sense to have a meeting of an organization dedicated to fighting AIDS on the continent where it had caused the most devastation.

The meeting went well, and at its conclusion I looked forward to an adventure that had been in the works for months.

That summer, a Wisconsin friend, Tom Still, visited me at my HHS office in Washington. Tom, whom I'd known since he was a reporter for the *Wisconsin State Journal*, was then (and is now) the president of the Wisconsin Technology Council. Tom brought along a good friend, Jay Handy, a Madison-based financial adviser and venture capitalist. The two of them wanted to talk to me about attracting more venture capital to Wisconsin.

During our discussion, it was mentioned that Jay had been a diabetic nearly all his life and was an educator and advocate for people with diabetes. Nevertheless, he had completed an Ironman triathlon and had once climbed a twenty-two-thousand-foot mountain in the Andes.

I was impressed. I also knew that coming up in a few months was my Global Fund trip to Tanzania, home of the famous Mount Kilimanjaro, a favorite for climbers and the setting of a great short story by Ernest Hemingway.

I asked Tom and Jay if they might want to meet me in Africa and climb Kilimanjaro. It would be a fun way to begin to close the book on my time at the Global Fund, and perhaps generate—particularly through Jay's participation—publicity about the many benefits of exercise and physical fitness, a goal of mine all along as HHS secretary.

They were game. Tom and Jay arrived a couple of days before the Global Fund meeting ended. The day before our climb, we took part in a photographic safari through the Arusha National Park and Ngorongoro Crater. The views were stunning and so was the wildlife—many animals were not shy about approaching the vehicles.

That night, November 19, there was a birthday party for me at a beautifully renovated hotel in Arusha, with a cake and candles and seafood stew. I had been very careful about what I was eating on the trip, but I felt I needed to have something of substance before undertaking the climb the next morning. With that in mind, I ate some food at the party, and it turned out to be a big mistake. Later that night I became violently sick. My security wanted to take me to the hospital, but I said I could weather it.

Early the next morning, I still wasn't doing well. We had to stop several times on the drive from the hotel to the mountain. I was dehydrated, but I was determined to make the climb, at least partway. I'd been training and looking forward to it for months.

Tom and Jay were there when my group arrived. I made it partway up the mountain. Tom remembers that I was too sick to start out. He's wrong about that. I got to maybe eighty-five hundred feet, but I was hurting. They were checking my pulse. I recall my favorite security guy, Mike Lonetto, saying, "Either we're going to go back, or you're going to die." We went back to the hotel.

All told, I visited thirty-seven countries during my time at HHS, including China, where I met with Chinese health officials in Beijing to try to encourage more openness in their dealings with AIDS and SARS. I went to the Greater Middle East, where Afghanistan, which I visited three times, proved to be both a rewarding and a frustrating experience. It was a priority for the Bush administration, in the wake of the October 2001 decision to launch attacks against the Taliban in Afghanistan. We needed to help the country recover from the destruction wrought by that brutal regime.

On December 12, 2001, in the National Museum of Women in the Arts in Washington, Bush signed the Afghan Women and Children Relief Act, bringing desperately needed education and health-care assistance to Afghanistan.

That same month, a remarkable woman, Dr. Sima Samar, was named the minister of women's affairs for the provisional Afghan government under interim leader Hamid Karzai.

I met Dr. Samar the following summer, when I hosted a reception for her in Washington during a visit to talk about what more the United States could do to help rebuild Afghanistan after the Taliban. Dr. Samar didn't speak English—she was always accompanied by an interpreter—but she became an important friend and adviser to me as we tried to assist the new government. HHS had in fact been active in Afghanistan since November 2001, providing immunizations and making general health-care assessments. We wanted to do more.

We recognized it was the women and children who had suffered the most under the Taliban, and Dr. Samar confirmed that grim reality. She had first-hand knowledge, having graduated from the Kabul University Medical School in 1987, after which she operated both schools and hospitals in Afghanistan before the Taliban finally forced her into exile in Pakistan. She shared extraordinary stories with me that day in Washington. When the Taliban first told her she had to close her school in Kabul—women were forbidden to work under the regime—Dr. Samar said, "Hang me and announce my crimes: She is giving pens and pencils and papers to the girls."

Dr. Samar wasn't very big and her voice was soft, but she was tough. She wore a scarf, not a burka. The most harrowing story she shared concerned the time the Taliban came to tell her she had to stop practicing medicine. There were several soldiers, but only one came inside to talk to her. When Dr. Samar insisted she had no intention of stopping, the soldier grabbed for her, but she managed to trip him and force him to the ground. This is as Dr. Samar told the story to me. She then grabbed a knife, sat on his chest, and told him if he didn't take his thugs and leave, she would slit his throat. "If they shoot me," she said, "I will kill you before I die." The soldiers left, muttering threats.

Eventually Dr. Samar did leave Afghanistan, returning with the fall of the Taliban. The situation was very bad, she told me—the Taliban had ravaged the country and traumatized the people. I asked how I could help. Money was needed, of course. And we talked about starting a program that would bring Afghan American doctors back to Afghanistan on a revolving basis to assist in reestablishing the health-care system.

It was only when I made my first visit to Afghanistan, in October 2002, that I saw how dire the situation truly was. The Taliban had destroyed so much—the medical schools, all the books. I talked to a medical professor whose *New England Journal of Medicine* dated 1978 was the most modern thing they had. If you were going to a hospital for an operation, you had to bring your own surgical thread for your sutures. There was no place for the doctors to scrub up. Many of them, we learned, needed glasses they did not have—the doctors couldn't see. Many others on staff had post-traumatic stress disorder. There was mold everywhere in the building and no running water—this was all at the most established women's hospital, Rabia Balkhi. Consequently, mortality rates for women associated with pregnancy and childbirth were shocking, as were the child mortality statistics. It was a disaster. I promised to try to help change that.

In hindsight, we may have been a little naïve or overly optimistic about how much we could accomplish in a short time. It was still a war zone, after all. But when I returned to the United States, I spoke to President Bush, whose wife, Laura, had already spoken out about the plight of Afghan women. (Laura Bush would remain involved in their cause to the extent of publishing a book about Afghan women in 2016.) The president pledged support for Rabia Balkhi, and then I talked to Donald Rumsfeld, who said if he couldn't find money in the defense budget, he'd write a personal check for $100,000.

We announced in January the Bush administration's intention to spend $5 million in 2003 to rebuild and expand Rabia Balkhi and also create satellite medical teaching units in other parts of the country.

That spring, I flew back to Afghanistan to officially open the refurbished hospital. On the way, we stopped in Italy. The opening was scheduled for Easter Sunday, so Bill Steiger and I decided to stop in Rome on Good Friday and attend Mass at the Vatican with Pope John Paul II. I wanted to meet the pope. That was a dream of mine. The pope walked past me, about six feet away, after the Good Friday services, and I gave some thought to trying to introduce myself. But I didn't want to jump in front of him and cause a scene. Just hearing him give the service was quite amazing.

Then, in April 2016, a remarkable thing happened. I was at the Vatican for a Stem for Life Foundation conference. They support adult stem cell research.

My son, Jason, was with me. Pope Francis addressed the gathering and afterward, unexpectedly, he walked down from the stage and met with people in the first three rows, including Jason and me. It was an unforgettable moment. He blessed us after shaking hands and gave us each rosary beads.

The opening of the rebuilt Rabia Balkhi in April 2003 in Kabul was remarkable too. Word had gotten around and several hundred women and children were on hand to offer thanks. They sang and gave me flowers and were very appreciative. I spoke and everyone had great hope that it was the start of a real turnaround in Afghan health care.

It certainly improved, I can say that with confidence. As time went by, after I left HHS, there were scattered news reports indicating the hospital was having problems, and then, in November 2007, a lengthy story in the *Atlanta Journal-Constitution*. The mortality rates of mothers in childbirth and their infants had not decreased as much as originally hoped. Yet even while knocking HHS efforts, the paper noted the hospital "is cleaner and provides better care since the project began, experts agree."

Bill Steiger, who stayed at HHS after I left, published a rebuttal in the *Journal-Constitution*. He was able to point out how the story had cherry-picked statistics in an effort to paint a gloomier picture, adding, "Make no mistake, Rabia Balkhi Hospital does not compare to a modern US hospital. But it is considered the best hospital in Afghanistan. It is clean and offers good health care."

In addition to the hospital, in 2004 HHS debuted a program to distribute pioneering interactive women's health books across Afghanistan. They were essentially talking picture books, which was vital, since at the time something like 80 percent of Afghan women couldn't read. We published them in both Dari and Pashto, Afghanistan's official languages.

The books offered information and advice on nineteen different health subjects, including childhood immunization, pregnancy, breastfeeding, sanitation, and water boiling. I believe we printed twenty thousand initially and distributed them in villages all over Afghanistan. That figure probably grew substantially. The books were a big hit.

I'm proud of numerous things we did during my time at HHS, but I think my true legacy is the work we did worldwide to combat HIV/AIDS. US government spending on HIV/AIDS increased by nearly $6 billion from fiscal year 2001 to fiscal year 2005—my time at HHS. A *Milwaukee Journal Sentinel* reporter who was along on the December 2003 trip to Africa spoke with Jong-Wook

Lee, director general of WHO, who predicted I would "be seen, when you look twenty years down the line, as somebody who saved millions of lives."

By the time of that trip I felt like we'd done a lot at HHS. It had been a tumultuous but productive three years. When we returned from Africa, I called Andy Card, Bush's chief of staff, and told him I wanted to talk about my future at HHS. I hadn't made any decisions but there were other things I wanted to do.

The president still had a year to go in his first term.

"Can you stay until after the election?" Card asked.

I told him I would.

There is a misconception, even among some friends of mine, that I regret having made the decision to leave the governor's job in 2001. There is no question—I've made it clear in these pages—that I found the bureaucracy in Washington challenging. It is much easier to get things done as a governor than as a cabinet secretary, and I like getting things done.

It's also true that for about the first six months at HHS, I missed Wisconsin dearly. I still have a framed cartoon that someone gave me that shows me pining for things like the Badgers and tailgating at games, wondering why I couldn't find a good bratwurst in Washington. That was an apt characterization of my first six months.

But after 9/11, and as that first year went on, I was too busy to have any regrets. It felt like the weight of the world was on my shoulders, and I had to respond. By the end of that first year at HHS, it was clear that the job was bigger than I'd ever imagined. I could see the magnitude of it each day. Every American—man, woman, child—is impacted by HHS every day. I rolled up my sleeves and got to work. There's no question I learned to love, respect, and appreciate the opportunity I had to run that department.

By late 2003, however, I had turned sixty-two years old. Frequently in the back of my mind I had wondered if I could be successful outside of government, in the business world. I had always wanted to run a business. And it just seemed to me that entering the private sector at sixty-two or sixty-three would be much different from—and preferable to—making that move when I was sixty-seven, which would have been the case if I'd stayed in the cabinet for President Bush's second term.

I was thinking, too, about Sue Ann and our children, how they had always supported me, and that while we'd done OK financially since my years as governor, I had never earned significant money, the kind you can make if you're successful in private business. Don't misunderstand me. We were comfortable, once I was elected governor. But there had never been much money in the bank, we still had mortgages, and I thought to myself that the time seemed right to see, in a manner of speaking, what my worth was. I'd been successful in state government and in federal government—could I be successful in business? Could I make some money?

I announced my resignation on December 3, 2004, in a formal letter to President Bush, and in a press conference in the Humphrey Building. In my letter I thanked the president for the opportunity to serve and remarked on what I thought were some of our significant achievements: fighting HIV/AIDS, passing the Medicare prescription drug benefit, spreading medical diplomacy around the globe, encouraging organ donation, and more.

"Mr. President," I wrote, "I do not tender my resignation easily. While these years have been challenging, they have been greatly rewarding."

Leaving the federal government was a much less emotional experience for me than resigning as governor. There was just no comparison. At the press conference, I seemed to surprise some of the reporters with my answers to a question about what concerned me most as I was leaving HHS. I suppose I was feeling a little more free to speak my mind without pushback from the White House. I said I was worried about the nation's food supply, along with the increase and spread of infectious diseases.

Our food supply seemed particularly vulnerable to attack. There is a bifurcated system in the federal government in which the Food and Drug Administration (FDA) and the Department of Agriculture (DOA) split the responsibility for food safety. But the split, at the time I left, gave the FDA most of the responsibility, while giving the DOA most of the resources. It didn't make sense. One or the other should have responsibility for the country's food safety—and I would argue for the FDA.

The amount of food coming into the United States is massive, and the percentage of it that is inspected is minute. We get a lot of honey coming out of the Middle East that would be easy to tamper with. That's just one example. We have food coming in from all over the world, all subject to tampering.

On two or three occasions while I was secretary, we made an effort to inspect all the prescription drugs that were coming into the country over a short, specific period of time. What we found was depressing. Many of the drugs had been tampered with or were simply counterfeit. A lot of medicines that were required to be refrigerated were not. Something was amiss with a high percentage of the prescription drugs we stopped and checked. My point is that if we had done it with food, I'm afraid we'd have found something similar. Our surveillance system for incoming food is grossly insufficient. We need to have it consolidated into one agency and make the inspection of both food and drugs more robust— which makes it a good fit for the FDA. The Food Safety Modernization Act that President Obama signed in 2011 was a step in the right direction, but more is needed.

I felt then, in 2004, and feel now that we also need to allocate more resources to combat infectious diseases, starting with the flu, which kills around thirty-six thousand Americans every year. We haven't found an effective system for controlling that. Other infectious diseases are coming into the United States from around the world and I fully expect to see an increase in zoonotic diseases— those spread from animals and birds to humans. The Centers for Disease Control (CDC) are the best in the world at what they do, but we need to buttress our immunizations and get the CDC the resources they need to monitor and fight these diseases.

At that last HHS press conference, I mentioned how pleased I was that we'd been able to get the Medicare prescription drug benefit passed, adding that I would like to see it somehow possible for the government to negotiate drug prices on behalf of the Medicare beneficiaries. That's a highly controversial subject, and one I know about firsthand.

In October 2001, during the anthrax scare, the Germany-based company Bayer A.G. was making an antianthrax antibiotic called Cipro. While anthrax did not turn out to be the widespread threat we feared it might, at the time at HHS we were looking to acquire enough of the drug to protect twelve million Americans. Bayer had a patent on Cipro and was charging what I felt was an exorbitant amount of money, per pill, for the drug. The offer to us at HHS was between $1.75 and $1.83 per pill.

I picked up the phone and called Helge Wehmeier, the chief executive and president of Bayer's American operation. I didn't have the authority to call the drug company, but once again I acted on my own instincts, made the call, and invited Wehmeier to a meeting at the Humphrey Building. There was a generic alternative that was not yet legally available—the Bayer patent extended to 2003—but I felt that despite my great respect for the company's patent rights, this was a national emergency, an extraordinary situation. If Bayer wouldn't negotiate, we'd have to think about the generic alternative.

Wehmeier and a few aides came to Washington. We sat down at a table and I gave them pen and paper and told them to write down a price. Meanwhile, I was writing down my own price: seventy-five cents a pill. I turned it over and said, "This is where you need to get to."

It didn't quite happen. But by the time they left the Humphrey Building that night, we had an agreement to buy Cipro from them for ninety-five cents a tablet.

I was pilloried in the conservative press. The *Wall Street Journal* ran an editorial titled "The Cipro Circus" that criticized me personally as well as the government of Canada, which had negotiated its own deal with Bayer for $1.30 a pill.

"Somebody might explain to the political grandstanders," the *Journal* wrote, "that drug patent rights aren't a menace to national security; they're essential to it."

I disagreed at the time and still do. Not only was it a unique situation, an anthrax scare on the heels of 9/11, but for the quantities we were looking at—*bulk* doesn't quite do it justice—some kind of price break is typical in business. I appreciated that Bayer saw it our way.

By the time I left HHS early in 2005, I felt my health-care sector bona fides were such that there would likely be opportunities for me in the private sector. I didn't know for certain. Very strict ethical restrictions prevented me from actively seeking business opportunities while I was still secretary. I'd had a long career and I think a good one in government, without any serious ethical screwups, and I certainly didn't want to leave under any kind of a cloud.

I asked some trusted friends, my former DOA secretary Jim Klauser, Madison attorney Steve Hurley, and another attorney and longtime associate, Chris Mohrman, for help.

I said, "If somebody contacts me, I can't talk to them. Is it OK if I have one of you talk to them, and then once I leave, we'll at least have had those discussions."

In early March 2005 I joined a major Washington law firm, Akin Gump, as a partner, and at the same time signed on with Deloitte and Touche USA, an accounting and consulting giant that was looking to start a center for health-care management. Later that month, I accepted an offer to become president of Logistics Health, Inc. (LHI), in La Crosse, Wisconsin, a company that provides medical readiness, occupational health, and homeland security services to both public and private sector clients.

It was too much too soon—which I will address momentarily—but one thing I didn't do for any of the businesses I worked for was lobby. I didn't have anything against lobbying. The fact is a lot of former governors and cabinet secretaries make a great deal of money lobbying. I had an opportunity to lobby for numerous organizations and I always turned those offers down. I thought about it and decided that I didn't want to be paid to go ask people to vote a particular way. Again, there is nothing wrong with it. Lobbyists play a useful role. I just didn't think I wanted to do it. It was written into my contracts with both Akin Gump and Deloitte that I would not register as a lobbyist.

It was a problem at Akin, which is a big lobbying shop. They wanted me to lobby, and I wouldn't. In the end, I think I served them well by bringing in new clients, mostly in the health-care sector. We would agree on a target number for new clients over a period of time, and I always exceeded that number.

The real problem in my first couple of years in the private sector was that I overextended myself. It was a serious mistake. Both Akin Gump and Deloitte wanted me full time, and I took both of those jobs. Then Don Weber, chairman of LHI in La Crosse, offered me the presidency of his company. I hadn't known him as governor, but he'd come to Washington to see me in July 2004 when I was HHS secretary. LHI had contracts with HHS. On that visit, Don was walking across Independence Avenue in front of the Humphrey Building when he was struck by a car that ran a red light. His pelvis was broken in four places. I went to see him the next day in the hospital—he was there three weeks. Less than a year later, he asked me to join his company, and I did.

If that wasn't enough—essentially three full-time positions—I also accepted adviser and director positions on many corporate boards of companies across the country. How I thought I could do all that I will never know. It has always been my personality to try to do too much. Then in the fall semester of 2005 I was the Roy M. and Barbara Goodman Family Visiting Professor of Practice in Public Service in the Kennedy School of Government at Harvard University.

What was I thinking? I leaned on Ed Sontag, who had worked for me as governor and secretary—and who taught at UW–Stevens Point—to help me prepare my classes. Ed was my researcher, and part of the money I was paid went to him for doing the research. I think we did all right for the students. I was able to get good guest speakers. Isadore Rosenfeld, a physician who was a regular guest on Fox News, spoke at my class. I learned three basic academic principles at Harvard: 1) students are really smart; 2) it's tough to be a professor and be fully prepared for each class; and 3) it doesn't pay very well.

The same could not be said of the fees I was paid for public speaking the first couple of years after I left HHS. Giving speeches around the country was the last piece of what was a schedule crowded to a ridiculous extreme when I first left the government. I would tell people I spent one-third of my time with Akin Gump, one-third with Deloitte, one-third on board service, one-third speaking, one-third teaching, and one-third looking at entrepreneurial opportunities, launching small businesses. Of course, that adds that up to six-thirds. Kevin Keane, my former communications director at HHS, told the *Milwaukee Journal Sentinel*, "He's doing so many things. You just worry that he's going to kill himself." Another former colleague, Bob Wood, was quoted in the same article: "He's just someone who doesn't have a third or fourth gear—he's always in fifth gear."

I was making money, real money, for the first time in my life. The speaking fees felt a little surreal. I signed on with the Washington Speakers Bureau and got a speech nearly every week somewhere in the country during my first year post-HHS. First-class air travel and accommodations—and a speaking fee of $25,000. It's incredibly good money. The check arrives a few days after you speak. I'm not sure I was worth that much money—who is?—but I spoke on health-care issues and worked hard to do a good job, mixing in some jokes and stories from what by then was a deep well of personal experience.

I will always be grateful for the money I made speaking because it allowed me to do something I'd been thinking about for a very long time. Earlier in these pages I spoke of the farm outside of Elroy that had been in my mother's family since the 1860s. When I first visited the farm as a boy in the 1940s, it was being operated by my mother's brother Len Dutton. Len had moved to Chicago and was hoping to be a lawyer when he got a call from his mother, my grandmother, saying he needed to come back to Elroy and run the farm. You may recall that another son, Len's brother Charles Jr., had been operating the farm, but after marrying a woman who was not a Catholic—Mildred was a Lutheran—Charles was effectively cast out by the tyrannical priest in Elroy, Father Murphy. Murphy insisted Charles not be allowed to run the farm, and the family acquiesced. Len returned from Chicago and took over.

Len had a son, Patrick, who was my cousin and about my age. Sometimes he stayed overnight with me in town, and occasionally I would go out to the farm and stay overnight with him. We had family gatherings and celebrated important occasions at the farm. We had a party there after my first communion. I hunted on the land, too, as a boy. It's beautiful country, and it became a part of who I am.

By the late 1950s, Len had around 275 acres of farmland and was raising Ayrshire Irish cattle, but he never really liked farming. An opportunity arose for him to purchase a woodworking operation in Onalaska, Wisconsin. By that time, my parents had married and were living in Elroy. Len came to them and explained that he was going to sell the farm. He hoped my parents might want to buy it, but he was selling regardless.

"I'll give you a good deal," Len said, "because I'd like it to stay in the family."

It made more sense than it otherwise might have for my father, since he had already invested in two small farms in the area and had a couple named Harold and Marcella Schultz managing them. My father decided to buy the Dutton farm from Len, and he eventually installed the Schultzes' son, Ervin, a friend of mine from high school, to run it. My understanding is that my dad paid less than $100,000 for the property, the cattle, and the machinery. Before long he added another two hundred acres adjacent to the Dutton farm.

Then, sometime in the mid-1960s, my dad came to me and said, "You know, the Schultzes want to buy the farm. I think I'm going to sell. They've been good renters. You're in law school—you're never going to come back and farm." He noted that my younger brothers weren't interested, either, and that our sister, Juliann, was living in California.

I was upset, but there was nothing I could do. My dad sold the farm and the two others he owned to the Schultzes for something like $75,000. It should have been considerably more. But he had his mind made up, the Schultzes had been good to him, and that was how it was going to be.

I became a lawyer and a legislator, and Erv Schultz—who eventually bought the Dutton farm from his parents—and I stayed in touch. I did some legal work for Erv. In the mid-1970s he told me he wanted to get bigger—buy more land and add a milking operation. My understanding is that he borrowed $200,000 for the expansion from the John Hancock Insurance Company. Erv worked hard but milk prices tumbled, and in the end, he couldn't make it go. He filed for bankruptcy in 1986.

This is where the story begins to come full circle.

I was elected governor in November of 1986. On December 7, 1986—I will always remember that date—I got a phone call in Madison from Dennis Schuh, my law partner in Juneau County.

I was in the transition office we had set up to interview people for jobs in my administration—I wouldn't take office until the following month. Chuck Thompson, John Tries, and Jim Klauser were helping me screen people, and we'd been putting in twelve-hour days trying to staff our new government.

Dennis called at eight thirty that morning and said, "Did you know your grandfather's old farm is going to be placed up at the sheriff's auction at noon today?"

I had not realized it. I think it's fair to say I was preoccupied being governor-elect. Talking to Dennis, I had various thoughts rushing through my head.

Finally, I said, "Go over and put in a bid for me of $200,000."

It pretty much just jumped out of my mouth. I didn't have any money. I'd been campaigning for a year. All I had was a little house in Elroy with a mortgage, a law office building, and an old car.

Dennis said, "Why do you want to do that? There's $350,000 owed against it. You're not going to get it for $200,000."

Then Dennis chuckled and said, "Plus, you don't have any money. I know you're broke."

I asked him to do it anyway. I think I wanted to be able to tell my kids that I put in a bid on the old family farm but lost it because I didn't have enough money. I wanted to be able to say at least I tried.

My team and I had lunch that noon with Tony Earl, the outgoing governor, and a few of his aides. Tony was gracious as always—we're friends to this day—as we talked about the transition. About one thirty, back at the transition office, I got another call from Dennis. I had completely forgotten his earlier call.

"We got it!" Dennis said.

"Got what?" I said.

"The family farm."

"What!" It dawned on me what he was saying. "How? I told you not to bid more than $200,000."

Dennis explained what had happened. He was bidding against some representatives from a financial institution. When the price got to $195,000, first Dennis, and then the other side, would bump the bid up by $1,000.

"When I bid $200,000," Dennis said, "they packed up their books and walked out."

Then Dennis said, "You have to have $50,000 in cash here by Monday."

That stopped me for a moment. I had virtually no assets, no real collateral for a loan.

"How are you going to get $50,000?" Dennis said.

I had the answer for that one. "I have no idea."

I did know that if I could come up with the $50,000—25 percent down on the purchase price—I would likely be able to find a bank that would loan me the rest. But how to get that first $50,000? It's not what I wanted to be thinking about as I was trying to put state government together.

There was, I felt, one possibility. I called my sister, Juliann, in California, and I didn't tiptoe around.

"Juliann, would you give me $50,000?"

"No," she said.

She thought I was calling for a campaign donation. I explained the situation and told her the story about what had happened at the auction. She thought for a minute and said, "I'll give you the $50,000, but I get half the farm."

It was smart of her, and, of course, I had no choice. I went to the Bank of Reedsburg—I'm not sure why I chose it—and, sure enough, they came through with the rest. "Of course we'll give you a loan. You're the governor."

Sue Ann was not pleased about my decision to buy the farm. Who could blame her? Here I was taking on a bunch of debt. I told her I would sell it in a year. And, well, that never happened. Let's just say it's not something I bring up to Sue Ann on a regular basis.

Eventually, I was able to buy out Juliann, and today I own the farm completely. While Sue Ann never truly warmed up to it, there was a time when she was part owner of some livestock on the farm. This began in the late 1990s. Sue Ann was talking with a friend, Mary Paul Long, who was with the Dane County Humane Society, and Mary Paul said her father had sold his herd of Belted

Galloway cattle in Colorado, but there were fourteen left and he wanted his daughter to take them.

Belted Galloways are rare Scottish cattle with a white belt around their middles—they look like Oreo cookies. When Mary Paul asked Sue Ann if she knew of any place that might want them, Sue Ann suggested my farm in Elroy. Which is how Sue Ann, Mary Paul, and Erv Schultz—who I retained to operate the farm for me—wound up as co-owners of the Belted Galloways.

I was out of it, except to field calls from one of the three co-owners complaining about one of the others. Erv and Mary Paul had kind of a love-hate relationship, although eventually they grew close. Erv taught Mary Paul how to drive a tractor. When Erv died, in 2011, Sue Ann was already out of the cattle business and I bought out Mary Paul. So now the Belted Galloways are owned by Erv's son, Scott Schultz, and me. Scott has taken over for his father and is in business with me at the farm. By summer 2017 we had one hundred Belted Galloways.

My farm is now over twelve hundred acres—nine hundred of them tillable—of corn, soybeans, and hay. It's not quite profitable yet, but we're going to make it profitable. Clearly it is about more than the money for me. My farm in Elroy is one of my favorites places in the world. I love everything about it, the history, and the Ireland connection. It is my little piece of heaven, aptly named Mount Haven by my great-grandfather Thomas Dutton.

I mentioned earlier how the speaking fees I began earning in 2005 eventually allowed me to do something I'd been thinking about for some time. It seemed like gravy on top of the other money I was bringing in, but I didn't want to just spend it without having something to show for it. Part of my farm—a few hundred acres, east of the original Dutton farmhouse—is the land where I used to hunt as a boy. It is singularly beautiful, sitting as it does on a rise with vistas in every direction, especially south. I'd always felt that if I ever got any money, I'd build a house there. It had been in the back of my mind forever.

When the speaking fees started coming in, I commissioned a contractor and told him it would be a job done in installments, as money allowed. I didn't tell Sue Ann. I think I might have been planning to surprise her when it was finished. That was unwise. She heard about it, of course, and she wasn't happy. Again, I couldn't blame her. In the end, my dream farmhouse was built, and Sue Ann found us a lovely property on Lake Wisconsin, and that lake house is where our kids and grandchildren—we now have nine grandchildren—love to come and enjoy the water.

I wish they enjoyed the farm more, and I think maybe they will, in time. I do ask each of our children to come up to the farm every year and, with the help of their own kids, plant one hundred trees each spring. I see it as a rite of passage. I want them to feel like they're a part of the farm, to see their trees growing, pick rocks, and learn about conservation. It's a weekend of work, but I hope it gives them an appreciation for the property. In the fall, they come up again and we pick apples and make apple cider. I put in a fishing pond that is so well stocked with fish that my grandkids can catch them without bait—just a bare hook. It's a lot more fun to fish when you catch something.

I am so proud of Kelli, Tommi, and Jason. They all have graduate degrees and have done well professionally. More important, they are good people, genuine, kind, and I give their mother a great deal of credit for that. When I was first elected governor, the girls were in high school and Jason was in sixth grade. They were playing sports in school and wanted to stay in Elroy. Sue Ann was still teaching. We decided as a family—led by Sue Ann—that they would stay in Elroy so the kids could finish school there. They'd come down to Madison on weekends, almost every Friday night, or I'd go to Elroy, especially when Jason and Tommi were playing basketball.

The fact that they stayed in Elroy, where nobody really cared if they were the governor's kids—there was no security—seems in hindsight a very good decision. Again, all credit to Sue Ann.

Our three children all have three children of their own. The grandchildren call me "Bunka," and each is amazing in her or his own way. I know you'll understand that I want to give them a shout-out. My daughter Kelli and her husband, Chris Iglar, have Sophie, Ellie, and Maggie. Sophie is the oldest grandchild: hardworking, smart, and an extremely driven young lady. Ellie is intelligent, athletic, and a sweet-natured soul. Maggie is spirited, funny, and very flexible.

My daughter Tommi and her husband, Brian Duffy, have Hayden, Eily, and Teddy (Thomas Edward). Hayden is talented in sports and the arts and has a wonderful sense of humor. Eily is bright, athletic, and extremely competitive. Teddy is the youngest grandchild. He came a little later than the rest. He is sweet and energetic—a ray of sunshine who completed our family.

My son, Jason, and his wife, Notesong Srisopark Thompson, have Jason Jr., Sabrene, and Juliana. Jason Jr. is outgoing, smart, and a great multisport athlete. Sabrene is sharp, determined, and a slightly wild child. Juliana is charming, engaging, nimble, and embraces all things girl.

Sue Ann and I could not love them more. They keep me young and moving quickly if I want to see all their games and activities on any given weekend day, and more than anything, I do.

One of my hopes is that those kids will always stand up for their siblings, just as Kelli, Tommi, and Jason have been there for each other over the years. That was never more evident than when Tommi was diagnosed with breast cancer, and Kelli carried Tommi's child, due to the cancer treatment.

It was a remarkable, profound, and at times scary experience for our whole family. There were complications. I recall being in La Crosse, working for Logistics Health, and going to a cathedral—it was Good Friday—and praying that everything would be all right.

It was. Kelli gave birth to a beautiful little girl. I have always thought of her as the "miracle baby."

It may sound like all I did when I left HHS was work—what with multiple jobs, board seats, and crisscrossing the country giving speeches—but I squeezed in some fun, too.

In 2005, I made my first trip to the Kentucky Derby, at Churchill Downs in Louisville. I had no experience with horse racing and no expectations other than to enjoy the spectacle. I'd been invited to sit in a suite by Terry Finley, president of West Point Thoroughbreds and a former army officer.

We were sipping mint juleps and he was explaining a little bit about the business to me. When a horse named Giacomo won the day's main event, the Kentucky Derby, Terry said he had a horse named Flashy Bull who had the same sire as Giacomo.

The bourbon may have got me. I said, "This is fun. I think I'd like to get into this business. What's involved?"

Terry said Flashy Bull was owned by a syndicate, and I could join the syndicate and receive an ownership interest in Flashy Bull for $5,000.

My good friend Dennis Markos, a Madison business executive who has traveled the world and is an ambassador for Wisconsin, had taken a group of friends down to the Derby on a train. He was somewhere on the grounds at Churchill Downs. I called his cell phone and he answered.

"Dennis?" I said. "I want you to know that you and I just bought a piece of a horse."

Dennis is a good sport. He wound up putting in more money than I did. Flashy Bull turned out to be the real deal. As a three-year-old, he finished second in the Fountain of Youth Stakes at Gulfstream Park, north of Miami, and he qualified—last horse in—for the 2006 Kentucky Derby. It doesn't get any better in horse racing than that.

Naturally I went to the Derby again, this time as part owner of a horse running in the race. Dennis and his wife, Carol, were there, too, and it was an amazing experience. We went down to the paddock and as owners got to stand in the middle of it all. Flashy Bull ran fourteenth, but the whole day was thrilling. Later, I thought about how I'd had the chance to ride my motorcycle around the track at the Indianapolis Motor Speedway, and now I'd been in the paddock at the Kentucky Derby watching the horses get saddled and the jockeys climb aboard. As I've reflected often in my life, it was a long way from Academy Street in Elroy.

Flashy Bull did not have a great 2006 racing season, but as a four-year-old in 2007 he won three of his first four starts, and then in June he won the Grade 1 Stakes Stephen Foster Handicap at Churchill Downs, a prestigious race named in honor of the songwriter who composed "My Old Kentucky Home." That win alone covered all our expenses related to Flashy Bull, and I've learned that if you break even as a racehorse owner, you're doing far better than most.

The following month at Saratoga in New York, Flashy Bull cracked an ankle bone and was retired to stud. Last I knew he was still at it, in Saudi Arabia, having been sold in 2014 to a stud farm in that country.

I had one more adventure in horse racing that proved very interesting. It developed out of the 2008 Kentucky Derby, which became a high-profile public-relations nightmare for the sport when a filly named Eight Belles, after finishing second in the race to Big Brown, broke down past the finish line and had to be euthanized. It brought to a head the criticism the industry was already receiving in the areas of safety and integrity.

The National Thoroughbred Racing Association (NTRA) reached out and asked if I would serve as independent counsel—in effect a monitor—for an initiative called the NTRA Safety and Integrity Alliance. The program would encourage racetracks across the country to reform in those areas, with accreditation bestowed on those that met the standards.

I agreed to take the job, partly because I was passionate about the sport and partly because I was assured I would be independent and able to tell the truth about the job the tracks were doing. In fact, after our initial press conference in New York City in October 2008, Alex Waldrop, the NTRA president, took me aside and told me I was sounding too much like a horse-racing fan.

"You're not an advocate," Alex said. "You monitor and report."

I stayed in the position for about eighteen months and in that time visited numerous racetracks around the country. In broad terms, we were looking for compliance in areas like injury reporting and prevention, wagering security and integrity, racing surface safety, medication uniformity and testing, and caring for the horses after retirement. It was an earnest attempt by the industry to clean up its act, and I feel it did improve safety for the horses and jockeys, whether I had much to do with it or not. I was the monitor. By 2016, twenty-three racetracks in the country had been accredited by the NTRA Safety and Integrity Alliance. Those tracks handled 94 percent of the Grade 1 stakes races and more than 70 percent of the pari-mutuel betting in North America.

Often in the years after I left HHS, whether I was at a racetrack or in an airport or restaurant, someone would come up and ask if I was thinking of running for office again. Or they'd wonder if I missed politics and government. If I was honest, the answer to both those questions was yes. While I certainly enjoyed and appreciated my early business career, I missed government. Some people get out of politics, breathe a sigh of relief, and say they'd never go back. That was not me. I felt like I'd accomplished a lot, both as governor and secretary. The truth is, I missed the action. There is more action in government, more big decisions that you make on a daily basis than in private business. Decisions that really impact people's lives. I missed that very much.

I'd given serious thought to running for governor of Wisconsin in 2006 against the Democratic incumbent, Jim Doyle. I had my announcement speech written in my head. I knew exactly what I wanted to say. In the end, I felt I was still too early in my business career to just set it aside. But after the elections, in which Doyle was reelected in Wisconsin and the Democrats claimed majorities in both houses of Congress, I started thinking even more seriously about running—this time for president.

As I've noted earlier, it was something I'd always wanted to do. I feel as if I missed my best chance, in 1996, when my closest colleagues were worn out after a decade in the governor's office and leery of the exhausting pace of a run for the presidency.

In December 2006 I established an exploratory committee to consider a presidential run and filed paperwork with the Federal Election Commission. I made my formal announcement in April 2007 with an appearance on ABC-TV's *This Week*. I knew money, or the lack of it, would be a problem, but my plan was to concentrate on Iowa and the caucuses, where actually getting out and meeting the voters—retail politics—was more important than buying TV time. I was good at retail politics. As for being an underdog, I had experience at that, from my first assembly race to my first run for governor. And I thought I had some good ideas to bring to the table, on Iraq—where my plan was to split the country into three parts, as it had been before Winston Churchill brought it together—and medical diplomacy, which I felt could be an enormously effective foreign policy tool. Domestically I had health-care and education initiatives that also set me apart.

My Iowa campaign manager, Steve Grubbs—he'd handled the state for Steve Forbes in 2000—said to me, "Tommy, we can win this thing. But you have to go to every county in Iowa."

I agreed to try. When in doubt, outwork everyone else. It proved especially grueling because my political advisers were telling me I needed to take a leave from all my business affiliations, and I wasn't going to do that. I was still just getting my mortgages paid off. So I was handling all my business duties and trying to visit ninety-nine counties in the state of Iowa. I didn't quite make it. I think I got to seventy-eight or eighty. Frankly, that was enough.

I still remember one morning, in a county way out in the southwestern part of the state. If Iowa is conservative, this county was conservative even by Iowa standards. Part of the deal with campaigning there was that they expected you to put on a breakfast or lunch, which you would pay for.

The morning I'm remembering was a breakfast at a country club at seven, maybe seven thirty in the morning. You could see the golf course out the window, and we had set up a buffet of bacon and eggs and pancakes. About twenty-five people were there, the kind of conservative voters who were likely to show up at the caucuses the following January.

About halfway through my speech, a distinguished-looking elderly couple came into the room. It was clear from the way the others reacted that they were big wheels in the community. People pulled out chairs for them. I smiled and nodded in welcome, and then when I was finished speaking, a campaign worker handed out pens and paper to everyone. While I was speaking I could see that I had this gentleman's attention. He was engaged, looking me in the eye. As I finished I said, "If you like what you've heard, please write down your name and address so we can stay in touch, and if you would like to do more than that"—meaning make a contribution—"that would be great, too."

Well, this gentleman was just kind of fiddling with the paper. He hadn't picked up the pen. I'm not sure what got into me—I'm sure I was tired—but I said to him, "Just sign the damn thing."

It was out of my mouth before I could stop it. His wife didn't miss a beat. "Watch your language, sonny," she said.

I have another Iowa campaign memory of a similar event, a pancake breakfast, in Ottumwa, the city best known as the hometown of the fictional character Radar on the TV series *M*A*S*H*.

The day before, I was out in California giving a speech at a health-care conference. We had planned my schedule so I could give the speech that afternoon and fly back to the Midwest in time for the breakfast the following morning. It could have worked. It was eighty and sunny in California. But in the Midwest—this must have been February or March, before my official announcement—there was a raging blizzard. I'd packed winter clothes in my suitcase, but my plane couldn't take off from California because of the conditions at O'Hare in Chicago, where I was supposed to land.

I had a campaign aide with me, and by the time we finally landed at O'Hare, we'd missed our connection to Des Moines, which is a ninety-minute drive from Ottumwa. There was one more flight to Des Moines that night, with one seat available, and it was about to depart. My aide couldn't go, and I knew my bag wouldn't make it, either, but I ran and made the flight.

The plane was able to land safely in Des Moines, and a driver was there to meet me, at probably two in the morning. The wind was howling. The roads were terrible. We found a twenty-four-hour Walmart on the way to Ottumwa, and I went in and bought some toiletries, a winter coat, a sweater, and a pair of Levi's jeans. As I walked out carrying them all in a Walmart bag, I had a flashback to the day I arrived at the University of Wisconsin with all my worldly possessions in a paper sack.

I managed to chuckle and thought, "Things really haven't changed much, have they?"

We got to the hotel in Ottumwa around four thirty. I slept for a couple hours, got up, put on my new clothes, and went to the pancake breakfast. The weather had doomed it. I don't think more than a dozen people showed up.

I worked hard in Iowa, and even though I was all-in with retail politics, canvassing the state, I still spent $750,000 of my own money, and my advisers wanted me to spend $1 million more. I refused. I would have had to borrow it and I wasn't going to do that. I felt I had enough money that if we skipped the straw poll in August, we could last until the caucuses the following January. But there was pressure, as an underdog, to enter the straw poll. It was a strange event—a day-long combination county fair/political convention, held on the campus of Iowa State University in Ames. It was a big money maker for the state Republican Party, in part because they charged exorbitant amounts for the candidates to have a presence.

Steve Grubbs advised me to skip the straw poll, and I almost did. Several of the front-runners had announced they weren't coming, and if I had followed suit, they might have called it off. (The party stopped having the event in 2015.) In the end, I went, and it was a strategic mistake.

Most things that could go wrong for me the day of the straw poll did. Mitt Romney and Mike Huckabee had secured the best spaces for their campaigns, near the front of the festivities, while our space was in the back, with the Ron Paul campaign. I remember Paul's volunteers coming over and helping themselves to our food. We were planning to arrive that day on motorcycles and they never showed up. My speech didn't go well. It was the hottest day of the summer—August in Iowa—and the general attendance for the event was down. Only people in the immediate area showed up, and my supporters were mostly from outstate.

I thought I had a good chance to come in second—but I finished sixth. I was surprised and disappointed, and I dropped out of the race the following morning.

But I still wasn't through with politics. It has been in my blood since I was a kid listening to my dad and his friends making deals about roads and bridges on Friday nights at the grocery store in Elroy. If it hasn't gone away by now, it's not going to, and that's OK, at least for me. My family is another matter.

I wanted very much to run against Russ Feingold for the United States Senate in 2010. My family was not enthusiastic. We had a family meeting and everyone, Sue Ann and the three kids, were all adamant that I not run. My older daughter, Kelli, was especially persuasive in her argument. She pointed out how well I was doing in business, adding that they were seeing more of me now, and they liked that. I was still on the fence.

As it happened, there was a Tax Day rally at the state capitol on April 15, 2010—not long after our family meeting about the US Senate race. I'd been invited to speak. I went up to the capitol that day with the intention of announcing either that I was running or that I would not run. I honestly wasn't sure, even driving over. Adding to the drama was that Kelli was with me.

Ron Johnson was at the Tax Day event—he hadn't announced yet as a Senate candidate, and he stood behind me while I addressed the gathering. I gave a passionate speech about the kind of taxpayer involvement and advocacy we were seeing in Wisconsin and the need to create the same thing at the federal level. It was an emotional speech and the crowd picked up on it, to the point where everybody started chanting, "Tommy for Senate!"

Later, a reporter told me he was absolutely certain that I was going to announce my candidacy in that moment. I almost did. As the crowd chanted, I glanced to my right and there was Kelli, looking directly at me with an expression that some might describe as a glare.

"After talking to my family," I said, as the chant grew quieter, "and I have my daughter, Kelli, here, and she's apoplectic about what I'm going to say next—I've decided not to run in 2010."

Two years later, when Herb Kohl decided to retire from the Senate—his term was up in 2012—there was no stopping me. Once again, my family tried to talk me out of it, but I was dismayed at having seen Wisconsin torn apart by the acrimony that had accompanied recent elections in the state. Everything had polarized. There was no middle ground, no chance for compromise. And while that was true when talking about the governor and the Democrats in the legislature, as well as Republican and Democratic legislators, what was worse was that by extension it pitted ordinary citizens against each other, forcing them to pick a side. Neighbors quit talking to each other. It was ugly. That's not the Wisconsin I knew.

I announced my intention to run for Herb Kohl's Senate seat and got broadsided almost immediately by the Tea Party, government-is-the-enemy tenor of the times. Maybe I deserved it for not seeing it coming. The Republican Party in Wisconsin, like the party nationally, had shifted to the right. I was surprised to have an opponent in the Republican primary—and ended up with three. It was as if people had forgotten what I'd done for the state, and that hurt. I was attacked by outside conservative groups in a barrage of television ads that tried to portray me as more Washington than Wisconsin, and not a true conservative. The primary was contentious. My family worked hard during the campaign—harder than they had in any of my previous races, which I appreciated—and I was able to prevail in the four-way race.

But it was a tough, wounding, and expensive primary. I started the general election campaign against Democrat Tammy Baldwin—who didn't have a primary opponent—with a financial disadvantage from which I never recovered. The national Republican Party assumed I was a lock to win—the first general election poll numbers were good for me—so they didn't want to give us any money. Early on I was fundraising when I should have been campaigning, while Baldwin was all over the state and up on television with ads attacking me in the manner of my Republican primary opponents. It was repeatedly suggested I had lost touch with Wisconsin. That wasn't true—I was back in Wisconsin all the time, even as HHS secretary—but to my disappointment they were able to sell that narrative.

Barack Obama won big in Wisconsin in November—the turnout in Milwaukee was one of the largest ever—and I lost the Senate race. Mitt Romney and Paul Ryan thought they were going to win Wisconsin, and instead they lost by seven percentage points. Had they lost by only three points, I'm confident I would have won the Senate race.

But let me be clear: losing hurt. It was my first statewide defeat, and it was a crushing blow. I felt bad, too, for the people who had worked so hard for me during the campaign, people who became friends, in some cases almost like family. I hosted an emotional lunch for them a week after the election.

In any event, I couldn't afford any real postelection funk. I had businesses to run and a considerable campaign debt to pay off. I am unlikely to run for office again—though I've learned never to say never—but my wounds healed and I stayed close to politics. As I've noted, it's in my blood.

I was involved in the overcrowded and contentious Republican presidential primaries in 2016 to the extent that I supported first Jeb Bush, and then John Kasich, for the Republican nomination. I chaired the Kasich campaign in Wisconsin. I like and respect John. But when it became clear that Donald Trump was going to be the nominee, I thought Kasich made a mistake by not coming to the national convention in Cleveland, which was, after all, his home state. I had differences with Trump, too, but I thought it was imperative that the Republicans come together to beat Hillary Clinton. I've known Hillary since 1987, and I did not think she would be a good president.

Do I like everything Trump says? No. Do I like everything he does? No. Do I wish he would tone down and not tweet so much? Yes. But the truth of the matter is, I thought—and think—his instincts as a businessman are far better for the future of this country than a Hillary Clinton presidency.

After Trump was nominated and the general election campaign began, I requested a half hour of his time during a visit he was making to La Crosse in August 2016. He gave me forty-five minutes. I know I surprised him from the start.

"You're not going to like what I have to say," I said.

We were in a room at the Charmant, the new hotel of my Logistics Health friend Don Weber, in La Crosse.

I told Trump that I wanted him to win the presidency, and in my opinion his time would be best served not returning to Wisconsin, because I did not feel he could win the state.

"Everyone else is going to tell you to spend a bunch of time in Wisconsin," I said. "But I believe—and I've never said this to any candidate, ever—that you're wasting your time here. You're not going to win Wisconsin. You need to be in Florida and Ohio. You need to win the presidency and that road does not run through Wisconsin."

I think Trump was taken aback. Late one afternoon two or three weeks later, I drove from my farm outside Elroy to Wausau to speak on behalf of a Republican assembly candidate. That drive was a revelation. Up through Portage County, Wood County, and Marathon County, I saw all kinds of Trump signs. I did not see one sign for Hillary Clinton. It really made an impression on me. Something was going on.

A day or two later—it was a Sunday afternoon—I called Trump.

"Donald, I was wrong," I said. "You need to come back to Wisconsin. You can win."

He did come back, but he has never let me forget that earlier conversation in La Crosse when I told him he had no chance. He mentioned it in late September when he came back to Wisconsin, and I introduced him at a rally in Waukesha.

On the afternoon of Election Day, I was driving to Milwaukee on business and decided to call Trump from the car. I just wanted to wish him well. It was 2:45, and all the polls were saying he had no chance, nationally or in Wisconsin. I just wanted to give him some encouragement.

Trump answered on the third ring, which surprised me—picking up right away on Election Day.

"Donald?"

"Who's this?"

"Tommy."

"Oh, Tommy. How are you?"

"I just called to wish you well."

Trump said, "Don't worry, Tommy. I'm going to win. I'm feeling good. How am I doing in Wisconsin?"

"Well, you know," I said, "Wisconsin is a tough state."

"Don't worry, Tommy," Trump said. "I'm going to win Wisconsin. Let's have a great victory."

I went down and visited Trump in Florida before he was inaugurated. He wanted to talk about health care. It wasn't a bad meeting, but it was a little surreal. We were in the large front room of his Mar-a-Lago resort, and the president-elect kept jumping up to greet guests while talking to me about health care. It was disconcerting. He gave me a lot of time, we talked in depth, and I think he's very astute. It was just an odd way to have a meeting.

I can't imagine a time when I won't have a hand in politics and government, but for the past several years my focus has been on Thompson Holdings, the company I organized in 2013 that serves as a kind of business umbrella under which I invest in and advise numerous private sector companies.

I left Akin Gump, the law firm that hired me after I left HHS, when I decided to run for the Senate. I'd parted with Deloitte some years earlier, having stayed an extra year beyond our original three-year deal. The health-care management center I helped initiate for them is now called the Deloitte Center for Health Solutions and is going strong. With Logistics Health (LHI), the La Crosse company that hired me in 2005, there came a time when TA Associates, the private equity firm that held a majority interest in LHI, decided to shop us. This was 2009. There is always a high level of uncertainty with any ownership change, so I suggested to Don Weber, the LHI founder and the man who brought me aboard, that we try to form a local group that could buy out TA and ensure we kept control and the company stayed in La Crosse. We contacted Gundersen Lutheran—it's now called Gundersen Health System—and it was interested. I was then able to go to US Bank and negotiate a loan that sealed the deal and allowed LHI to stay in La Crosse. When Don—who remains a close friend—subsequently sold to UnitedHealth Group, I left the company.

Thompson Holdings has allowed me to work with my son, Jason, who is an attorney and savvy businessman. When I am approached about a new company—and there was a time when it happened almost weekly—I have Jason do the vetting, giving it either a thumbs-up or thumbs-down. We've invested in around thirty companies across the country, almost all of them health care related. Sometimes I sit on the board, sometimes Jason sits on the board, and some we just take a management interest.

One company that stands out among our interests, in part because it is headquartered in Wisconsin, is Physicians Realty Trust. I am very active in the company and chairman of the board of trustees. The company has quite a story that has never really been told, at least as this is written.

Physicians Realty Trust is a real estate company organized to acquire, selectively develop, own, and manage health-care properties that are leased to physicians, hospitals, and health-care delivery systems. The company invests nationwide in real estate that is integral to providing high quality health care. We completed our IPO on the New York Stock Exchange at $11.50 per share in July 2013 and got "DOC" for our trading symbol—perfect for what we were doing.

The company started with just nineteen buildings totaling nearly 528,000 square feet that were acquired from the Ziegler Healthcare Real Estate Funds. In total we raised $134 million in the IPO to acquire these properties and grow the company through new investments. Today, Physicians Realty Trust has over $4 billion in medical office investments.

I knew the business model for Physicians Realty Trust was solid, but no one could have anticipated how fast it has grown. The average age of doctors is fifty-five. They have a lot of their money in their office buildings—their clinics. We go in and offer to buy the buildings, often in a sale-leaseback transaction. When selecting Physicians Realty Trust as their partner in health-care real estate, the selling physicians can choose to receive cash, stock in our company, or a combination of both. They usually want cash. They also want to keep practicing medicine. They just want to take the money out of the building and live. We give them the money, and they typically give us a ten- or fifteen-year, triple net lease, which means they pay the real estate taxes, insurance, and all maintenance expenses. It works for them, and it is great for us.

As of the second quarter in 2017, we have over thirteen million square feet of medical office space in 262 buildings in thirty states across America. We own some of the largest cancer centers in the country. I am particularly proud of the fact that we paid our first quarterly dividend sixty-seven days after we went public and just recently raised the quarterly dividend payment for the first time. As we grow a long-term company in Wisconsin, our goal is to continue growing at nearly $1 billion per year in new health-care real estate investments that provide reliable, rising dividends for investors and offer high-quality health care for the patients and providers we serve. The company's future couldn't be brighter.

I still see a lot of airports these days. I travel for business as much as, or more than, when I was governor and cabinet secretary. People ask me when I'm going to slow down, and I ask how I can slow down when there is still so much I want to do? My personality has never been to be particularly reflective. I want to know what we're going to do tomorrow.

Still, having lived a life, I'd like to offer ten principles I've learned—the hard way in some cases—on my journey. Some are my own, some I've adopted from others. Call them Tommy's Tenets.

1. Love life and have fun.
2. Today is the best day of the rest of your life.
3. Spend time with your family and love them. They're the only ones who will always be there for you.
4. Never trade in an old friend for a new friend.
5. You have two ears and one mouth. Use them in that proportion. (From my dad.)
6. Never forget where you come from. (From George H. W. Bush.)
7. If they don't say yes, it's no. (From Tim Cullen, who got it from Bill Bablitch.)
8. Never discuss a subject you know little about until you gather the facts. (Learned the hard way at a Washington press conference.)
9. Always vet and know the person you're appointing to any position. (Which I failed to do once as governor.)

Finally, courtesy of the distinguished Warren Knowles, former governor of Wisconsin:

10. Never pass up the chance to use a restroom.

These days, when my batteries need recharging, and sometimes when they don't, I head for my farm, outside Elroy. It's my go-to spot on weekends. We have big machinery now, tractors and a bulldozer, and I can climb on one and make myself useful. It clears my head, and on occasion in those moments, I reflect.

One day in the summer of 2016 I cut twenty-five acres of hay by myself. Nobody was around. It was sweltering. I wiped the sweat off my face, looked back over my shoulder, and felt a sense of accomplishment out of proportion to what I had done. After all, I'd just cut a bunch of hay. But it felt good. I smiled to myself and thought, "I did that—nobody else."

That year—2016—was an important one for me, in numerous ways. It marked the fiftieth anniversary of my first being elected to the assembly and the thirtieth anniversary of my first being elected governor. In November of that year, I turned seventy-five.

Six months earlier, in May, I returned to the University of Wisconsin–Madison to receive an honorary doctorate of laws degree at the spring commencement. As I've noted in these pages, it was a great honor. Toward the end of the lengthy graduation ceremony, I was asked to speak.

"I can see," I said, after being introduced by Chancellor Rebecca Blank, "how excited these students are for one more speech."

I didn't speak long, ten minutes or so. Primarily I wanted to thank the university for what it had given me—much more than an honorary degree—and once again make the case for how very valuable our great university is to the entire state of Wisconsin, as an economic engine and more.

I thought it was important to tell the graduating students in the audience a little about myself. How I came from a small city called Elroy, where if you dialed a wrong number on the phone you talked to whoever answered, because of course everyone knew everyone else. I talked about coming down to Madison for school with nothing but some dreams, and I told them how, with a lot of hard work, a lot of help, and a bit of luck, I'd been elected to the Wisconsin assembly and then elected governor. I'd gone to Washington and served a president in his cabinet. It still seemed so improbable, talking about it all these years later.

What I really wanted to convey was that my story, so much a Wisconsin story, could be their story, too, if they dreamt big enough, and reached high enough.

Later, Chancellor Blank asked me if it would be possible to get a copy of my speech. I had to tell her there were no copies. I'd written nothing down. It came from the heart.

Acknowledgments

This book has been a journey that began with a handshake in early 2011 at the Esquire Club on Madison's north side. I asked longtime Madison journalist and author Doug Moe to collaborate with me on my autobiography. Our handshake sealed the deal. We never needed a more formal agreement.

Which is not to say it was easy. It's seven years later now that our book is being published. In the years between I worked hard—the only way I know how—on numerous business ventures, traveled extensively, gave speeches, viewed—sometimes in dismay—the shifting political landscape in Wisconsin and across the country, and, most significantly, watched my grandchildren grow and blossom. It doesn't get any better than that.

I also found time to reflect on my life, and in doing so I realized just how fortunate I have been. Fortunate to have been born and raised in a small town in the greatest state in the United States. Fortunate to have had a loving family, both as a child and as a husband and father. And fortunate to have found a passion—politics and government—that propelled me onto stages a kid from Elroy could hardly dare imagine.

At every point I've been blessed with help from family, friends, and colleagues, and that includes in the writing of this book.

While the story consists of my recollections of my life, many people shared their own memories of various times, places, and events, and in doing so helped clarify my own remembrances. Thanks to Ave Bie, Ed Brown, Carl Gulbrand-sen, Steve Hurley, Kevin Keane, Jim Klauser, Bill Kraus, John Matthews, Bill McCoshen, Stewart Simonson, Bill Steiger, Dean Stensberg, Tom Still, Dr. Michael Sussman, and Bob Wood. Members of my family also helped by sharing memories. Thanks to my wife, Sue Ann; our children, Kelli, Tommi, and Jason; and my sister, Juliann Martin.

The quotations in the book are for the most part drawn from my memory of the conversations described, abetted in some instances by newspaper accounts, notes, and the recollections of others. The quotes are represented as I remember them, while realizing an exact word for word reproduction may not be possible.

Once a draft of the manuscript was completed, numerous people took time to read portions of it and make suggestions. Thanks to Jason Denby, Steve Hurley, Kevin Keane, Jim Klauser, Scott Klug, Bill McCoshen, Jeanan Yasiri Moe, Brian Nemoir, Stewart Simonson, Bill Steiger, Dean Stensberg, and Bob Wood. Once again, family members assisted as well. Thanks to Sue Ann, Kelli, Tommi, and Jason; my sons-in-law, Chris Iglar and Brian Duffy; daughter-in-law, Notesong Srisopark Thompson; and my sister, Juliann Martin.

In recollecting my professional life, no single resource was more valuable than the Tommy G. Thompson Collection at Marquette University in Milwau-kee. Archivist Bill Fliss, curator of the collection, was eager to help and served as a matchless guide through the extensive holdings that I donated after leaving government service.

Thanks to everyone at the University of Wisconsin Press for their good work in the editing, design, and production of this book.

Numerous other friends and colleagues helped in ways small and large, not just with this book but throughout my life. Many will find their names in these pages. I wish there had been space to include everyone, but you know who you are. I'm grateful to everyone I've known or worked with, for each of you gave me the ability to serve, making tomorrow better than today.

Two people deserving of special mention are my friend and assistant Patricia Hackett, who cheerfully handled the thankless task of coordinating schedules so the coauthors could get together and do their work, and Jason Denby, my close associate and scheduler who also worked wonders with logistics.

Regarding my coauthor, Doug Moe, it has been said that getting two people together to write a book can be problematic. It wasn't like that for us. Doug and I began this project as friendly acquaintances and ended it as very good friends.

I've thanked my family already in these acknowledgments, but I want to do so again, because they are everything to me: Kelli and Chris, Tommi and Brian, Jason and Notesong, and Sue Ann and our wonderful grandchildren— Sophie, Ellie, Maggie, Jason Jr., Sabrene, Juliana, Hayden, Eily, and Teddy— thank you from the bottom of my heart. I love you.

Finally, I would like to thank the great people of Wisconsin for allowing me to have served them as governor for fourteen years. What a joy and privilege that was. It is to the people of Wisconsin that this book is dedicated.

Index

Page references in italics indicate an illustration. "TGT" refers to Tommy Thompson.

263